CLASS AND STATUS
IN FRANCE

CLASS AND STATUS IN FRANCE

Economic Change and Social Immobility
1945–1975

JANE MARCEAU

CLARENDON PRESS · OXFORD
1977

Oxford University Press, Walton Street, Oxford OX2 6DP

OXFORD LONDON GLASGOW NEW YORK
TORONTO MELBOURNE WELLINGTON CAPE TOWN
IBADAN NAIROBI DAR ES SALAAM LUSAKA ADDIS ABABA
KUALA LUMPUR SINGAPORE JAKARTA HONG KONG TOKYO
DELHI BOMBAY CALCUTTA MADRAS KARACHI

British Library Cataloging in Publication Data
Marceau, Jane
  Class and status in France: economic change and social immobility, 1945–1975.
  1. Social classes—France 2. Social structure
  3. France—Economic conditions—1945–
  I. Title
  301.4′00944   HN440.S6

ISBN 0 19 827217 0

*Set by Hope Services, Wantage, and
Printed in Great Britain, by
Billing & Sons Limited, Guildford and London*

To my parents
To André
To Didier

PREFACE

The writing of a book of this nature involves much research and much discussion. I have benefited greatly from comments from colleagues at the University of Essex, particularly Colin Bell, Howard Newby, and Adrian Sinfield, who all read an early draft of the manuscript, and from conversations with colleagues in France at the Maison des Sciences de l'Homme and the Institut Européen d'Administration des Affaires and with my students at the Université de Paris X, Nanterre. Detailed and invaluable comments on the text were made by Roy MacLeod of the University of Sussex. Richard Whitley, of Manchester Business School, helped me avoid some theoretical confusions. My husband was a constant source of intellectual, moral, and financial support. Last, but not least, Marcia Brown most patiently typed and retyped the manuscipt. May they all find my thanks here. Errors, of course, are my own responsibility.

ACKNOWLEDGEMENTS

I should like to thank the persons and publishers listed below for their kind permission to reproduce copyright material: Institut National d'Études Démographiques for tables drawn from articles published in *Population*; H.-C. de Bettignies and D. Hall; Mme J. Frisch and the *Année sociologique*; Pierre Bourdieu and J-C Passeron; Éditions François Maspéro and C. Baudelot and R. Establet; Éditions A. Colin and G. Dupeux; J.J. Carré, P. Dubois, and E. Malinvaud and the Editions du Seuil. R. Salais, N. Triballat-Seligman, and the editors of the *Revue d'économie politique*; E.-H. Lacombe and *Éditions économie et humanisme*; Union des Industries Métallurgiques et Minières; M. Dogan; F. Le Reclus and the editors of *Politique*.

CONTENTS

LIST OF TABLES

LIST OF TABLES

ABBREVIATIONS

ANPE	Agence Nationale pour l'Emploi
ASSEDIC	Association pour l'Emploi dans l'Industrie et le Commerce
BUS	Bureau Universitaire de Statistiques
CERC	Centre d'Études des Revenus et des Coûts
CFDT	Confédération Française des Travailleurs Démocratiques
CFTC	Confédération Française des Travailleurs Chrétiens
CGT	Confédération Générale du Travail
CREDOC	Centre de Recherche et de Documentation sur la Consommation
INED	Institut National d'Études Démographiques
INSEE	Institut National de la Statistique et des Études Économiques
MRP	Mouvement Républicain Populaire
OP	*Ouvrier professionnel*
OQ	*Ouvrier qualifié*
OS	*Ouvrier spécialisé*
PDM	Progrès et Démocratie Moderne
UDR	Union des Démocrates pour la République
UNEDIC	Union Nationale pour l'Emploi dans l'Industrie et le Commerce

INTRODUCTION

Economic growth is frequently considered by observers to contain inherent mechanisms which, by increasing the general level of economic prosperity, decrease unequal participation by citizens in a nation's wealth. Increasingly close examination of modern Western capitalist societies has cast doubt on such assumptions, a doubt thrown into special relief by the reappearance of deep economic difficulties in the 1970s.

Social and economic inequality and inequalities have become a problem of increased political salience, and their reduction appears on many political party platforms. Frequently, however, the discussion centres only on particular inequalities such as those of income or access to particular services. Rarely is the inequality structure as a whole the centre of attention; too rarely is the accumulation of all or most aspects of inequality by members of particular sections of the society brought to light. The systematic nature of inequality and its fundamental relationship to the position of an individual and group in the production process are too often left obscure. The present book takes a different approach. Through an exploration of the effects of prolonged and rapid economic growth on the social structure of a particular modern European country, France, the book focuses on the socio-economic conditions prevalent there over the thirty years between 1945 and 1975. Examination of these conditions shows that, although after 1945 economic changes, allied to certain social and political ones, greatly improved the living standards of the mass of French people they nevertheless did little to modify the shape of the social structure. In spite of economic growth, examination of specific inequalities, whether concerning the distribution of rewards, material and symbolic, or probabilities of professional and social mobility, of access to various forms of education, to culture or to power, reveals the persistence of two phenomena, closely interlinked. On the one hand, it becomes evident that individuals situated in certain groups occupying specific positions in the opportunity structure accumulated and continued to accumulate advantages or disadvantages. Those groups relatively worst placed in terms of any one aspect of well-being were to be found equally badly off in terms of virtually all the others. The arrangement of social groups into such a hierarchy received symbolic recognition in terms of a hierarchy of prestige and power, 'justified' on the basis of rewards accruing to individual 'contributions' to the production of material goods and presented as returns on relative scarcity of important skills.

Examination of all the aspects of inequality makes it evident that the real basis for the presence and the persistence of these patterned inequalities between groups was the place held by each group in the production process. France, in common with other countries in and outside Europe, to which it was linked through trade, imperialism, and war, began a capitalist form of industrial economic development in the nineteenth century. In spite of some modifications, common to most advanced western European countries, and a form of 'indicative planning', introduced after the Liberation, France retained all the essential features of a capitalist economy after 1945. In the society the division between manual and non-manual labour, and within the 'non-manual' section the division between the owners and controllers of the productive process and the executive and services branches are crucial. Around these are clustered the various aspects of inequality discussed in this book. While those divisions persist, and while the dominant value system in the society which justifies them persists, the example of the situation in France over thirty years of rapid economic growth and transformation suggests that little fundamental change in the shape of the social structure is possible.

An attempt is made in this book to examine the structure of a society in its totality. That 'totality' does not, of course, include the details of everyday life or such matters as internal family relationships. It is seen as composed of elements, institutions, and groups, of which certain are dominant, linked together in patterned ways. These elements have historical, social, and economic roots, and are the subject of a specific process of historical development. On that process are dependent the state of the elements, the shape of the society, at any given time. It is difficult to assign exact dates to the beginning of a process or to dissect a 'slice' of a society for examination at any specific moment. This book, while concentrating on the period after 1945, therefore has a longer historical dimension and discusses both the development of industrialization in the nineteenth and twentieth centuries and the establishment of the major groups and classes in French society over the period. Throughout I take the economic system, the mode of production, as basic, and the social, political, and ideological systems as in important senses derived from economic relationships. However, I am more concerned here with the description of the consequences of the economic system in relation to an over-all structure of inequality than to a detailed analysis of the relationships between them. The book is primarily an empirical work, though not an empiricist one. Rather it is intended both to confront the reader with detailed evidence on the non-accidental and essentially systematic nature of inequality in French society and to suggest that the situation in France may be taken as a case study showing mechanisms undoubtedly at work in most other advanced industrial societies, in Europe and elsewhere.

A word of explanation about data sources may be useful here. The study of a 'whole' social structure and, in particular, of a class structure, involves a number of problems, exacerbated by the use, inevitable in such an enterprise, of secondary sources of information. Many sociological concepts refer to constructs of social reality which are part of a wider explicit or implicit theoretical framework and often involve specific notions about the kind of evidence admissible and the terminology to be employed. These constructs contain emphases on some aspects of 'reality' rather than others, and involve representations of that reality which do not all refer to the same level. The data available to a study such as this have frequently been obtained with different aims in mind. In order to unify the categories used in the analysis and to make comparable internally data referring to different phenomena I have used official statistics as far as possible.[1] The framework used here to fit the data together owes much to that developed by Pierre Bourdieu and his colleagues at the Ecole des Hautes Études en Sciences Sociales (formerly École Pratique des Hautes Etudes). They have devised a theoretical perspective which emphasizes the importance to the shape of a social structure of the differential distribution between groups within it of three major forms of capital—economic (shares, businesses, money, etc.), social (composed mainly of networks of relationships), and cultural (diplomas and cultural knowledge). Analysis of the distribution of these types of capital forms the skeleton on which discussion of the socio-economic structure in France after 1945 is hung in the chapters which follow here.

Before beginning the major part of the text, the reader may be interested in two further points. One of the original objectives of this book had been to present the work of modern French sociologists analysing their own society, particularly in relation to social 'stratification'. This proved to be difficult, for authors writing about their own

[1]   I am, of course, aware of the inadequacies of official statistics for sociological analysis; for instance, they frequently underestimate certain 'undesirable' phenomena. However, as the picture of inequality in France emerges so strongly in spite of this, the use of official statistics serves here rather to emphasize the situation.

culture take so much knowledge for granted in their readers that each
work builds on implicit assumptions which are not always easy to
decipher. The intellectual roots and the development of French
sociology were, and are, far more grounded in philosophy and theory
than those of their more empiricist English counterparts, and, as a
result, the whole style of discourse and exegesis of French writers is as
different from that of the English as is their intellectual universe. This
poses important problems of 'translation' in the widest sense. More
specifically, inequality in the whole society, and its persistence in the
face of economic growth, has rarely been treated directly by French
sociologists, although there have been important symposia on the
subject, and each different aspect of the theme has been treated by
French observers in varying ways. Although, on the whole, sociologists
in France seem to have retained a more critical view of their society
and social institutions than did their colleagues in some other countries
over the same period, nevertheless there were important gaps in the
literature and much that was done remained partial and in many senses
incoherent. These gaps remain to be filled, particularly concerning such
institutions as the family and the description of the interaction and
interdependence of the economic and social (and political) sectors of
the society.

On the other hand, the foreign sociologist approaching French
society does find certain native institutions useful. The *patron* tradition
in French higher education and research has had the positive side of
ensuring a flow of studies on the same or related themes over a considerable period of time. Pierre Bourdieu and his team have perhaps been the
most productive, producing a steady stream of reports, using the same
basic framework, linking different specific elements studies to a common
theme; the legitimation of society, the reproduction of social relations
and the maintenance in power of a dominant class. These studies covered
almost all parts of the education system, élites in business and other
fields of power, and extended to farmers and other social groups.
Similarly, at INED Alain Girard for long directed a team interested in
education and the professions which produced a long series of studies.
Unfortunately, both for the foreign and the native observer, all these
teams keep their work largely separate and it is rare that the work of
one is used by others. Each group tends to monopolize specific journals
and frequently opportunities for cross-fertilization are missed.

For these reasons the book is not primarily a map of recent trends in French sociology.[2] It is a selection of largely sociological work supplemented by official data, made by the present writer in relation to a specific theme, and is a selection which reflects my biases and centres of interest. The choice of the data is entirely my responsibility and does not necessarily reflect the views of any of the authors otherwise cited. All translations of quotations in the text below are my own unless otherwise indicated.

Finally, it should perhaps be emphasized that this book, while containing much of relevance to other modern Western industrial capitalist societies, is about France. Very little French work on the subjects covered here has been directly comparative and in the present text space permits only brief references to other societies and to sociological debates developed in relation to them.

[2] However, the spectrum of themes of sociological interest covered here is wide and the major themes and conclusions of the works used in the book are presented in some detail; they also cover a thirty-year period which saw not only economic growth but also (and perhaps not accidentally?) the rapid development of French sociology. The reader of this book will, therefore, become familiar with much of the landscape of French sociology of the time. Readers especially interested in this may usefully consult Bourdieu and Passeron's selection of sociological texts (1966). The long bibliography has, moreover, been drawn up so as to allow the reader to find as much further information as possible, or at least the sources for it, on any particular aspect of the subject.

1. CLASS AND STATUS

Class structure

France between 1945 and 19'/5 remained a country of many local traditions and variations. An observer who speaks of a class system or structure implies a certain over-all national unity. Many French observers have drawn imaginary lines across their country, dividing it into regions north and south of the river Loire, for instance, or east and west of a line Caen-Nîmes (e.g. Gervais, *et al.,* 1965), on the basis of degree of industrialization or urbanization, or by farm size or religious affiliation, each division expressing a part of French social reality and affecting the class structure of the time. During the thirty years after 1945, however, each area became increasingly subject to the centralizing forces emanating from the dominant economic base of industrial capitalism in an internal expansionist phase. As within each region there developed large towns, sometimes based on the expansion of existing industries, sometimes on the creation of new ones, so there also developed a manual working class in both industry and tertiary sectors of the economy. The same forces in each area, starting from the metropolis, Paris, but spreading everywhere, affected small producers, artisans and shopkeepers, and marginal industrial employers and the agricultural sectors which acted as a reservoir of labour for either local or Parisian industry. Within each region the rural notables, unless they operated successful reconversion strategies, largely gave way to the influence of their urban counterparts. Although not affected at the same rate nor at the same period, the exact timing depending on a multitude of factors, both national and local, each area was subject to the same pull and push forces with very similar effects.[1]

In sum, each region came to contain the same fundamental social classes, although in different numerical proportions, and each to be dominated by a fraction, or several fractions, of the same class, the bourgeoisie. For these reasons it seems justified to speak of a national social structure and a national class stratification system.

[1] Paradoxically, the renewed strength of 'nationalist' movements which became apparent towards the end of the period until 1975, particularly in Corsica and Brittany, was evidence of the weakness rather than the strength of the regions, and a protest against the dominant centralizing forces and their effects on the local population, particularly the lack of employment opportunities and the frequent necessity for migration to Paris or major cities in other areas of France. An excellent analysis of the effects of the industrialization process on the outer regions of France has been made by Dulong (1975) in relation to Brittany.

In the class system, we may distinguish three major social classes of which two, bourgeoisie and working class, are the major ones, the third, the middle class, being essentially a zone of transition. Poulantzas argues that social classes are

groups of social agents, of men defined *principally* but not exclusively by their place in the *production process*, that is, by their place in the economic sphere . . . a social class is defined by its place in the *ensemble* of social practices, that is, by its place in the *ensemble* of the division of labour, which includes political and ideological relations . . . The economic sphere is determined by the *production process* and the place of the agents, their distribution into social classes, by the *relations of production*. (1973: 27–8.)

The groups thus defined coincide closely with the three major units discernible on the basis of position in the opportunity structure and relative possession of the three kinds of capital—economic, social, cultural—distinguished by Bourdieu. The upper and dominant class, the bourgeoisie (*classe supérieure*), was composed mainly of owners (employers) in industry and commerce, members of the liberal professions, senior civil servants, political leaders and senior university teachers, and also included senior managers in industry and commerce for 'they shared with other members of the dominant class the ideological and political relations implied by the relations of production; they fulfilled the functions of capital, exercised power based on capital, and tended to subscribe to the justification of their activity, and hence to the existing form of economic and social life, in terms of "expansion" and "efficiency", which appeared in the period as the dominant variant of bourgeois ideology' (Poulantzas, 1974: 195).

With Boltanski (1973) we distinguish five *champs de pouvoir*, fields of power; the economic, political, administrative, academic (*universitaire*), and that of cultural diffusion. For positional and personal, as well as structural, reasons the 'significant' personnel in each constituted fractions of the dominant class.

Defined by its place in the production process and its structural 'opposition' to the bourgeoisie, the second major class was formed by the working class (*classe populaire* or *classe ouvrière*). The principal element within it was the manual working class, particularly composed of urban industrial workers, who grew fast in numbers. Inside the class there existed a number of divisions based first on skill—unskilled (*manœuvres*), semi-skilled (*ouvriers spécialisés*, OS), and the skilled (*ouvriers professionnels*, O.P. or *qualifiés*, OQ), then on type of plant (production line, continuous process, etc.), and lastly on national, ethnic, and regional origin. In spite of internal divisions, whichever aspect of the distribution of rewards or power is considered, members of the manual working class find themselves in a fundamentally similar and stable situation.

It seems useful for the kind of analysis undertaken in this book to follow the example of Bertaux (1970) and include also in the working class, rural farm workers, and indeed small farmers. The conditions of life and production of the latter as they evolved throughout the period after 1945 meant, for example, decreased autonomy, due to the development both of vertical integration contracts with firms transforming farm products into industrial ones (canning, etc.) and of horizontal integration through co-operatives, buying groups and so on, which largely acted as capitalist entrepreneurs in relation to their adherents. To place small farmers in the working class is not to deny that there remained important differences between industrial workers and small independent farm producers, but the statistics concerning their participation in the society, in the symbolic and material rewards with which one is dealing here, show clear similarities between the two situations which justify their inclusion in the same group.

Between the bourgeoisie and the working class, and structurally linked to both, came the middle class (*classe moyenne*), composed of two, in certain ways distinct, parts. On the one hand, there still existed the more traditional elements of the petty bourgeoisie, artisans and small independent shopkeepers. These remained closely linked to the grander bourgeoisie throughout most of the period concerned here, the links being expressed, for instance, in voting behaviour and political attitudes, in spite of occasional protest movements such as that led by Poujade in the early 1950s (although this solidarity became increasingly threatened by the effects of the concentration process in industry and commerce which accelerated throughout the 1960s). On the other hand, changes in the economy called into existence and augmented the number of *cadres moyens*, middle supervisory personnel and technical staff, technicians, and in some cases engineers, and intellectural workers such as primary school teachers. In terms of participation in the rewards generated by the economy and in the major institutions of the society, such as the education system, both sections of the *classe moyenne*[2] appeared as in the 'middle' between an upper and a working class but particularly they appeared as 'transition' classes (*classes charnières*)

---

[2] It should be noted that the French terminology differs slightly from the English, the *classe moyenne* appearing lower in the power and prestige scales than the English middle class.

through which people, frequently over two generations, were socially mobile upwards or downwards.

These then are the major groups with whose place in French society this book is concerned. Describing that place has been complicated by the absence of large-scale sociological studies using my framework and terminology. For all their limitations, the most comprehensive and accessible data on the social and economic conditions of France are those gathered by INSEE, whose major categories I, as do many French observers, regroup as follows:

| (2)[3] | patrons of industry and commerce | Bourgeoisie, upper class |
| (3) | liberal professions and cadres supérieurs[4] | (classe supérieure) |

| (4) | cadres moyens—middle and lower management | middle class |
| (5) | white-collar workers, artisans and shopkeepers | (classe moyenne) |

(0)	farmers	working class
(1)	agricultural workers	(classe populaire)
(6)	manual workers	

The above scale may be compared to that of Hall and Jones, and to the Registrar-General's scale used in Britain, and to the new five-point scale developed, also for Britain, by John Goldthorpe and his colleagues carrying out the latest large-scale British style of mobility in England and Wales (Goldthorpe and Hope, 1974).

Status and power

Status in France, with some regional variations in terms of class fraction or stratum concerned, remained over the period very largely correlated with class position in the sense used above. Where finer distinctions

---

[3] The numbers refer to the INSEE code numbers. Groups 7 and 8 are miscellaneous and not counted here.

[4] Cadre has no single English equivalent. Cadres share a broad 'status' reflected in a national pension fund and a trade union, but are much divided. They may be described as representing management in some capacity, but vary from the high level cadres supérieurs (senior executives), though the cadres moyens (middle supervisory staff), down to plant foremen who are often but not always included. The term cadres supérieurs is also used in a wider sense to refer to the élite of the nation. A similar translation problem arises also for the important ingénieurs. 'Engineers' is both too wide and too narrow to render ingénieurs, who acquire their title from the diplomas obtained from one of the technical Grandes Écoles (another translation problem: élite specialist school), and it means broadly that they have specialized in a technical subject at a very high level. As well as a qualification, the term ingénieur also denotes a status or title which in certain firms may be acquired through promotion. In this book both the terms cadre and ingénieur will be left in the original where appropriate.

needed to be made, particularly within the bourgeoisie, status was associated with degree of possession of the *culture générale* and synthesizing minds supposedly imparted by the very highest levels of the education system and which could go far towards 'making a man what he is', recognized as such by his peers. Status change in France largely meant occupational movement which, if upwards, should be accompanied if possible by a diploma, particularly one 'guaranteed' by the State and acquired in the 'proper' fashion through 'normal' progress through the school system. This aspect of status change contributed to making long-distance intra-generational status mobility difficult and its importance did not lessen over the period after 1945. While in the 1930s Goblot could describe possession of the *baccalauréat* examination as the *sine qua non* of bourgeois status, as both the *barrière* and the *niveau*, the post-war growth in numbers in the schools pushed the *barrière* upward towards the Grandes Écoles, particularly the State engineering ones at the highest level, such as the famed École Polytechnique, but also a host of minor ones, whose fight for recognition rather resembled the sans-kritization process used for caste mobility in India.

All aspects of a person's social position may not be entirely congruent and may not change simultaneously, but in French society over the period considered, occupation and social status seem to have been closely linked. As Parkin says, speaking generally of European industrialized countries:

the backbone of the class structure, and indeed the entire reward system of modern western society, is the occupational order. Other sources of economic and symbolic advantage do co-exist alongside the occupational order, but for the great majority of the population these tend to be secondary to those deriving from the division of labour . . . (1972: 18).

In France as elsewhere, material and symbolic rewards were so closely associated that

it is plausible to regard status honour as an emergent property generated by the class system. More concisely, we can consider it as a system of social evaluation arising from the moral judgements of those who occupy dominant positions in the class structure . . . those who control the major agencies of socialisation typically occupy privileged class positions; As a consequence, their definitions of social reality and their moral judgements are far more likely to be blessed with the stamp of public legitimacy than are the social and moral constructs of those in subordinate class positions. (Parkin, 1972: 42)

Evaluation of the place of different groups in French society remained that of the bourgeoisie and it was principally bourgeois constructs which were 'blessed with the stamp of public legitimacy'.

Economic, Social, and Cultural Capital

Analysis of the means by which dominant groups in a society maintain their power in periods of change necessitates analysis of the reproduction of the system of relations within the social structure. In France some such analyses have emphasized the important role of education and cultural inequalities in maintaining the overlap of the three kinds of capital (economic, social, cultural) held by the dominant groups.[5] In the more Marxian tradition, and especially its Althusserian variant, studies made in the late 1960s and especially the early 1970s emphasized the role of other institutions, those of the economic system and those of an ideological kind, such as the mass media and the Catholic Church. Here we use both.

In both, possession of capital is crucial. In Bourdieu's view, 'capital attracts capital' in all three forms, and each form of capital can be used to the maximum only when in conjunction with the others. The basic, and thereby most independent and most powerful, is economic capital, and it alone can be 'cashed' in almost any sector of the society. Social capital assists social placement in all spheres but cultural capital, if unsupported by capital of the other kinds, is only fully effective within the education system. There it is used in its turn in the reproduction not only of cultural capital but also of the whole system. The education system is seen, in modern societies, as the crucial legitimating mechanism; it has the specific function of turning 'natural' attributes into 'social' ones and, even more important, of disguising 'social' attributes as 'natural' ones, thereby hiding the true basis for the distribution of power and privilege in French and other Western advanced industrial societies. Education thus has a legitimating effect as well as being a real mechanism for the transition of privileges and hence of the reproduction of the socio-economic structure.

In any society the distribution and the particular forms and configurations of the different types of capital vary over time with specific economic and social (as well as legal) circumstances. These changes lead to modifications in the ways used by the dominant class to maintain

[5] See especially Bourdieu, 1966a; and 1966b; Bourdieu and Passeron, 1970; Bourdieu, 1971; Bourdieu et al., 1973.

its position and involve groups and individuals, therefore, not only in reproductive but also in 'reconversion' strategies.

The strategies of reproduction through which members, or fractions, of the capital holding classes tend, consciously or unconsciously, to maintain or improve their position in the structure of class relationships, by safeguarding or increasing their capital, constitute a system. The system functions and transforms itself, being the product of one and the same unifying and generating principle. This principle is the class's disposition in relation to the future, which is itself determined by the objective chances of group reproduction, that is, by the class's objective future. The strategies used depend first on the volume and the structure of the capital to be reproduced, that is to say, on the actual and potential volume of the economic, cultural, and social capital possessed by the group and the relative weights of these forms of capital in the patrimonial structure; secondly, they depend on the state (itself a function of the state of relations of force between the social classes) of the system of the instruments of reproduction, institutionalized or not. More precisely, they depend on the relation established at any moment between the patrimony of the different groups and the different instruments of reproduction, which define the transmissibility of the patrimony by fixing the conditions of its transmission, that is to say, the differential return that the different instruments of reproduction are able to offer on the investments of each class or class fraction. (Bourdieu *et al.*, 1973: 61)

In other words, the possibilities of class reproduction depend on the use that can be made in socially defined (institutional and public) situations which surround and determine the varying capital forms available, including in those forms the class's belief in its own future, which belief is itself defined by the system. The uses of capital constitute a system, in which the different parts are interlinked, and the possibilities of use largely determined by the class structure. Bourdieu and his colleagues go on to suggest that:

because strategies of reproduction [also] constitute a system and depend both on the state of the system of the instruments of reproduction (including custom, inheritance laws, labour market, education systems etc.) and on the volume and structure of the capital to reproduce, all change in any of these elements leads to a restructuring of the entire system of reproduction strategies. This restructuring, for the price of a reconversion of the currencies of capital held into other currencies which are more acceptable, profitable, and legitimate [at that time], itself tends to cause a transformation of the patrimonial structure. (Ibid. 61).

This approach, on the one hand, helps us to understand changes such as the explosion in the social demand for education in the 1950s and 1960s in France, and also suggests the importance of the analysis of the power structure, of the interlinking both of the different fields of power and of persons who hold power within them; for the conditions determining the state of the instruments of reproduction are subject to determination by political and economic pressures, which themselves form part of the system of reproduction.

In any society the configurations of capital of the three types may be considered to be in part inherited and in part acquired in each generation.[6] Each type of capital constitutes resources available to families and individuals in differing quantities, which may be used to a greater or lesser degree and with more or less intensity. Resources available at the time were used in specific and different ways by members of the different social classes, both as strategies for change (particularly by individuals) and as strategies for the reproduction of social position (particularly by families, although the distinction between individuals and families here is somewhat artificial), and frequently involved reconversion strategies (Bourdieu *et al.*, 1973).[7]

The social inertia, immobility, of French society of the period, which will be apparent throughout the book, illustrates clearly the narrowness within which such strategies could be exercised by any but the dominant classes. Indeed, the strategies used by the dominant classes effectively limited the chances of success of those of members of the petty bourgeoisie, while rendering those of the working class marginal. At one and the same time the predominance of bourgeois ideology encouraged and legitimated the attempt at movement (for instance, social mobility based on professional mobility made possible through use of the school system, in theory open to all), while making that attempt 'objectively' forlorn and legitimating the 'failure' at the bottom of the social scale by the same criterion as it legitimated 'success' at the top.

---

[6] One may also consider resources as in part private but also in part public; the relationship between the two in terms of use is as important as the quantity of each available.

[7] Analysis in terms of such strategies does not necessarily imply conscious use of them by the actor concerned (indeed their very ˙automatic' nature is frequently an essential ingredient to their full success because it renders them 'invisible' and thereby less vulnerable), but is a heuristic device intended to illustrate the consequences and meanings of certain forms of social action in relation to the configurations of capital available to the actors. The society was not, of course, entirely rigid. There was room for manoeuvre at all levels, for attempts at betterment of oneself or one's children, even where that manoeuvre did not lead to a clear change of class. Investment could be made in a more highly paid job, in better housing, in more 'valuable' cultural activities, and, especially, in education for one's offspring.

2. THE SOCIO-ECONOMIC SYSTEM: THE DISTRIBUTION OF RESOURCES

Changed economic and political circumstances after 1945 in France and Europe generally provided a favourable environment for a rapid and radical transformation of the French economy. A far greater proportion of the population than previously came to be employed in manufacturing industry and in commerce with a correspondingly lesser proportion in agriculture, fisheries, and the extractive industries, with a concomitant geographical movement from country to town. 'Industrialization' as a process has historically tended to involve certain changes, but it does not necessarily have a specific internal momentum; rather it is a social and economic process, with important political components. In each country it takes place in specific social and political conditions and is subject to direct and indirect national and international pressures. From the early nineteenth century industrialization in France was essentially carried out under the control of the industrial and commercial bourgeoisie who were largely also dominant in the political process: after 1945, in spite of the intentions of many members of French society, the important role played by that class remained substantially unchanged.

France in 1945 was a war-ravaged country, both in terms of the destruction of the means of production and the political and social re-ordering made necessary by the years of German occupation and the *Résistance* and, indeed, the repercussions of the pre-war existence, and ultimate failure, of the Popular Front. The precise political manœuvres, divisions, and decisions of the immediate post-war governments and the early years of the Fourth Republic have been well described elsewhere (see for example, Williams, 1964; Werth, 1956). Suffice it to emphasize here the importance of the re-emergence of the internal political divisions almost immediately after the Liberation. The *Résistance* had been an association of Frenchmen not of one but of many political persuasions, who had joined it for a variety of reasons. Even before the Liberation there were splits between the government 'in exile' in Algiers and the *Conseil National de la Résistance* (C.N.R.), to which a number of political parties were affiliated.

The C.N.R. Charter was intended by its authors to become the basic programme of political action after the Liberation, and to make fundamental changes. It involved a programme of far-reaching reforms touching most aspects of French society. On the economic side, there was to be a 'true economic and social democracy', whose establishment involved the removal from the management of the economy of the great bourgeois families and the nationalization of the major means of production, principally sources of energy, minerals, and also insurance and banking. On the social side these economic changes were to be accompanied particularly by a system of social protection, social security and pension provisions, and by an education system open to all according to ability. Both public and private sectors of the economy were to be regulated by a Plan drawn up by the Government after consultation with the major interested parties. Many of the Charter's intentions were, however, stillborn. If it constituted a minimum programme for much of the Left, including, notably, the Communists, who were soon to show their electoral strength and local organisational ability, it threatened many still powerful French sectional interests on certain of whom de Gaulle depended and whose interests he shared, thus ensuring that their representatives would be heard.

Even more important the programme involved enormous capital outlay and investment in productive equipment of all kinds as well as in housing, hospitals, and schools. Only one country seemed able to supply the necessary aid. With the development of the Cold War, American interest in the establishment of a prosperous western Europe intensified and the Marshall Plan finally afforded the capital needed. There were, however, costs to this aid. Although some of the major provisions of the Liberation Charter were indeed carried out—nationalization of, principally, the major banks and insurance companies, of Renault (for collaboration), of gas, electricity, coal, and cement took place, and important social provisions were introduced—the presence of the Communists in the government became impossible, and soon afterwards the power of the unions grouped in the CGT was curtailed by the creation, actively enouraged by the U.S.A. (Godson, 1973–4), of the anti-Communist union confederation Force Ouvrière (FO), which effectively split the labour movement. Moreover, the basic structure of industries, both nationalized and independent, remained virtually unchanged and companies were frequently run by men who had been in power, either as civil servants or business men, before and even during the war. The French sociologist, Raymond Aron, summed up the situation of the time as favourable to the U.S.A. rather than the U.S.S.R. as principal ally for France and suggested the importance of American aid to France even before the Marshall Plan. Aron wrote:

it is not true to say that we depend *equally* on both the giants. For reconstruction we are largely dependent on the U.S.A. Without

American credits even the present mediocre standard of living of the French people would be impossible. Without them there could be no Monnet Plan. Even if the U.S.S.R. wanted to it could not replace the U.S.A. Also, our Empire is dependent on American goodwill. (25 Jan 1947, quoted in Werth, 1956: 350)

Gradually the Communists lost popularity and the Socialists separated from them. American and French government statements constantly harped on the Communist danger and the successful infiltration of their warnings to the public mind was seen in the success of the right-wing Gaullist Rassemblement du Peuple Français (RPF.) In the 1947 elections. The political strength of the RPF. was greatly modified in the polls of 1951, but by that time French public attention was on the Empire abroad, and economic growth at home, in spite of a number of setbacks, to which widespread strikes were a reaction, was beginning to make its effect felt.

The Plan, too, was set up in the early years of the Liberation, and functioned from then on, but the objective of the Plan was technical efficiency through a maximum of information about economic conditions rather than any profound structural reforms, and in any case its provisions were purely indicative.

It is thus apparent that in the crucial early years of the post-war era of 'modernization', the industrialization of the French economy was carried out in a social and political situation which meant little fundamental change in the class structure and left the power balance, both in public and private sectors of the society and economy, much in favour of the bourgeoisie and the upper and middle classes. The labour movement in the 1950s was hampered by strong anti-Communist feeling, by low recruitment and poor finances, as well as by the concentration of public attention on the colonial situation. The very success of the industrialization policy contributed to a weakening labour self-conciousness, as it meant, on the one hand, the dilution of the established working class with many recent migrants from the rural areas and later from abroad, and, on the other, a rise in the standard of living made possible by increased productivity and a high rate of economic growth. The general effects of the reconstruction of cities and the enormous development of numbers in education to some extent offered an image of egalitarianism and fostered the acceptance of notions of progress towards a 'better' society while justifying the apparent transfer of power away from the politicians towards the efficient and 'neutral' technocrats controlling that progress. The effects of economic growth engendered in France, as in Britain, notions such as 'the progressive disappearance of poverty', of 'social mobility through education', and discouraged direct attempts by organized labour to change the class and social structures. In order to examine this more closely, some indication of the major phases of the industrialization process and its important social effects is necessary. The description, like Gaul, is divided into three parts: the history and major features of French economic growth before and after 1945; demographic changes and urbanization; and modifications to occupational groups.

Early and late industrialization: class and social structures

The industrialization of France was, relative to England and Belgium or Germany, late and patchy. What the French historian, George Dupeux (1964), calls the 'massive and generalized union of work and steam power', in other words, the first part of the industrial revolution, principally the growth of the textile industry, began in France late in the first half of the nineteenth century. The revolution in transport—railways and canals—came only well after 1850. Once the industrialization process started it was associated with a series of changes familiar to students of the development of other countries; that is, an internal migration of workers from the countryside to the towns and a consequent increase in the proportion of the urbanized population; a separation of family and work and home work place; and a rise in population migration of workers from the countryside to the towns and a consequent increase in the proportion of the urbanized population; a separation of family and work and home and work place; and a rise in population Industrial and urban development was very uneven, both in intensity and in geographical distribution, and whole areas of France and the lives of the French remained in many ways largely unaffected. As George Dupeux insists, the principal characteristic of French industrial production for most of the nineteenth and early twentieth centuries was the co-existence of archaic, master-man relationships in small workshops of the eighteenth-century type and the modern type of factory. The urban population, too, was clustered in a few large towns while the majority remained in small, largely rural *communes.*[1]

This is not to say that there were not extremely important social consequences of these early movements. In many ways the early days of the industrialization process were fundamental in the formation of the post-1945 social and class structures. During the nineteenth century the industrial and banking bourgeoisie grew and became solidly

---

[1]   The *commune* is the smallest adminstrative unit.

entrenched, spreading sons and influence into politics, the central administration, the education system, and, of course, the dominant ideology, thereby establishing the enduring class basis of French society. Leading families, such as the Schneiders, who grew to predominance in heavy industry in the nineteenth century, still affected the lives of thousands of Frenchmen and women in the post-war period. The great textile families and their affines described by Lambert-Dansette (1954) were still not only directly part of the working lives of the men and women of the north and east of France, but also, indirectly, through their sons who moved into other sectors of the society, continued to affect the destinies of French people everywhere through their political, admininistrative, and cultural activies. To many they still represented a model of French values and ways of life and to many Frenchmen they constituted an archetype of employer, for though the great bourgeois families were few, there existed many who were smaller, more localized, replicas.

Formed at the same time as the bourgeoisie, in the nineteenth century, was the urban, industrial proletariat, beginning in the iron and steel works and textile mills of north, east, and centre, and spreading to allied industries, especially transportation of all kinds. At first the sons of farm workers and small farmers, unused to the conditions of factory work and urban living, soon there were new generations for whom this was their only experience. Their miserable conditions of employment and housing in the iron age of industrial development forged in France a very strong anarcho-syndicalist tradition and a strong belief in class warfare and the desirability of a change from bourgeois capitalism to another type of social and economic organization. The events of the Commune and the formation of the left-wing political parties and trade union movements under the Third Republic, and the ideology of at least the more vociferous parts of these movements, were manifestations of the early and continuing experience of a society based on concepts of work and the distribution of rewards which continued to be predominantly those of bourgeois capitalism, oriented to family control of the means of production and hence of the lives of the workers. This largely continued unchanged throughout the seventy years of the Third Republic and the capitulation of France to Germany in 1940.

After the Second World War, after 1945, for the first time in French history industrialization was on such a massive scale and so far-reaching that it affected the lives of all workers in France. As elsewhere in Europe, there was a gigantic increase in the gross national product, in the productivity of labour and capital, accompanied by considerable income improvement overall, by a move to the towns and urban employment, a growth in population and a change in its distribution by economic sector. Some observers were even led to declare that France changed more in twenty-five years after 1945 than in the preceding hundred years, while others wrote of 'the new French revolution' (Ardagh, 1970).

After 1945, in sharp contradistinction to the early period, rapid economic growth created a mass consumption society. Living standards for the mass of people rose enormously. Important changes in production techniques and the dominance of American economic expansion and of international markets encouraged the formation, and in some crucial sectors domination, of large enterprises, frequently multinational or linked together in vast financial groups (Morin, 1974). Bourgeois capitalism began to give way to monopoly capitalism as the economic form determining the shape of both economy and society. It is important to emphasize, however, that the elements particular to monopoly capitalism were to an important extent superimposed on an economic and social structure which still contained many aspects of the bourgeois capitalism which preceded it. Market conditions, and to that extent production conditions, became determined by the newer forces, but within that framework the organization of much of the productive and distributive process remained bourgeois and petty bourgeois.[2] The working-class movement had still to deal not only with newcomers to its ranks who had recently left the countryside, but also with widely varying working conditions and ideology related to the type of ownership and control of the enterprise, to its size and to the technology used. Further, after the beginning of the economic crisis in 1973, widely differing market conditions of the firm and large-scale unemployment had important effects on union strategies.

The movement from one kind of economy to another was not straightforward and regular and it will be useful to look briefly at the major aspects of the industrialization process.

Industry and economy: growth and stagnation

In France, as in England, industrial development in its first decades was

[2] Government policy, particularly under George Pompidou, was largely favourable to the growth of monopoly capital. The policy had important political repercussions which could be seen in political dissensions between different fractions of the bourgeoisie acting in local and national political instances. See Biarez *et al.* (1973) who analyse the situation in Roanne, a town in the Rhône valley.

begun by iron, coal, and steel and developments in the textile, cotton, wool, and silk industries, and was concentrated in the eastern, northern, and central regions of France, where raw materials and the sources of energy were to be found. While such areas grew rapidly, their industrialization and urbanization (allied to that of the English) were the ruin of such older textile cities as Rouen (Quoist, 1952) and even to some extent of Lyon.

The early industrial initiatives, however, were not substained. Even in the nineteenth century the movement was cyclical; industry grew and then stagnated, grew a little and then declined, and did not immediately lead to major economic and social changes. By 1850 the cotton and silk industries were already growing much more slowly (Dupeux, 1964: 46), although the English inventions (spinning jenny, waterloom, etc.) had only recently and sporadically been introduced. The major factor of growth after 1850 was the construction of railways and allied industries such as coal, steel, and metallurgy. Railways stimulated the growth of the regions which they penetrated, but industrial enterprises largely remained small and geographically concentrated and the depression of the last decades of the nineteenth century slowed development. Urbanization, very rapid between 1851 and 1866, slowed down and became almost stationary in the late nineteenth and the first years of the twentieth centuries. Heavy industry remained concentrated in certain areas and its influence limited. At the end of the nineteenth century France still had many of the characteristics of an agricultural country. The 1891 Census showed that the population living from agriculture was 17·5 million while only 9·5 million lived from industry. In other words, 46 per cent of the population gained its livelihood from agricultural activities while only 25 per cent did so from industry. At the same time five million people lived from income from commerce and transport, two and a half million from the liberal professions, and two million from their *rentes,* mainly from land at home and investment abroad. In 1891, therefore, agriculture provided a source of income for the same number of people as all other activities put together (Dupeux, 1964: 168).

Thus, not only was the France of the late nineteenth and early twentieth centuries not very industrialized in terms of its productive base, but the scale and structure of its enterprises remained small and old-fashioned. Over half of all farms were less than five *hectares*[3] in size, while in industry, in 1906, half the industrial workforce worked in

---

[3] One *hectare* equals two and a half acres.

establishments employing less than five people. Small enterprises continued to proliferate. In 1906 nearly three million persons worked 'alone' (or with their families), and only one million employed one or more workers. Of the industrial workforce 44 per cent were workers and 42 per cent owners. 'On the eve of the first world war the predominant form of enterprise in France was that of the individual or family employing no labour' (Dupeux, 1964: 175).

Capital was placed less in industrial ventures than in securities, particularly land, in foreign banks and shares, or abroad in the newly acquired colonies. By such a bias, capital was turned away from a direct contribution to the productive process. 'This export of capital . . . was largely responsible for the slow development of French industry by depriving it of a part of the capital needed to maintain growth at the same rhythm as that of other European powers and the United States' (Dupeux, 1964: 42). Agriculture, too, developed only very slowly. After the depression and crisis of the 1860s Jules Méline (then Minister of Agriculture) began a policy of protectionsism behind high-tariff walls which permitted small farms to survive with little capital and few improvements. French farmers fed only three to four people when in Britain and the U.S.A. they were feeding ten or more. The conclusion drawn from the experience of this period is that 'the protectionist policy . . . contributed to the sclerosis of the productive structures of the country and in the long run slowed the growth rate of the French economy' (Marczewski, quoted Dupeux, 1964: 44). This was to some extent a deliberate political decision of the time for, after the social upheavals of the middle years of the century and the Paris *Commune* of 1870, Méline and his followers wished to preserve a country of small producers and traders as a 'guarantee' of a stable society. The boom of the first decade of the twentieth century was largely due to the appearance of new textile industries, rayon and artificial fibres, and the development of new industrial sectors such as the mechanical industries, but they were not of a kind or scale to create far-reaching changes and did little to encourage modernization of plant and equipment or of methods of work.

The First World War and its aftermath—boom and bust

In France, as in England, the First World War marked the decline of the old industries. After the war came the development of new industries and sources of energy, especially electricity. New techniques transformed methods of work, with important social consequences for, from 1918 on, the introduction of factories with production-lines involving the 'Taylorization' of the production process led to the birth of a new and important type of worker, the semi-skilled, known as the *ouvrier spécialisé* (or O.S.), and, thus, to a change in the nature of the working class. The main impulse for economic change seems to have been the necessity after the First World War for French industry (and agriculture) to supply a mass market with a reduced labour force: of every ten men between twenty and forty five years of age in 1914, six were either dead or incapacitated in 1918, only four capable of working. At the time of the Armistice, France had mobilized eight million men, 20·5 per cent of her population (against 12·5 per cent in Britain and 3·7 per cent in the U.S.A.) and of these had lost 1,400,000, to which should be added three million wounded, of whom 750,000 were henceforth permanent invalids.

Other factors, too, were crucial. A new source of energy, electricity, began to be developed, and for the first time the State began to interfere between employers and the market mechanisms. There occurred, simultaneously, a loss of monetary stability and a rise in inflation so dramatic that the holders of fixed incomes were ruined by 85 per cent. The social climate began to change. With inflation came periods of boom, slump, and then in the late 1920s a prolonged boom.

A prolonged boom there was but still not a strong economy for, 'hit later than other countries, France was not less gravely hit [by the Depression] and a kind of permanent crisis set in which lasted until the outbreak of the Second World War. In 1938 the volume of industrial production was 15–17 per cent lower than that of 1928 and from 1935–9 the numbers of the unemployed never fell below 350,000' (Dupeux, 1964: 231). Incomes to all productive sectors fell and remained low. The social upheavals, seen in strikes and in the election of the Popular Front Government in 1936, led to apparently spectacular wage rises and increased social benefits for the working class, but because of inflation and the ways in which the social measures were applied real wage rates increased by only about 5 per cent, and Alfred Sauvy has been led to conclude that 'the social results of the policies of the Popular Front were extremely modest, if not negative. No deep or durable reform accompanied them' (quoted by Fohlen, 1966: 155). Opposition from employers, social unrest, inflation, and monetary instability forced successive devaluations. By 1937 industrial production had fallen to less than 25 per cent of that of 1929 and 375,000 persons remained unemployed. Members of the bourgeoisie, who had felt themselves threatened in 1936, immediately afterwards sabotaged all efforts at reform and, with the rise of fascism in Germany, feeling the international climate favourable to them, increased their resistance.

The period after 1945—the 'French miracle'

After 1945, however, France rapidly became an urbanized, indus-trialized country, with a young and increasingly educated population. The 'French miracle', about which many qualified observers in the 1950s still had doubts, was the creation of a modern, widespread industrial base, an improved agriculture, and an urbanized society. An impression of these complex changes can be gained from some figures.

First, we can examine the distribution of the economically active population. Economists often use the proportions of persons employed in the different economic sectors to gauge roughly the development of the economy. The primary sector is composed of agriculture and extractive industries, the secondary of manufacturing industry, and the tertiary of the service sector.

TABLE 2.1.

Distribution of active population by sector percentages

Sector	1851	1901	1931	1936	1954	1962	1968
Primary	53	42	37	37	28	21	16
Secondary	25	31	33	30	36	38	39
Tertiary	22	27	30	33	36	41	45

Source: Adapted from Dupeux, 1964: 33, and 'Données essentielles sur l'économie française., *Écon. & stat.,* 1970: 14.

Agriculture and mining remained important sources of employment right up to the 1960s. Only in 1936 did the secondary sector overtake the importance of the tertiary, but even then agriculture employed more than either of the other two. The real change began to be apparent in 1954 and became more accentuated in 1962 and 1968; agriculture and mining were in clear regression and the tertiary sector progressing particularly fast, but it should be emphasized that although the tertiary sector was growing fast, the secondary sector was also growing and employing increasing numbers of people. International comparisons show that France was not alone in undergoing such changes but also that it was doing so considerably later than the other more advanced countries. France was, therefore, throughout this period, more like Italy and Japan, where agriculture remained more important, than Germany, which had greater concentration on the secondary sector, and England, where more than half the active population belonged to the secondary sector and two fifths to the tertiary, leaving only one tenth in agriculture in 1960 (Dupeux, 1964: 33). In terms of growth of production, too, France's development was more similar to that of Japan and Italy than to that of the U.S.A. and Great Britain, which grew more slowly after 1945. The same picture emerges if one considers productivity per man-hour.

TABLE 2.2.
Rate of annual growth of French economy: percentages

Period	Industry	All prod. activities	Prod. branches and non-prod. services
1896–1913	2·4	1·9	1·8
1913–29	2·6	1·7	1·5
1929–38	−1·1	−0·4	−0·3
1938–49	0·8	0·8	1·1
1949–63	5·3	5·0	4·6
(1949–69)	(5·3)	(5·0)	(4·7)

Source: J. J. Carré. P. Dubois, E. Malinvaud, 1972, 32.

TABLE 2.3.
Growth of production, 1896–1963

Country	Indices–base 100 in 1938							
	1896	1913	1920	1929	1938	1946	1951	1963
Germany*	+70%		+28%				+114%	
						(1945)		
U.S.A.	28	61	72	102	100	177	197	284
France	56	78	67	102	100	79	122	218
	(1902)						(1952)	
Italy	44	67	70	89	100	88	116	231
Japan	8	17	49	58	100		93	250
Great Britain	62	77		82	100	114	126	171

* No detailed figures because of territorial changes
Source: P. Dubois, 1966: 52.

The tables show the importance of the expansion which took place between 1946 and 1969. 'Such rapid growth over twenty years has no precedent in our economic history, neither since the beginning of this century nor probably before' (Carré *et al.*, 1972: 39). This growth took place in phases. First, there was a period of very fast growth 1945–51, due, suggest Carré and his colleagues, to the return to work of home-coming prisoners, to an end to rationing, and to the development of heavy industry. From then on, the development of goods for consumption grew too and overall there were three further periods, 1951–7, 1957–63, 1963–9,[4] each characterized by fast growing, inflation, deflationary intervention by the government in an attempt to stabilize prices, a drop in the rate of growth for a year or two, and then a new start. Gross Product doubled over the period 1949–62 in both industry and agriculture, and household income increased by 130 per cent, but political divisions and compromises and a series of booms, slumps, and inflation, culminating in a series of widespread strikes in the early 1950s, indicated that early growth was uneven and did not benefit all sections of the population equally. Each phase was accompanied by social and industrial unrest, of which the events of 1968 were the most dramatic and widespread example but by no means the only one.

Population–growth in numbers

After 1945 population, particularly through a spectacular increase in the birth rate, grew fast. In the last decade of the eighteenth century the French population numbered twenty seven million. By 1950 it had risen to forty-seven million, and by the census of 1968 to fifty million. France's share of the European population of France, however, dropped. In the 1790s, western Europe numbered 180 million people and by 1950, 550 million; in 1800 the French accounted for 15 per cent of the people of Europe but by 1950 only 7·8 per cent. In the first half of the twentieth century the French population increased by only 7·5 per cent, while during the same period that of Europe grew by one third (Dupeux, 1964: 10), but after 1945 it grew extremely fast, so fast that by the mid-1960s one third of the entire population was in school.

The history of French population changes has been similar to that of industrial growth–periods of boom, slump and stagnation. After a period of growth in the nineteenth century the 1914–18 war dealt a severe blow to the growth in numbers, for many women remained unmarried and those who did marry tended to have small families, which has led to their being called the 'empty classes', the *classes creuses*. In the 1930s the economic crisis caused a drop in both birth-

---

[4]   From 1973 France was, of course, affected by the results of the oil crisis, as well as other longer-term trends in the international economy, and economic growth dropped radically while inflation remained high and unemployment rose, and this may constitute a fourth period.

and marriage-rates and during the ten years from 1935 to 1945 the death-rate actually exceeded the birth-rate. During the Second World War, almost a million people lost their lives but nevertheless after the war the birth-rate swung dramatically upward, to 40 per cent above that of 1939. Between 1860 and 1946 the French population grew by three million persons—between 1946 and 1961 by five million. After 1972, however, the birth-rate began again to fall, to the expressed alarm of the Government.

To the rise in the birth-rate was added the increased rate of immigration to France of the ten to fifteen years after 1960. At the end of the Algerian war 90,000 French Algerians and *harkis*[5] were repatriated to France and after 1960 increased worker immigration from southern Europe, North Africa, and black Africa was such that by 1970 immigrants probably accounted for about two million people, 4 per cent of the population of France, constituting nearly 10 per cent of all employed persons and an important sector of the working class.[6]

Size of labour force

The economic growth of France was achieved with an active population virtually unchanged in size since the beginning of the century. Only in the late 1960s did the number of employed people increase to any real extent, with young people born after 1945 coming into the labour market and marked increases in the proportion of women, especially

TABLE 2.4.
Evolution of the total employed population, 1896–1968

Years	No. millions	%
1896	19·5	51
1906	19·8	51
1926	20·3	50·5
1936	19·3	47
1946	19·4	48·5
1954	19·6	45·5
1962	19·7	42·5
1968	20·6	41

Source: Carré *et al.*, 1972:77.

[5] *Harkis* are the Muslim Algerians who fought on the side of the French in the Algerian war and after the war mostly had to leave Algeria.
[6] Immigrants came off badly on most counts where inequality was concerned. Until the mid-1960s, however, many immigrants, notably North Africans, were counted as French and did not appear separately in the statistics on income, etc.

married women, in paid employment. It is notable that the proportion of the employed in the total population declined over the period, being smaller in 1968 than in 1896.

Not only did French economic growth occur without any significant increase in the active population, but it occurred with a heavy proportion of inactive persons to be supported by the active and at a time when the cost of such inactive persons was increasing fast with the increased investment in education, rise in social security payments, etc. Such figures clearly translate the increases in labour productivity that occurred throughout the period and indicate the causes of some of the social problems encountered.

Economic structure: enterprises and labour market

Fundamental changes in the economic base of a society necessarily involve changes in the structure of employment—the kind of jobs available—and an analysis of these both suggests the possibilities open to an individual and indicates the shape of the over-all structure. The employment market is partly a function of the size and type of firm, the technology employed, and the legal mode of ownership and control. Particularly in the 1960s Government policy, supported by men such as Georges Pompidou, encouraged considerable American investment in French companies, and brought with it a series of mergers and the formation of new important industrial and financial groups. Crucial enterprises in important sectors of the economy—such as electronics, the electrical industry, petro-chemicals, etc.—thus became part of American controlled corporations[7] or, through mergers and sales, came to be the dominant few in their sector in a situation of oligopoly, or effective monopoly. This process involved the disappearance of a number of medium-sized firms, in particular in such sectors as the textile industry, which had previously been important in their field. It also meant the disappearance of many small ventures while many others, though remaining in existence, became effectively dominated by the larger ones, or indeed legally so dominated, the previous owner staying on as manager (*gérant*), for instance. After a first wave of concentration of medium-sized firms came a new wave after 1965 of the merging of large ones (Carré *et al.*, 1972: 226–8). Particular sectors were especially affected, whether considered in terms of the numbers employed or as percentage of production in the sector.

[7] See for instance the case of the only major French computer firm, Bull, taken over by the American firm of Honeywell.

Moreover, many of these firms, including all the two hundred biggest industrial firms and the forty biggest banking ones, were at the head of important groups and control led the financial co-ordination of their many sub-units. Morin (1974: 24) quotes the 1966 INSEE census of industrial firms as showing that 529 firms, 0·01 per cent of all firms (those employing more than 1,000 people) employed two million persons, nearly 40 per cent of all persons in industry. A very large proportion of industrial workers thus depend directly on a very few firms. The same survey also showed that half of the turnover of all French industry was realized by 0·2 per cent of firms. The annual report of the Commission des Opérations en Bourse also showed that in 1972 the thirty-one French companies with a capital of more than one thousand million francs represented 40 per cent of all the stock-exchange capitalization (Morin, 1974: 24). The grouping into this form of monopoly capital essentially took place in the late 1960s and was especially brought about, not only by foreign capital, but also by firms controlled by managers rather than families (*sous contrôle technocratique*) (ibid.: 25), and particularly under the impulsion of finance capital (Diman, 1972), which process has itself accelerated since 1971 (Morin, 1974).

Many medium-sized firms, then, disappeared along with the very small in the late 1950s and early 1960s, even before the great concentration movement at the top. Many, however, remained, and had their own 'union' organization, that of the Petites et Moyennes Entreprises (P.M.E.), and in the last Messmer Government under President Pompidou the small firms had their own Minister, Monsieur Royer, and retained an important place in the French economy and in the working lives of French people as 60 per cent of the non-agricultural labour force continued to work in such firms.

The few very large firms employed almost half of the active population in industry. Here it is also important to distinguish between size of enterprise and size of establishment. In the latter, on the contrary, a very large proportion of the population was employed in small to medium establishments as well as in small firms. The following three tables show first the change in the industrial sector (by establishment) in France over forty years and then some international comparisons and, finally and most important, the distribution by size of industrial *enterprise* in France in 1968.

The first table shows the striking immobility between 1926 and 1966 of numbers employed in industrial enterprises of any given size, in spite of the enormous production changes of the period; it is especially striking that in 1966 a smaller proportion of economically active people

TABLE 2.5.
Population employed in industrial establishments: percentage

No. of persons employed	1926	1931	1936	1954	1962	1966
11–20	10	10	10	8	8	8
21–50	15	15	15	16	15	16
51–100	12	12	12	12	13	13
101–200	30	30	13	14	14	14
201–500			17	17	18	19
501–1000	33	33	11	12	12	12
+1000			22	21	20	18
Total	100	100	100	100	100	100

Source: Carré *et al.*, 1972:220.

TABLE 2.6.
Population in industrial enterprises, international comparisons: percentage

No. workers per establishment	France 1862	FRG* 1961	Belgium 1963	USA 1963	Italy 1961	Japan 1963	Netherlands 1962
10–49	21	16	17	13	26	32	17
50–99	12	10	11	10	14	13	24
100–499	34	29	31	32	30	26	15
500–999	12	12	14	13	11	11	13
1000 +	21	33	27	32	19	18	31
Total	100	100	100	100	100	100	100

* Federal Republic of Germany.
Source: Carré *et al.*, 1972: 223.

TABLE 2.7.
1968 population employed by size of industrial enterprise

Industry (not bldg.)	Total	0–9	10–44	50–199	200–499	500–999	1000–4999	5000 +
No. of enterprises	351,603	302,739	34,878	10,301	2,350	776	478	81
No. of workers	5,476,500	421,800	766,600	975,700	712,100	532,600	901,900	1,165,300
No. of workers %	100	7·7	14·0	17·8	13·0	9·7	16·5	21·3

Source: 'Données essentielles sur l'industrie française', *Écon. et stat*', 1970, No. 14, p. 46.

worked in establishments of more than 1,000 people than did in 1954 or even 1936. Similarly, in relation to size of enterprises (Table 1.7) although one cannot compare over time, out of 350,000 industrial enterprises in France in 1968, 345,000 employed fewer than 200 people and 300,000 fewer than ten people. Even in terms of proportion of the industrial labour force alone, nearly 40 per cent worked in enterprises employing less than 200 people. (If to this are added the building trades, not included above but employing one in ten of all French active persons, there emerges the true social and economic importance of the smaller enterprise.) On the other hand, those with more than 1,000 employees employed another 40 per cent. That is, there occurred a considerable amount of polarization with the small and medium-sized enterprises and establishments on the one hand and the very large on the other, each constituting the framework of their working life for nearly half the French population employed in industry.

The petty bourgeoisie in the traditional sense of small owners, therefore, could be seen to still be very much in existence between 1945 and 1975, and their enterprises formed the framework for the working life of slightly more than half of the French population active in industry and a similar proportion in commerce.

The peasantry were very hard pressed by economic changes after 1945, and the policy of both the Government and the Common Market authorities was for long to encourage, while also to some extent trying to 'soften', the flight from the land, first of farm workers and then of small farmers, which became known as the 'rural exodus'. In spite of the drastic fall in the proportion of farmers in the active population (from 21 per cent in 1954 to 12 per cent in 1968) farm size remained on the whole very small, and farms were overwhelmingly worked only by members of the owners' families. In the mid-1960s Salais shows that average farm size was seventeen *hectares* but also that in 1967 one third of the cultivable land was in holdings of less than twenty *hectares* (50 acres); only 30 per cent of farms had more than fifty *hectares*, including 13 per cent with more than 100 *hectares*. Two thirds, 65 per cent of farms were run by the owner, with 27 per cent being rented from one or more landlords under *fermage* (lease) agreements and 8 per cent worked under the old system of *métayage* (share-cropping) whereby 'rent' for the land worked is paid in kind. Of the nearly two million or so farms existing in the early 1960s only 100,000 employed workers from outside the family and of these 85 per cent had only one to two workers (Maillet, 1967: 9). There still existed, therefore, in France a fairly numerous class of small peasant farmers, and the proportions of holdings of 1–20 *hectares*, 20–50 *hectares*, and more than 50 *hectares* remained virtually unchanged at least until 1955 (Carré *et al*, 1972: 230). On the other hand, the class of agricultural workers was tiny. These small units showed themselves unable to compete in an open market for agricultural produce, and the crisis in agriculture became again more serious in the early 1970s after the period of relative calm which followed the riots of the late 1950s and the agricultural orientation laws of 1960 and 1962.

The employed population

Linked to the phenomena described above, the employed population underwent a number of important changes. The most important of these was the rise to predominance of salaried workers. Out of twenty and a half million active persons in 1968, 15,215,000 were salaried, 2,700,000 more than in 1954. Between 1954 and 1969 the proportion of salaried persons grew from 62 to 74–6 per cent, increasing fast both proportionately and in absolute terms, (Le Capitalisme monopoliste d'état, 1972: 193). The following table shows their distribution by socio-professional category and sex in relation to that of employers and independents. Some groups were increasing, other declining, both in absolute and in proportionate terms.

TABLE 2.8.
Structure of active population, 1954–68: percentage

Socio-professional category	Men and Women			Men			Women		
	1954	1962	1968	1954	1962	1968	1954	1962	1968
Employers–industry and commerce	12	11	10	12	10	10	13	11	10
Liberal professions– *cadres supérieurs*	3	4	5	4	5	6	1	2	3
Cadres moyens	6	8	10	6	7	9	6	9	11·5
White-collar workers	11	12·5	15	8	8	9	16	21	26
Manual workers	34	37	38	40	44	46	22	23	22
Service personnel	5	5	6	2	2	2	12	13	13
Farmers	21	16	12	19	15	11·5	25	18	13
Farm workers	6	4	3	8	6	4	3	1	1
Others	3	3	3	3	3	3	2	2	1·5
Total	100	100	100	100	100	100	100	100	100

Source: Adapted from R. Salais, 1969: 889.

Groups in decline

Agriculture and mining   The major occupational groups in decline were, of course, those in the extractive industries and agriculture. Miners lost 25 per cent of their number between 1962 and 1968. Agriculture lost 15 per cent of its labour force between 1954 and 1962 and another 25 per cent between 1962 and 1968. The early migrants were farm labourers, and particularly women, but soon came to include large numbers of farmers. The great majority of farm migrants joined the manual working class as holders of unskilled jobs—30 per cent became labourers, *manoeuvres*, 20 per cent went into the building trades and 14 per cent into transport, so that the proletarianization of these migrants was rapid and almost total. Only 7,500 out of the 80,000 persons leaving agriculture each year could be accommodated on Government re-training schemes, and there were no means whereby agricultural diplomas could be converted into equivalents useful elsewhere (de Farcy, 1971: 22). Of the women who left farming, the great majority were absorbed into the category 'service personnel' which covers cleaners, waitresses, and other basically unskilled jobs, as well as the skilled such as nursing and social work which, although growing fast, did not allow much possibility for entrants with the low general education usually possessed by farm migrants. Essentially, then, migrants from agriculture went to swell the numbers of the urban manual working class.

Entrepreneurs and employers   Small entrepreneurs and employers in industry and commerce also decreased in numbers. 'Independents' declined by 12 per cent between 1954 and 1962 and after that dropped further. They still constituted, however, about 6–7 per cent of the active population in the late 1960s and were important both as a reference group for many workers and to some extent as a real means of upward social mobility through a change of status from 'wage-earner' to 'independent' (Andrieux and Lignon, 1960; Frisch, 1966). Although the over-all number of small enterprises, particularly in commerce, declined, it did not decline very fast and there were important differences among the different kinds of enterprises. While food and haberdashery shops decreased in number, do-it-yourself, furniture, clothing and other very specialized *boutiques* did well (Parodi, 1971: 200). Over the period 1954–1968 the number of *patrons* in industry and commerce fell only by 340,000, whereas two million persons left agriculture. These figures support the contention of Poulantzas (1974) and Baudelot *et al.* (1974) that the petty bourgeoisie still existed as a significant sub-class in French society and that the independent and small employers formed a major part of it over the period considered here.

The expanding groups

Technicians   Massive industrialization and 'modernization' of the economic infrastructure created new kinds of jobs and greatly expanded certain varieties of existing employment. Much sociological attention particularly in France has been concentrated on the increase in demand for technicians and *cadres* of all kinds, whose ranks are often thought to constitute an avenue of social mobility *par excellence* for sons of the working classes into the lower sections of the *classe moyenne* as technicians and for the sons of the *classe moyenne* to rise and become *cadres supérieurs*. There indeed took place a considerable rise in their numbers, but the consequences of it have been greatly exaggerated. The ranks of the technicians, defined as persons playing an intermediary role between the *ingénieurs* and the lower echelons of the productive system, grew by 67 per cent between 1954 and 1962, and continued to grow afterwards, though more slowly (d'Hugues and Peslier, 1969: 267), so that by 1968 there were more than 500,000. Such growth is impressive, but in order to consider their importance for social mobility, and hence the effect they might have on the class system, what is important is their proportion in the total labour force, and, especially in France, their geographical distribution. For since not all industries expanded their numbers of technicians and *cadres*, the opportunities were not evenly spread over the country as a whole. Not only were they particularly concentrated in such industries as aerospace and petro-chemicals and particularly located in the Paris area (Legoux, 1959), but the total group of technicians constituted only around 2–4 per cent of the active non-agricultural population over the period concerned. The capacity of the category to absorb newcomers was not, therefore, very considerable in relation to the total labour force and by no means constituted a major avenue for professional and hence social advancement.

Ingénieurs and cadres   The same is true of *ingénieurs*, for although their numbers rose by 25 per cent between 1954 and 1962, by the latter date they constituted less than 1 per cent of the active non-farm population, including both those with diplomas and the self-taught. Geographically, they were at least as concentrated as the technicians.

The administrative hierarchy could theoretically be important for social mobility in the middle levels. However, although middle administrative personnel, *cadres administratifs moyens*, increased by 34 per cent between 1962 and 1968, they then constituted only 2·5 per cent of the active non-farm population, and other supervisory personnel were in a similar position.

Considerable growth occurred, too, at the more general higher levels, to the extent that in the 1968 Census nearly one million *cadres supérieurs* could be found. However, this figure is highly misleading as the INSEE category in use at the time was very diverse and included members of the liberal professions, bankers, librarians, magistrates and police officers, senior management, including *ingénieurs,* and teachers in secondary and higher education. It is clear that in total, the *cadres supérieurs* were still a very small percentage of the active population—4·8 per cent in 1968 as against 3 per cent in 1954. Moreover, the different professions included grew at different rates; while between 1962 and 1968 the whole category grew by 30 per cent, the highest growth rate was found among the teaching and scientific professions, which grew by two thirds (*Écon. & stat.* 40, 1972: 53) but which do not, because of their reliance on high-level educational diplomas, offer much opportunity for children from working class homes.

Two further points of importance deserve emphasis in the context of the present book. The first is that access to positions of power in organizations, through the growth of power (decision-making) positions, represented by *cadres suérieurs* in the more limited sense, grew only by 26–30 per cent; in other words, it did not widen considerably. The second is that one of the major results of the high level of education was to renew and increase the ranks of the educators, a 'reproductive effect' as Bourdieu points out.

White-collar workers   Even where opportunities at lower levels were concerned they remained limited. Thus, while the category of white-collar, non-manual workers grew fastest of all, its biggest sector was that of office workers which by 1962 involved more than one and a half million people, 10 per cent of the active population excluding those engaged in agriculture. This was a sector which largely employed women—one in every five of all working women—and was well known as one with few or no chances of promotion. Moreover, as work by French sociologists such as Crozier (1965) has shown, the conditions of work and payment of many persons in that category were deteriorating and brought them closer to those of the manual working class—a situation for which Lockwood (1958) found parallels in England in the 1950s.

Manual workers   The manual working class grew throughout the period. Increased employment in other sectors by no means diminished the numbers employed in manual occupations. While half the new jobs created were in the tertiary sector, many of these were for *ouvriers* and frequently basically unskilled. Between 1962 and 1968, workers' numbers increased by 9 per cent (nearly 11 per cent if men are counted alone), comprising 7,698,000 out of a total labour force (including agriculture) of 20,439,160 persons, about 38 per cent of the active population, excluding agricultural workers. Indeed, workers' numbers were not only increasing but they were also increasing faster than the labour force, 9 per cent as against 6 per cent (men alone nearly 11 per cent). It is clear therefore that a greater proportion of the population than ever before found itself within the manual working class.

Closer examination of the composition of that class shows that although it was the élite, foremen (*contre-maîtres*), whose numbers increased most, by 16–17 per cent, skilled workers' numbers also increased, by 14 per cent, and were closely followed by those of the semi-skilled, the OS, which grew by 13 per cent. The unskilled *manoeuvres* declined but only by one half of one per cent (Parodi, 1971: 268–9). Moreover, the 1971 INSEE survey carried out on industrial enterprises employing more than ten people showed that, of industry's salaried employees, *ouvriers* formed 70 per cent and, of these, one-half (one-third male) were either *ouvriers spécialisés* or *manœuvres*, that is, semi- or unskilled (Cézard, 1972: 49–51). As many of the jobs offered on the labour market were still unskilled or of low skill requirement, there persisted considerable limitations on upward movement within the working class. This remains true even though many of the two million immigrant workers undertook the least skilled work while the French workers essentially competed for the more skilled, better-paid jobs, at least in the more urbanized and industrialized areas of France, for in some regions foreign workers were concentrated in certain industries such as building and public works (Minces, 1973; Granotier, 1973 edn).

Urbanization

The industrialization process also involved a change of habitat and a geographical re-distribution of the population. People had to migrate not only from rural areas to towns but also between regions and particularly to to the Paris area which came to contain about one fifth of the total population. This re-distribution and its speed are important to an understanding of the social structure of France after 1945 and the social problems apparent. Following industrial growth, in the nineteenth century there was rapid movement away from the countryside into pre-existing towns, which grew in size, and the creation of new towns in areas previously largely rural. As industrialization slowed, so too did the drift to the the towns. In 1800 the French urban population was 20 per cent and in 1846 was still less than one quarter of the population; by 1901 only 40 per cent of the population was urban, reaching barely more than 50 per cent of the late 1940s. In 1968, however, 70 per cent of French people were living in urban centres of more than 2,000 inhabitants.

Northern towns and other major manufacturing centres and some ports grew first. Until about the mid-point of the last century the population of all *départements* increased, but due to changing employment and communication conditions some regions began to lose both relatively and absolutely. First mountainous but later all rural regions became, though unequally, adversely affected. Especially Aquitaine, the west, the east, and the Paris basin decline; those areas which already contained a big town tended to grow. The process of urbanization and regional migration was thus everywhere intense but not equally distributed. A pattern of 'swallow migration', familiar to students of urbanization in Latin America, developed, with migrants going from country to small town and small town to city or capital, as well as directly from country and small town to capital, Paris, which in the 1950s grew at the tremendous rate of 120,000 families a year. Small towns lost to the bigger ones, creating an important disequilibrium and exacerbating the crisis in housing, education, and other public services.

TABLE 2.9.
Growth of the urban population, 1946–62

	Population in thousands		Rate of growth %
	1946	1962	
Urban population (towns of more than 2000)	21,724	28,105	+ 29
Communes of:			
5,000–9,999	3,246	3,875	+ 19
10,000–19,999	3,043	3,974	+ 31
20,000–49,999	3,922	5,918	+ 50
50,000–99,999	2,195	2,195	+ 45
100,000–199,999	1,843	3,097	+ 68
200,000 + (not Paris)	4,750	5,293	+ 15
Paris	2,725	2,753	+ 1

Source: Dupeux, 1969: 16.

TABLE 2.10.

Urban population and total population: percentages

Year	Total population (millions)	Urban population	
		% total population	millions of inhabitants
1901	39·0	40·9	16,0
1921	39·1	46·3	18,1
1946	40·1	54·7	22
1962	46·2	64·0	29,5
1968	50·8	66·2	33,6
1985*	60·0	77·0	44

* projected
Source: Lacombe, 1971: 132.

By 1968 thirty-seven towns of more than 100,000 inhabitants included 19 per cent of the population, and half the French population lived in towns of more than 10,000 inhabitants. By 1985 the proportion of urban-dwellers will probably be double that of 1946. Massive urbanization, due both to 'pull' factors from the big towns, where most new jobs were created, and to 'push' factors from the countryside and very small towns, where the increasingly unfavourable conditions for small farmers and very small businesses meant that the only possibility was migration, exacerbated transportation, housing, and other difficulties, unsolved by Government policies, which hit the poorer sections of the population particuarly hard.

Regional opportunities

Already by the late 1950s technicians were principally to be found in the energy and chemical industries (Legoux, 1959), and in 1971 it was the energy sector which employed the lowest proportion of OS and *manœuvres,* less than 10 per cent as against 25 per cent *cadres,* (Cézard: 1972), while in industries such as mining, textiles, and furniture, the proportion of unskilled and semi-skilled workers could be as much as half and seldom less than 25–30 per cent (ibid.). These industries tended to be concentrated in certain regions. The Paris region in 1962 contained 18 per cent of the population but employed 49 per cent of the *ingénieurs* and 70 per cent of all research personnel (Praderie, 1968: 55). Big towns were the least 'manual'. Service industry towns tended to grow fastest. While very few industrial jobs were created in Paris, and while manufacturing industrial towns in general—textile, steel, and heavy engineering—tended to lose population or remain stable, towns such as

Grenoble, with its high technology industries, and tourist towns such as Annecy, or Montpellier grew extremely fast. Many people, however, remained in small urban areas and relatively isolated from the centres of non-manual employment and modern amenities of all kinds. If in the late 1960s 50 per cent of the French population lived in towns of over 10,000, in 1968 30 per cent lived in *communes* of less than 2,000, and of those one third in *communes* of less than 500 (Hémery, 1972: 872).

Summary

In sum, then, the French economy changed, in terms of its own history, exceptionally fast after 1945. These changes involved a certain redistribution of population in terms of occupation—fewer peasants, fewer *patrons* and independents, more *cadres* and white-collar workers but also, importantly, more manual workers. The wave of concentration of enterprises hit first small and medium-sized firms and then large ones, so that by 1975 the structure was dominated in certain key sectors by a few giant organizations (some of which were nationalized industries), while nevertheless there continued to exist alongside a powerful national bourgeoisie, a petty bourgeoisie, an *artisanat*, and a class of peasant farmers all of whom remained important in the political life of the country. The industrialization process, accompanied by demographic increase for the first time in several decades, also involved a radical geographical redistribution of the population into urban centres and thus the creation of urban social problems on a massive scale.

3. ACCESS TO REWARDS

Two features remained particularly salient in French society between 1945 and 1975. The first was unequal access by individuals to nearly all the socially available 'rewards' generated by the socio-economic system, an inequality patterned by the place of the recipient in the productive process. Secondly, there was a clear clustering of rewards; individuals who had privileged access to income also did well in relation not only to rewards directly purchasable, such as housing or consumer goods, but even to those supposedly 'redistributed' by specific social intervention such as social transfer payments. At the same time, those who were privileged where receipt of rewards was concerned were inversely privileged in relation to the distribution of 'risks', such as unemployment, accident, or sickness. The diagram on p. 40 may serve as a useful summary. The nature-culture dichotomy which crowns the diagram indicates the principal way in which the system was justified, that is, through the education system and the attempted creation of meritocracy such that each person, and hence group, appears in its 'natural' place. The schema is not intended to be exhaustive and each column does not necessarily correspond to its opposite. It indicates the areas of clustering which can be related to particular places in the occupation structure of the period.

Capital and patrimony

The ownership of productive capital is crucial not only to the class structure but also to the distribution of income, but French official statistics on this are almost totally lacking. It is evident, however, that where there exist small businesses there exist small capital-holders, and the same is probably true of the medium-sized firms of which there continued to be many. Moreover, many large companies were owned and/or controlled by individual families. A study by François Morin shows that even in the late 1960s and early 1970s, of the two hundred biggest French industrial companies, half were family controlled and of these, thirty-six had absolute family majority control and forty-three absolute minority control (Morin, 1974: 65). Of the twenty biggest firms, six were controlled by single families (ibid: 91). Morin's data show, too, that many more families were involved as important shareholders in the remaining largest firms. Family control and concentrated family interests were particularly important in merchant banking and

The diagram reads from the bottom to the top.

culture	nature
participation in collective life	
+	−
leisure holidays	delinquency punishment
consumption expenditure	working conditions hours worked
housing	life expectancy
tax { social security	sickness accident
revenues	unemployment chances/length
occupation	
income { labour capital	

textiles. Unfortunately, although many books appeared in the ten years after 1960, analysing the process of concentration within French industry and commerce, little attention was paid to the distribution of shareholding, landholding, etc. in relation to individual members of the French bourgeoisie and aristocracy, and few data are available.

Similarly, although a first attempt was made at the examination of capital-holding through 'savings surveys' carried out by INSEE on 2,000–3,000 families in 1967 and 1969, the surveys do not cover precisely the people who are likely to own the most capital, the *patrons* of industry and commerce and members of the liberal professions. Data exist only on employed person (*salariés*) and the inactive, mainly the retired. However, even with these severe limitations, the studies shed some light on the distribution of at least certain forms of capital, and by pointing to the concentration in the higher income ranges may give some indication of the sections not covered directly. The results are summarized in Table 3.1.

TABLE 3.1.

*Distribution of different types of capital
by socio-professional category, 1966: percentages*

Socio-professional category	% of households*	Real Estate	Life Insurance	Loans and Obligations	Shares	Bonds	Savings Accounts	Bank accounts (cheque)	Real Estate debts	Average Value total capital F
Manual workers	32	18	36	4	1	12	21	9	39	35,000
White-collar workers	10·5	8	9	2	1	2	11·5	13	15	46,000
Cadres moyens	14	22	22	8	17	6	16	29·5	26	92,000
Cadres supérieurs	5	14	24	16	46	7	10	20·5	13	214,000
Inactive	36	34	6	54	29	69	40	23	3	61,000

* employed and inactive only.
Source: L'Hardy, 1973: 8–9.

Commenting on this table L'Hardy points out that 'stratification by social status shows up strong inequalities. The most typical case is that of shares: *cadres supérieurs* (5 per cent households) hold 46 per cent of all shares while manual workers (32% households) only hold 10 per cent of them. The weight of the *cadres supérieurs* can be seen, moreover, for all forms of capital, although in varying degrees: high for shares, low for bonds which are mainly held by other households, and savings accounts which are distributed very equally. The other social categories seem each to prefer different forms of saving; life insurance for manual workers, savings accounts and bank accounts for white-collar workers and *cadres moyens*, bonds etc., for the inactive.' For the lower income group, debts for real estate—home-ownership mainly—weighed heavy.

Even with the limitations on the data noted above, the concentration of the different forms of saving in the higher income groups is very clear; households declaring annual incomes of more than 50,000 f. represented only 2·6 per cent of the population studied but held 43 per cent shares, 24 per cent bank accounts, 21 per cent loans and obligations, 18 per cent of life insurance, and 11·5 per cent of real estate.[1]

[1] In relation to the shares, however, it must be emphasized that the percentages relate only to the shares owned by the households in the study—*not* to the totality of shares which cannot be estimated from these data.

This book was finished when new studies on patrimony and capital ownership appeared. Presenting them under the title, 'Inequality of fortunes in France is greater than imagined' (*Le Monde*, 18 June 1976: 21 and 25), Mathieu points out that 5 per cent of shareholders hold 42 per cent of all shares and 37 per cent of all other forms of financial participation. Indeed, the same 5 per cent also own 35 per cent of all bank current accounts and 30 per cent of all immovable property. Nine per cent of French households own 60 per cent of all financial titles (shares, bonds, etc.) while 60 per cent of the population own only 8 per cent. The number of shares and bonds held by members of the liberal professions is seventy-five times greater than that held by workers and twenty times greater than that held by *cadres moyens*. Members of the liberal professions and *cadres supérieurs*, less than 7 per cent of the population, own 39 per cent of all shares, bonds and other titles, a portfolio six times heavier than their weight in the population. Workers, 33 per cent of the population, only own 5 per cent of the portfolio. These figures are striking, even though much capital owned is in fact left out of account in the studies—INSEE did not include capital owned by individuals considered as part of their enterprises, i.e. the value of the business (*fonds de commerce*, etc.), business premises, some housing and bank accounts, land, buildings, and equipment belonging to farmers. Moreover, INSEE only included principal residences and not holiday houses nor even buildings owned and rented out. Gold, foreign currency, and money was excluded. Mathieu concludes that comparison with earlier studies suggests that in this way, nearly half, 40 per cent, of the total patrimony held by the French is excluded from the study. Were this to be included the range of inequality in capital-holding would undoubtedly be far greater still. The situation changed little between 1966 and 1972, essentially, according to INSEE, because of family property passed on through gift and inheritance.

Capital gains

The amount of capital held at one time is important, but so too is the rate at which it grows. In 1962 Gilbert Mathieu (1962, 15) quoted M. Martin, an investor invented by the financial journal *La Vie française*, who invested one million old francs in 1947 in shares and saw his invest-ment grow to over twenty million A.F.[2] by March 1962, although it

---

[2] A.F. = *anciens francs*, old francs, before the 1959 devaluation; N.F. = *nouveaux francs*, as from 1959. 100 A.F. = 1 N.F. f. in the text below always refers to new francs.

fell back to eighteen million as Wall Street dropped. In all probability many investments grew similarly over the same period, although 1962 was a high point and many have done less well since, and although the 1970s may be less favourable to capital they will probably not be very favourable to salaries either. M. Martin perhaps did better than many other investors but INSEE studies on French share prices also showed that between 1953 and 1961 the nominal value of shares had risen 315 per cent, a real rise of 203 per cent, whereas salaries only rose by two thirds over the same period. The revenues gained from these investments rose at a real rate of 23 per cent (68 per cent nominal increase) which, as Mathieu points out, is 'not bad for their owners who have merely had to leave their share titles in the bank'. The average real salary rises at the same time for full-time workers were around 25 per cent.

The rise in capital values can be further seen by examining the rise in life assurance values and above all of gold, held by many French investors, and finally of land. Many families who owned other forms of capital also owned life insurance which, on a with-profits basis, grew particularly fast during the 1960s. Gold, which, according to recent INSEE surveys, had a negative rate of interest in the early 1960s, later had a positive one, and represented a very considerable capital gain. Land prices, too, began to rise fast as investors sought a *valeur refuge; Le Monde* of 21 November 1972 pointed out that the price of agricultural land had more than doubled in ten years and in 1973 it rose more than in the ten preceding years. Farmers, after a couple of good years, were trying to extend their holdings but, as a study by the Ministry of Agriculture showed:

more than specifically agricultural circumstances, it is the whole monetary situation which explains the size of the price rises. As almost always in periods of all-round price rises, land appeared to be the safe-value (*valeur refuge*) *par excellence*, allowing investors to protect themselves against inflation. This is not new but seems to have played a particularly important role in 1973 and has led to an increase in demand for land from non-farm sources. . .' (*Écon. & stat.* 59, 1974: 48)

Thus, capital holders largely managed to increase their capital assets (and frequently their incomes) at a greater rate than did salaried personnel, an increase greatly facilitated by the absence of a capital gains tax in France. Indeed holders of shares which made, often nominal, losses could set those losses against their income tax, as did M. Chaban-Delmas amongst other notables, thus diminishing their tax burden and contributing doubly to the perpetuation of fiscal inequality.

The division of reward—income

Breadth and depth—salary and income ranges

A historical perspective is essential to any discussion of the 'sharing of fruits of growth', to use the French Government phrase, and to an analysis of the extent to which different sections of the population benefited from economic changes after 1945. It is, however, difficult to provide this, as Mathieu (1962) points out, for until 1961, official statistics on income distribution were lacking, as only one third of the population even filled in a tax form. The only reasonable information available was on salaries as employers made the declarations.

Before, however, discussing changes in the range of incomes over time, some basic data[3] must be given.

In the social reforms of the Liberation period in France a guaranteed minimum wage was introduced, first for industrial and tertiary sector workers, the SMIG (Salaire Minimum Interprofessionnel Garanti), and then for agricultural workers, the SMAG (Salaire Minimum Agricole Garanti), both of which were transformed in 1969 into the SMIC (Salaire Minimum Interprofessionnel de Croissance). These were periodically readjusted, at first following the cost of living index, later automatically when inflation reached a certain point; these readjustments affected the range of incomes as they raised the base line, often triggering differential maintenance rises just above, but did not affect the top levels.

The first important study of incomes in France was carried out by CREDOC and INSEE in 1956 on a representative sample of 20,000

[3] Here a word of warning is required. French income statistics of the period were generally less reliable when referring to upper income levels. This is because they mainly dealt with *salaries* and covered only very sketchily income from property, shares etc. The calculations for salaries were based on declared income on tax return forms and employers' declarations and were probably accurate, except perhaps at the very top. However, it should be remembered that there remained in France a larger class of self-employed persons and small employers than in most other advanced European countries, and that the revenues of these people were often the most difficult to obtain. Many, including the great majority of small farmers and shopkeepers, did not declare their income at all and paid tax on a forfeit basis. Further, it is sometimes difficult to be sure whether the statistics concerned refer to before or after tax income. This is very important as half the French population paid no tax at all while others paid up to 70 per cent. One of these warnings was voiced by Gilbert Mathieu as long ago as 1962, when he pointed out that there were four sets of salary statistics, all official, drawn up by various Government bodies; the situation has not substantially changed since. Hence, whenever statistics are given, their source will be noted and every effort made to ensure comparability. An even greater problem of reliability is evident when one attempts to talk of real income and hence of the relationship between money income and prices, essential to any discussion over time.

families. The data were brought up to date in 1960 by the Ministry of Finance and rendered comparable to its own data on high incomes. The results were startling.

Using official figures alone, Mathieu points out (1962: 411 ff.) that one discovered an *income* (not only salaries) hierarchy of 1–700 before tax and 1–400 after tax.[4] Even assuming that the very low incomes were underestimated, a factor probably compensated for by the under-estimation of the highest incomes (the latter were estimated by the Finance Ministry to be understated by approximately 30 per cent), this suggests a considerable dimension of inequality, varying from the poorest farmers (75 N.F. per month) to the 48,000 N.F. declared by the highest income receivers. Three major groups could be distinguished, although, as Mathieu says, the 'great mass of incomes are to be found in the lowest ranges; 73 per cent of households have less than 100,000 A.F. (1,000 N.F.) of fiscal revenue per month, i.e. less than 135,000 A.F. effective income' (ibid.: 413). Nearly two million more households had less than 25,000 A.F. (£20.00 approximately) per month; although many were the households of the retired, many more were persons on low salaries, notably agricultural workers, and farmers, and many industrial workers, especially women. In the medium incomes group three million households had 50,000–75,000 A.F. fiscal revenue per month. This group covered the majority of the working population in-cluding the more 'privileged' manual workers, the majority of white-collar workers, farmers and 'supervisors' (*petits cadres*). More favoured were the 3·2 million households with 75–112,000 A.F. per month which covered the remaining white-collar workers, middle-management (*cadres moyens*) and many women in senior management (*cadres supérieurs*). Thus, 80 per cent of the total population had effective incomes of less than 150,000 A.F. (£110·00) per month. There then remained 20 per cent which were the 'privileged' familes whose incomes varied enormously, with fiscal incomes ranging from 112,500 A.F. to more than 625,800 A.F., that is, real incomes of 150,000 to more than 800,000 A.F. (£100–700·00 approximately in 1960). Another 14,000 households earned more than that, with the top 800 receiving 4,800,000 A.F. per month on average (£4,000) (ibid.: 414).

Where *salaries* alone were concerned official differences between the highest and the lowest were a great deal less pronounced, being roughly

[4] Inevitably income data appear somewhat dated. What is important, how-ever, is less the absolute figures than the reward *structure* revealed by the figures. This structure, it will be seen, changed little over the period after Mathieu was writing.

1 to 12 but this is certainly an underestimation as the top category of the 1962 INSEE study was 'more than 3,259 f.' and the bottom figures only covered persons who worked the whole year for the same employer; those with less stable employment, 3 million persons in all, approximately one sixth of the then labour force, almost certainly earned less. Moreover, the study excluded the known lowest paid as it did not cover farm workers, domestic servants and state employees. The study covered 6 million salaried persons, about one third of the total employed population, of whom 4,380,000 were manual workers and 1,320,000 white-collar workers. Even so when we look at the salary figures we find that the higher salary levels only concerned 280,000 and the medium ones 590,000 persons, the remaining 5 million earning below 100,000 A.F. per month (1962).

Ten years on

The figure of 100,000 A.F., or 1,000 N.F., per month is a good point at which to make comparisons. Ten years later, in 1972, the major trade union federations, and in particular the CGT., were agitating for this to be made the SMIC (guaranteed minimum wage) and that demand provoked a good deal of controversy over whether the nation could 'afford' it.

Incomes did not increase at an equal rate after 1945. There were periods of fast increases followed, as in the late 1950s and mid-1960s, by Government deflationary measures which slowed income growth. Further, changes in income and its distribution throughout the total active population are linked to changes in the distribution of the population itself, the growth of certain professional categories and the decline of others, of which Table 3.2 may be a convenient summary form. It refers only to the period ending in 1965, but the trends can be seen and may be assumed to have continued. The active population also increased as did the *salaried* population, reaching 15·3 million in 1968, of which 11·5 million were in the private sector, 2·7 million in state service, and 1 million in the nationalized industries (Perrot, 1971: 15).

Note in particular the diminution in the number of those employed in agriculture and as small shopkeepers but the *increase* in manual workers, both skilled and unskilled, as well as that of *cadres* of all levels and the 'inactive', principally the retired. Note further that the occupations counted are those of the *head of the household* and *not* the total in each sector of the population. This means an underestimation of the number of persons actually employed in all sectors, especially those in domestic service whose real numbers were found to be 500,000 in 1968.

TABLE 3.2.

Number of households in each socio-professional category: thousands

	1956	1965
Farmers	2,740	1,420
Farm workers	460	280
Patrons industry and big commerce	150	130
Artisans	570	570
Small shopkeepers	710	580
Cadres supérieurs and liberal professionals	440	680
Cadres moyens	740	1,090
White-collar workers	1,010	1,040
Foremen/supervisors	190	370
Manual workers	3,050	3,580
Unskilled manual workers	480	510
Domestic servants	180	150
Miscellaneous	450	660
Inactive	3,390	4,290
Total	13,610	15,350

Source: Vangrevelinghe, 1969: 8.

The present data and the information on income evolution since 1962 are derived from an INSEE study carried out in 1972 on 1970 data, and based on the income declared by households to the income tax inspectors, a declaration probably below the reality. They do *not* count transfer payments through social insurance nor tax-free or tax-paid share income etc., which revenues in all probably constituted about 20 per cent total household income. Non-salaried incomes were probably under-declared by about one third, a situation little different from that referred to by Mathieu in 1962 (Banderier, 1974). 'Households' are defined by the INSEE as 'persons occupying together an individual dwelling whether they are related to each other or not'. The tax inspectors base themselves on the notion of *foyer fiscal*, composed of household head and the persons he/she is financially responsible for, which is not the same as the INSEE household; the tax data have been reconstituted (by Banderier) to fit the INSEE definitions and he did this for the representative sample of 45,000 dwellings covered by the study.

1962–70

Presenting the main results of the INSEE income studies over the period 1962–70, Banderier gives a summary table of income distribution (Table 3.3). This gives some indication of the dispersion of income, but it calls for greater emphasis to be given to a number of features. First,

TABLE 3.3.

Distribution of annual income by socio-professional category, 1970: %

Socio-professional category	Distribution total income in Francs (annual income)									%
	3000FF	3000–6,499	6,500–9,999	10,000–14,999	15,000–19,999	20,000–29,999	30,000–59,999	60,000–99,999	100,000+	100
Independent professions*	2	4	6	12	12	20·5	28	9	6	100
Cadres supérieurs	–	–	0·4	1	2	11	51	26	8	
Cadres moyens	–	0·6	1	6	12·5	32	42	5	1	
White-collar workers	1	3	6	21	20	27	19·5	2	–	
Manual workers	1	4	10	25	22	26	13	–	–	
Farmers	21	26	16	14	8	7	6	1	–	
Farm workers	2	14	29	28	12	11	4	–	–	
Inactive	13	23	17·5	17	10	10	7·5	1	–	
Average Total	6	11	11	17	14	19	18	3	1	

* The new INSEE classifications put together *patrons* and members of the liberal professions and also the top-level *cadres dirigeants*.
Source: Slightly adapted from Banderier, 1974: 52(22).

the figures given refer to annual income and include all bonuses, over-time pay, etc. received by households, which may mean considerable variation from month to month. Secondly, they refer to fiscal income per household. This means that effective income is slightly under-estimated because of allowances etc., but the effect of tax payments is not allowed for. It also means that the figures do not relate to average salaries but to household income and there may well be more than one wage-earner, and therefore any one salary may well be considerably below what is recorded here.

From the data given in the table, the importance of *low incomes* is striking. Banderier warns that farm incomes were grossly underestimated (48 per cent of farmers declared in 1970 an annual income of less than 6,500 f. (£600.00) of which 21 per cent declared less than 3,000 f., and one fifth of the farm population declared 150 f. per month of income, and nearly half, 541 f. or less.) But even assuming an underestimation of 50 per cent farm incomes appear still as staggeringly low, especially since that income was likely to be the return on the work of more than one person, and probably earned over very long hours. Farm workers too were extremely poor, although appearing to do slightly better than farmers, probably because salaries were more accurately known; 46 per cent earned less than 541 f. per month and 66 per cent less than 1,250 f., again probably for very long hours, in 1970. These figures *include* estimates of income in kind. After the farm sector, and again extremely poor, came the 'inactive', principally composed of households of the retired, of whom 36 per cent received less than 541 f., per month.

Considerable proportions of households employed in the industrial and commercial spheres had very low incomes. In 1970, 40 per cent of the households of manual workers' (*ouvriers*, including domestic servants) had incomes of less than 15,000 f. *per year*, 1,250 f. per month; 62 per cent had less han 20,000 f., per year, 1,666 f. per month; and 88 per cent received less than 30,000 f. per year, 2,500 f. per month. It is common in this sector to find that the annual salary includes a thirteenth month (as well as other bonuses impossible to estimate here), and dividing the annual salary by thirteen instead of twelve shows 40 per cent with less than 1,153 f. per month, 62 per cent with less than 1,538 f., and 88 per cent with less than 2,307 f. No manual workers earned more than 60,000 f. per year, 5,000 f. per month, while 34 per cent of *cadres supérieurs*, a third of the total, had household incomes in that range.

The middle incomes were received by the households of white-collar workers and *cadres moyens*, and at first sight the two set of households seem to have much in common. However, in fact there are important differences. While the same proportions, 52 per cent in each case, had incomes of less than 30,000 f. per year, within that range they were distributed differently. Thus, a fifth of white-collar workers were to be found in the range 10,000–15,000 f. and a fifth in that of 15,000–20,000 f., that is to say, 41 per cent with an income below 20,000 f. and only 27 per cent in the range 20,000–30,000 f. while only a quarter of *cadres moyens* had such low incomes (one third of the *cadres moyens* were in the 20,000–30,000 f. range and 42 per cent in the range above, 30,000–60,000 f.). It seems likely that the lower salaries in each professional group were in part a question of the age of the main income earner, the young receiving less, so probably virtually all *cadre moyen* incomes were in the higher ranges.

The top two social categories and in particular that of *cadres supérieurs* stand out clearly in terms of income. Of these households only 15 per cent received an income of less than 30,000 f. per year (of which only 1·5 per cent was below 20,000 f.), and this again may be a question of age. On the other hand, 37 per cent received between 30,000 and 60,000 f. (2,500–5,000 f. per month) and 26 per cent earned 60,000–99,000 f., and a further 8 per cent more than 100,000 f. In other words, 77 per cent, more than three quarters, earned more than 30,000 f., and one quarter more than 60,000 f. The independent professions are slightly problematic here as they include industrialists and large commercial businessmen as well as members of the liberal and subsidiary liberal professions, the last section probably accounting for most of the lower incomes in the category. Of these groups 56 per cent declared household incomes of less than 30,000 f., including 38 per cent under 20,000 f.; 28 per cent declared between 30,000 f. and 60,000 f.; and nearly 16 per cent more than 60,000 f. However, the incomes of such persons are reckoned by INSEE to be underestimated by 30 per cent, so allowance should be made for that.

Throughout the data there is a clear clustering—manual workers, including farmers and farm workers, members of the *classe populaire*, then those in white-collar jobs of the lower grades, and finally the upper groups, largely bourgeois by origin and function.

Dispersal

In relation to these figures it is important to notice that the dispersal of income is quite different for the different categories. The higher incomes tended to be concentrated within a few ranges, although this may be somewhat accentuated by the fact that at those levels the ranges

presented by INSEE are themselves much wider than at the bottom—
30,000 f. difference instead of 3,500 f., or 5,000 f.—which may disguise
other concentrations. On the other hand, the incomes of the manual
workers were fairly evenly distributed among three categories and a
further two at each end of that range, suggesting the more limited nature
of their income possibilities.

The effects of economic growth

Data gathered by INSEE and published by Banderier in the article
quoted above, showed an average increase in income per household
per year between 1962 and 1970 of 9·3 per cent per year, a virtual
doubling of nominal fiscal income over the period considered.

TABLE 3.4.
Evolution of household annual incomes, 1962–70

Socio-professional category of household head	Income in Francs		Annual rate of increase %
	1962	1970	
Independent professions	19,383	37,894	8·7
Cadres supérieurs	33,769	57,229	6·8
Cadres moyens	18,035	32,770	7·7
White-collar workers	11,324	22,546	9·0
Manual workers	9,685	19,171	8·9
Farmers	4,030	11,339	13·8
Farm workers	5,796	12,706	10·3
Inactive	6,328	13,201	9·6
All categories*	10,823	22,013	9·3

* The 'all category' figures are weighted averages and not simple 'averages of
averages', the latter calculation giving rather higher but less accurate figures.
Source: Slightly adapted from Banderier, 1974: 26.

As Table 3.4 shows, not all socio-professional categories benefited
equally from the increase in the national cake. At first sight it suggests
that on the whole it was those categories which previously had the
lowest incomes which benefited proportionately most, and Banderier
concludes that 'the average differentials between categories and the
inequalities within categories have tended to decrease slightly over the
period' (ibid.: 27).

The figures, however, deserve more careful scrutiny. First, there are
the influences of changes in the proportion of the active population
within each category summarized in Table 3.2 above. One of the
principal reasons why farm incomes have increased so fast is the disappearance of the marginal farms which brought the earlier averages

down (the professional migration of many farm workers also contributed to the rapid rate of increase in income of those remaining). Many of those leaving agriculture went into the less skilled manual jobs in commerce and industry. Not only was average farm income thus raised, but it was raised faster than the income of individual households in the category.

Secondly, it is important to emphasize that the differences in percentage increase across the categories are very small, being for salaried persons only between 7 per cent and 10 per cent per year. This means that the ratio of high to low salaries remained almost static over the period, that while the low paid benefited, the highly paid benefited too. Further, percentage increases in income may mask *increasing* income inequality. All incomes may increase by 25 per cent but 25 per cent of a high income is, in francs, in purchasing power, more than 25 per cent of a low income. Thus, if incomes rise between 7 and 10 per cent overall, the *ratio* of high to low incomes remains basically the same, for example, 1:10, but the purchasing power of the high increases considerably more, an increase sometimes representing 50 per cent of a low salary. There has therefore in fact been an *increase* in inequality in a certain sense.

The tables above have indicated the evolution of household incomes over a period of eight years, 1962 to 1970; that period was one of boom and relative stability after the years of rapid change in the 1950s and, equally important, at the end of the colonial wars, including the last, that of Algeria. In order to examine changes made by the industrialization process one must include the 'pre-boom' years. Here again the INSEE data are most accessible (see Table 3.4).

Overall increases in revenue in the periods 1956–65 and 1962–1970 were very similar, around 9 per cent. Exact comparisons, group by group, are not easy to make here as, unfortunately, the earlier figures are coded in the classic way, which puts liberal professions with *cadres supérieurs*, whereas in the later figures the former group forms part of the independent professions. Here, as before, farmers increased (15 per cent), as did farm workers (10 per cent) and *patrons* of industry and commerce (11·5 per cent), the other categories being all contained between 9 per cent and 10·5 per cent, except the inactive (8 per cent). These figures suggest that over the whole period of boom (there are no figures recent enough to situate the results of the crisis of the 1970s) the different categories of the nation maintained their relative shares of the national cake in much the same *proportions*, each increasing at approximately the same rate. There was no basic change in the structure of income distribution to different social groups.

TABLE 3.5.

Evolution of average annual incomes, 1956–65
by socio-professional category of household head

Socio-professional Category	Average incomes (francs)		Rate of annual increase %
	1956	1965	
Patrons in industry and commerce	8,148	21,757	11·5
Cadres supérieurs and liberal professions	21,139	46,334	9·1
Cadres moyens	11,752	24,694	8·6
White-collar workers	6,820	15,130	9·3
Manual workers	6,002	13,344	9·3
Service personnel	4,587	10,031	9·1
Farmers	1,695	5,858	14·8
Farm workers	3,077	7,454	10·3
Other actively employed	6,705	16,156	10·5
Inactive	4,352	8,626	7·9
All categories	6,660	14,641	9·1

Source: Slightly adapted from Banderier, 1970: 40.

Periods of growth and income change; the stability of income structure

Income changes do not occur as an even flow to each category over time. The period covered includes times when different categories, usually as a result of militant collective action, differentially increased their shares of the cake, and one may, by taking certain baseline dates, come to varying conclusions. Thus, for instance, the period 1968–70 suggests that the range of incomes, at least as far as salaries are concerned, was decreasing. This is because, between 1968 and 1971, salaries increased by more than 30 per cent and 'the lowest-paid workers received the highest increases, in both the public and private sectors' (Perrot, 1971: 15). The Accords de Grenelle of 1968, which sharply increased the SMIG. (minimum salary, now SMIC.), were responsible for salary rises for several million workers, either directly, because they were paid on the SMIG., or indirectly by the maintenance of differentials; but since the former were more numerous than the latter, the range was reduced. It is by no means certain that such special measures leave durable results, and it seems most likely that the range subsequently widened again.

What do these figures mean? Available statistics seem to support the argument that industrialization and economic growth in France benefited all sections of the community in an absolute sense by raising all income levels. All sections of the French population were better off in 1975, in absolute terms and in terms of real purchasing power, than they were in 1950 or 1955, and all sections of the population benefited roughly equally in proportion over the period.

However, there are important provisos in this. First, it seems likely that differentials in monetary terms increased. Secondly, and more important, large sections of the population were not paid the proportion of salaries which corresponded to their proportion in the active population. While structural changes—the elimination of many small farmers, for example—meant fast increases in the revenue of the remaining members of the group, they did not always mean an appropriate transfer to the other sectors. The result of the economic changes was an increase in the numbers of manual workers, but their proportion in the active population was not reflected in income received. For instance, in 1968 manual workers constituted 64 per cent of the salaried personnel of the private sector but only received 53 per cent of the total salary bill in that sector. Similarly, white-collar workers constituted then 20 per cent of all such personnel but received only 18 per cent of salaries. However, where *cadres* salaries were concerned the position was the reverse: *cadres moyens* and supervisors constituted 11 per cent of personnel but received 14 per cent of salaries. At the top level the difference was even clearer: *cadres supérieurs* formed in 1968 only 5 per cent of the work force but received 15 per cent of all salary payments made.

To class inequalities in relation to income and job must be added inequalities based on sex. The annual net salary received by a woman was approximately *one third lower* than that received by a man in each profession sector, or, expressed so as to underline the reality, a man earned on average *50 per cent more* than a woman: if a woman earned £60·00 per month, a man earned £90·00. Less than ten salaried women in a hundred acceded to *cadre* positions where nearly one fifth of men did so. Within the manual working class women overwhelmingly occupied the least qualified and lowest paid positions (Charraud and Saada, 1974: 3–17).

Income security

While the amount of income received is extremely important, its regularity, its certainty, are by no means less vital. The higher socio-professional categories throughout the period since 1945 had not only the higher incomes but also the most certain. Most *cadres*, of all levels, were not only paid by the month as opposed to by actual number of hours worked, but also did not have to sacrifice salary for the first three days of any illness, and usually benefited from contracts guaranteeing a certain security of employment and, in case of prolonged sickness, at least six months on full pay and probably another six months on half pay. Moreover, by the very nature of the jobs, they were far less subject to seasonal and cyclical fluctuations in demand, and were the last to be made redundant in recession or mergers. White-collar workers to some extent shared their privileges (not only in security, but also in work conditions, canteens, lack of obligation to 'clock-in', some flexibility of hours, etc.). Manual workers on the other hand, until the late 1960s at least, were often subject to considerable fluctuations of income from month to month. They were usually paid by the hour[5] and hours not worked were not paid, so that in times of slack demand there may not even have been full-time work, let alone the overtime which, for many, was a crucial part of their income. Even where regular hours were worked they were often not the only basis on which wages were calculated, there being in addition a whole series of bonuses, according to production, often so complex that a worker could not be sure how his or her income was made up[6] (see for example Minces, 1969).

Tax deductions and transfer payment

The gross figures on income distribution and the range of nominal incomes do not show the real, available, incomes of households. On the other hand, many incomes are reduced by income tax, and, on the other, are increased by various social transfer payments, such as pensions, unemployment and sickness benefits, and child and other

[5] Workers were also subject to discriminating time division practices; three minutes late could lose a person fifteen minutes' pay, but less than thirty minutes' overtime was not always counted, even in 1975.

[6] In the later years, however, some collective agreements brought manual workers onto monthly salaries, and an over-all agreement was concluded in April 1970. The effectiveness of these agreements was very varied, but it was thought that by 1971 about 50 per cent of manual workers would be paid by the month. Workers did not by that token necessarily receive the same amount each month, as frequently the number of hours actually worked was still calculated so that the forty hours basic were paid separately from any overtime. The measure did, however, have the great advantage of bringing the manual worker the promise that in case of sickness he or she would be paid in full for the first three days and for a period after that, rather than the half-pay or less offered by the social security system. To some extent, too, such agreements instituted a system of salary rises per period of service which did not exist before, the payment for official holidays such as New Year's Day, and an improvement in redundancy payments. In spite of the added cost of such agreements, studies suggested that the over-all cost of each hour worked in France remained the lowest in the Common Market, and equally that hours worked in France were also the longest.

allowances. These may be expected to reduce over-all inequality, but analysing the net results of such transfers is complicated, especially since it makes most sense to examine the changes over a period of time. The task is made more difficult by the profusion of statistics referring to different base units and different periods of time. What follows can only be an approximation and provide a broad outline.

Transfer payments

Transfer payments in most countries include principally sickness, maternity, and unemployment benefits, family allowances, and pensions, that is, payments which are, in a certain way, a return on contributions paid but which also include non-contributory payments made by State and local authorities, such as various subsidies and scholarships for school children and students as well as certain kinds of non-contributory pensions and allowances, such as *aide sociale*. Virtually all French households received some of these payments but they did so in varying amounts according to their over-all financial and family situations, number of contributions etc. Expressed as a percentage of total revenues, the proportions received by different socio-professional groups towards the end of our period were as indicated in Table 3.6, with groups at the bottom of the scale, farmers and workers, receiving approximately one third of their income from that source.

TABLE 3.6.
Structure of average household incomes, 1970: percentages

	Indep. profs.	Cadres sups.	Cadres moyens	White-collar workers	Manual workers	Farmers	Farm workers	Inactive	Average Total
1. Primary resources of which:	104	99	87	81	74	89	69	44	80
Income from labour	13	87	81	73	68	4·5	58	14	45
Income from capital	12	7	4	5	3	7	7	22	9
Income from enterprise	79	5	2	3	2	77·5	3	7	26
2. Transfer income	6	13	19	24	29	15	34	62	26
3. Total income	110	112	166	155	103	104	102	105	106
4. Direct taxes	−10	−12	−6	−5	−3	−4	−2	−5	−6
5. Disposable income					100				

Source: Adapted from Roze, 1974, 21.

The percentage of income derived from transfer payments was high. The percentage *increase* in income from this source (over the period 1962–70) was almost certainly higher, as is seen in the following example. Household A had a total income of 600 f.; of this 150 f. was transfer payment, in other words, 25 per cent of total income. *But* income before transfer payments was 450 f. (600 f. less 150 f.). Therefore the increase in income due to transfer payments was 33 per cent and not 25 per cent. This should be borne in mind when examining Table 3.7.

TABLE 3.7.

Household income increase due to transfer payments
as percentage of primary income

Socio-professional group of household head	1962	1965	1970
Independent professions	7	6	6
Cadres supérieurs	17	12	13
Cadres moyens	24	21	22
White-collar workers	31	32	29·5
Manual workers	40	40	40
Farmers	12	16	17
Farm workers	42	44	49
Inactive	113	132	141
Total	29	30·5	33

Source: Adapted from Roze, 1974: 25.

Over the period 1962–70, transfer payments affected differently the income of the various social groups; there was an *increase* in the proportion of incomes due to transfer payments for the worst-off sections of the population (farmers, farm workers, and especially the inactive), *stability* where manual workers are concerned, and a *decrease* in the proportion at the upper levels. This suggests an effort made on behalf of the lower income groups, but it should be noted that the percentage *changes* were not very great in most cases (except where farmers were concerned, and this largely because new schemes became applicable to them in the course of the period). From these figures Roze concludes that the net result of these changes over the period 1962–70 was a decrease in economic inequality in the sense of a regular decrease in the range of incomes, but it would seem from other sources and from the categorization used by INSEE itself that these figures *underestimate* real income differences.

Taxation

Direct taxation Here one can deal in detail only with the effects of direct taxation, and then only to the degree to which taxable incomes are known to the tax authorities or appear in national accounts. In France between 1945 and 1975, income tax payments represented a much lower proportion of total income than in Britain; the tax rates were lower, they came into operation higher up the income scale and the 'children's allowance' (*quotient familial*) both brought many people out of the tax range and reduced the burden enormously on families with children as against the unmarried and childless couples (which did not, however, necessarily mean that it contributed to social justice).

According to Roze (op. cit.) direct taxes on income represented 6 per cent of primary income of households in 1962, 7 per cent in 1965, and 8 per cent in 1970. This represents a slight increase over the period, largely due to the fact that money incomes increased enormously while the point at which households became liable for tax altered less. On the whole, the tax burden on the higher incomes increased faster than on the lower ones but only to a small degree. Moreover, direct taxation over-all had only a small equalizing effect, as can be seen in Table 3.8.

TABLE 3.8.
Percentage decrease in incomes due to direct taxes

Date	Indep. profs.	Cadres sups.	Cadres moyens	White-collar workers	Manual workers	Farmers	Farm workers	Inactive
1962	− 9	−10	−5	−4·5	−3	−3	−3	−11
1965	−10	−11	−6	−5	−4	−3	−3	−13
1970	−10	−12	−7	−6·5	−4	−4	−3	−12

Source: Slightly adapted from Roze, 1974: 27.

Roze concludes that the relationship between the highest incomes derived from work (independent professions) and the lowest (farm workers) dropped marginally from 4·9 in 1962 to 4·8 in 1970. But these are tiny changes, so its seems that while transfer payments and direct tax deductions did work to reduce the range of income available to households, especially as transfer payments increased income by as much as 49 per cent (farm workers, workers 40 per cent), they did not, in spite of this, drastically reduce disposable income differentials.

What are the reasons for this? First, at the lower levels, in 1972 only one in four French families paid income tax at all. On the other hand, of the low incomes which were taxable, most hit were salaried workers and not farmers and small shopkeepers (taxed on a forfeit basis), creating inequality within the same real income brackets.[7] At the high-income levels there existed considerable opportunities for reducing taxable income enormously. Not only were many fringe benefits such as shares, use of car, housing etc., not declared, but many legal ways existed of making paper share losses and setting them against tax. These, however, were relatively marginal in relation to the most widespread tax reduction mechanism—the child allowance, *quotient familial.* This, of course, was open to all families and brought many lower incomes out of the taxable range, but it was fiscally most useful at high income levels. This is because in France there was no flat rate child 'allowance' to set against tax, such as existed in most European countries. Instead, there was the *quotient familial,* which meant that a person's income was divided by the number of members of the family—a spouse counted as a whole share and each dependent child a half share. As the number of shares was the same regardless of income, the net effect was to make wives and children financially much more valuable high on the income scale than lower down. This is especially important as it was families high on the scale rather than in the middle that had larger families. Over the last few years of our period a number of bodies, including the Plan's Committee, recommended replacing the *quotient familial* by a forfeit system, but successive Governments refused. The Conseil des Impôts published a series of figures, reproduced in *Le Monde,* on the differential effects of the allowance (see Table 3.9).

TABLE 3.9.

Differential tax reductions per child for a disposable income of X francs

No. of children \ Annual income	12,500 f.	25,000 f.	50,000 f.	70,000 f.	100,000 f.	200,000 f.
1st child	229 f.	657 f.	2,002 f.	2,503 f.	4,237 f.	6,394 f.
3rd child	229 f.	410 f.	1,187 f.	1,802 f.	2,503 f.	4.819 f.
5th child	229 f.	250 f.	658 f.	1,403 f.	2,503 f.	4,819 f.

Source: Le Monde, 22 Aug. 1973: 15.

Gilbert Mathieu, commenting in *Le Monde*, pointed out that

thus, for an income eight times higher (200,000 f. instead of 25,000 f.), the tax reduction per child, from the second on, is eleven to fourteen

[7] The figures do not show the real amount of inequality because of the known underestimation of particularly high incomes, and it is not known whether that is compensated by underestimation of certain lower categories of income such as that of farmers and small shopkeepers, taxed on a forfeit basis.

times higher . . . For the first child, and comparing with a lower income (12,500 f.) per year, the difference is much greater, twenty-eight times (it is still nine times if one compares taxable incomes going from one to four—12,500 f. to 50,000 f.).

Put differently, the *quotient familial* was equivalent to a net tax reduction equal to nearly three-quarters of one month's total salary at the higher levels (from 8,000 f. approximately taxable income per month) for the first child. This system, added to the fact that income tax rates were fairly steeply regressive, meant that the *cadres supérieurs*, for instance, in 1970 still only lost an average just over 12 per cent of their income in tax (Roze, 1974: 27).

Moreover, while direct tax imposition undoubtedly reduced the range of incomes, the tax burden went on growing unequally. For some the tax burden even dropped: members of the independent professions (where we find many people with the highest incomes) paid 21 per cent of their income in 1965 but only 19 per cent in 1970. At the other end of the scale, because of rapid inflation and associated fiscal drag, the number of families of farm workers, manual workers, and white-collar workers subject to tax not only augmented, but the percentage rate of increase in the tax they paid increased faster than the percentage increase in salary (Banderier, 1974: 28).

Indirect taxation Indirect taxation is more regressive in its applica-tion than direct tax. It is, therefore, important to note here that the rate of value added tax (TVA.) in France was higher than in other European countries and applied to food and children's clothes as well as other basic items.

Net effects of taxation and transfer payments

Transfer payments in most modern countries have an equalizing effect on income, but the major transfers in France, as frequently else-where, tended to be between households within the same social category and principally between the different groups within the manual working class. There was also even some transfer from that class to higher social groups. The evidence available on this is unsystematic but provides some indications.

First, although social security contributions were a percentage of salary (for those who earned salaries), there was a ceiling beyond which income was not subject to these payments. This meant that proportion-ately to total incomes the lower salaries were paying most. In absolute terms the working class (farm, manual, and white-collar workers) was numerically greatest and contributed most to the common pool.

Secondly, although the working class contributed most, its members did not by that token get most back. Family allowances are a significant example, as they were given according to family size and not income. Through family allowances there was some tranfer from the skilled and white-collar fractions of the working class to unskilled workers and farm labourers, as the latter had the larger families (those of the white-collar workers were particularly small), but, also, there was some transfer 'up', to members of the independent professions in particular, as they also had more children. Such allowances were a net gain in greater proportion for the latter, since they were not taxable in France as they were at the same time in England. Thus, while family allowances formed a greater part of the revenue of low-income families, the real gain to high-income families for the same sum was greater.

The differences only appear marginal but they become significant in conjunction with other factors. Other allowances, such as single income allowances, housing allowances etc., were paid only to those families with lower range incomes but, as the income ceiling for receiving such payments covered most working class and many *cadre* families, it seems that any redistribution took place largely *within that class*, from those without children to those with children, rather than from outside the class.

Use of collective services

Much of the tax collected by the Government was used, in France as elsewhere, for the provision of collective services. Of these the most important, in that it concerned every family with children and indeed also concerned every young family who had yet to have children, was education. Chapter Five below will spell out in detail the social selectivity of educational institutions, particularly beyond primary level. Here suffice it to underline the fact that while the least expensive schools, the *maternelle* and primary schools, were used by virtually all the population in the secondary level and above, the most expensive elements of the system, working-class children were progressively less represented and children of the upper middle classes overwhelmingly more so, involving a net transfer of benefit from the working class to the more privileged sectors of the population.

Social security benefits, too, in some ways were similarly distributed. Although after the introduction of the system, many more working class families sought medical aid than before, there is evidence that it was middle- and upper-class individuals who used the system most, thus getting out of it proportionately more than they contributed.

The distribution of rewards—distinctive class positions

The real increases in purchasing power of members of the different social classes did not basically alter their position either in economic terms in relation to each other or in terms of other aspects of material and cultural conditions and ways of life. Private affluence was still highly relative for members of the working class (and small farmers), and did not obscure the distinctive position of that class in relation to public amenities or to 'private' conditions of life such as housing. The over-all situation of members of that class in relation to others could be summarized in 1975 as follows:

> They contributed most to transfer payments
> They earned least
> They had least income security
> They were most subject to unemployment
> They owned least capital
> They received the lowest pensions
> They look fewest holidays
> They lived the shortest lives
> They were most subject to illness and accident
> They had the poorest housing
> They bought fewest consumer goods
> They participated least in collective services
> They participated least in leisure/cultural activies
> Above all, they 'knew' least about inequalities in French society.

After an examination of monetary rewards it will be useful to turn now to the wider conditions of life and work.

Life expectancy

First, how long could people expect to live at all?

In spite of some slight changes of order between the ages of seventy and seventy-five years, indicating different mortality rates between those ages, INSEE data show the overwhelming importance of occupation as a determinant of life expectancy (Durieux and Seibel, 1973; Desplanques, 1973). In 1970 *cadres* at thirty-five years could expect to live a further 39·4 years, while workers (including white-collar, farms, and blue-collar) would live only 36·1 years, with the small independents, farmers and shopkeepers, in the middle with 37·4 years. Considering only workers, average white-collar life-expectancy at thirty-five years old was 37·5 years but blue-collar only 35·8 years. There were similar differences between the public and private sectors, it being advantageous to be a worker in the public sector (37·2 years against 35·5 years). Thus, at thirty-five years a teacher could, on average, expect to live nearly forty-one years more, but an unskilled worker could only expect 34·5 years of life. The shorter-lived members of a society contribute to the better-off. Moreover, these figures do not include certain high-risk professions, such as mining and fishing, and foreign workers nearly all had a higher mortality rate than those in the sample. It should also be noted that members of the less skilled professions commonly began work ten or more years earlier than *cadres* and others and, therefore, contributed to pension funds over a much longer period.[8]

Sickness and accident

The same INSEE study provides some information on the reasons for differential mortality by occupation. Some risks were particularly linked directly to the type of job as such—building sites are far more dangerous places than primary school classrooms—but many were linked directly to occupation via the income received and the conditions of life money income gave access to. The study separated causes of death into two groups—those clearly linked to profession and those more independent, though in fact still showing variations by profession. Most linked to profession were tuberculosis, alcoholism, accidents, and suicides. Contrary to popular impression, high-level *cadres* were not particularly subject to cardiac diseases—indeed the *cadres supérieurs* and liberal professions were well down the list for deaths from these causes, although technicians and lower-management were quite high. The figures are indeed striking, with the top-income groups showing

[8] Retirement is a major cause of poverty in many countries and France is no exception. Indeed, pensions were for long low in France relative to most other European countries and until relatively late in our period many sections of the population were not covered (de la Gorce, 1965). The pension system remained extremely complicated, with individuals frequently having rights to pensions from a number of different sources. This being so, it is likely that many people were eligible for higher pensions than they actually received. The rate at which they did receive them varied considerably according to the type of job they had had when working—with civil servants (remembering this category is very wide in France) doing best and farmers and farm workers least well (approximately one eighth of the former's rate). Further, Scardigli (1970) calculated that low incomes in France in 1966 were those of 6,000 f. per year. Eight years later, in 1974, the Government raised pensions to 6,300 f. per year, or 550 f. per month (*Le Monde*, 21 June 1974: 36), the second increase in the year, but this is a sum which still barely represents half the guaranteed minimum wage. The social isolation of pensioners, especially the poorer and less educated ones, contributed to their economic difficulties (cf. Guillemard, 1972.).

the lowest rates on nearly every cause of death studied by INSEE. Comparing only *cadres supérieurs* and unskilled workers, the frequency of cause of death per cause was as indicated in Table 3.10.

TABLE 3.10.
Mortality rates—X per 100,000, 1955—65

| | Cause of death: | | | | | |
| | said to INSEE to be linked to profession | | | | said to be independent of profession | |
Age 35–44	T.B.	Alcohol	Accidents	Suicide	Cancer	Heart disease
Cadres supérieurs/ lib. professions	5	5	45	9	33	26
Unskilled workers	36	88	109	49	49	36
Age 45–54						
Cadres supérieurs/ lib. professions	11	23	49	13	119	113
Unskilled workers	74	200	212	79	247	122

Source: Adapted from Desplanques, 1973: 12–13.

The risks of dying of T.B. were, thus, (age group 35—44) over seven times higher for an unskilled worker than for a *cadre,* of alcohol nearly eighteen times greater, of accidents between two and three times greater, of suicide between six and seven times greater. At age 45—54 the respective differences were seven times greater for T.B., for alcohol nine times greater, for accident between four and five times greater and for suicide six times greater. These causes of death were undoubtedly linked to the conditions of work, especially those causing accidents at work, which meant one death every forty minutes in 1969, (*Le Monde,* 10 Sept. 1969), conditions of housing, especially sanitation (T.B.), and other aspects of the typical unskilled, low-paid job, which encouraged alcoholism and could lead to suicide.

Unemployment

Perhaps one of the crucial factors differentiating the life-styles and life-chances of the different socio-professional groups is unemployment. Unemployment and underemployment were among the factors causing first farm workers and then farmers to flee the countryside, and in an industrial society most men are dependent on the remuneration of their labour. On the whole, the thirty years considered here were a period of boom, and although there were sub-periods of stagnation or even recession, overall it was a period of 'full' employment, at least when the whole of France is considered. On the other hand, there were significant variations by region (with the decline and replacement of important sectors such as mining and steel) and by category of job. Not all sections of society were equally touched nor, with the recession days of the mid-1970s, will they be, although the crisis promises to be so deep that all sections of the labour force will be affected to some degree. Particularly in 1974 and 1975 the numbers of the unemployed were much greater but comparison of the early years and the late years of our period shows that the structure of unemployment remained very similar.

There is always considerable debate about the numbers of the unemployed because of the various criteria on which the calculations are based. In France three major categories were used throughout our period. The first was that of persons drawing unemployment pay and registered with national employment exchanges, giving the Demandes d'Emploi Non Satisfaites (DENS). The second was composed of people spontaneously declaring themselves unemployed during interviews (by INSEE etc.) on a sample survey basis. This comprised the Population Disponible à la Recherche d'un Emploi (PDRE), whether they were registered as unemployed or not. The third, and much disputed category, was that made up of persons declaring themselves to be without a job and seeking one when *asked specifically* during interviews. The last category was largely composed of women and the young and known as the Population Marginale Disponible à la Recherche d'un Emploi (PMDRE). The published information on unemployment amongst these categories is based on statistics drawn from the National Employment Agencies (ANPE) and unemployment assistance offices (ASSEDIC), the Ministry of Labour, censuses, and INSEE employment surveys. Over-all numbers of the unemployed are important, but equally so are two other dimensions of unemployment—risks of being unemployed, that is, rate of unemployment per socio-professional category, and length of time unemployed, on the same basis.

Information drawn from a number of sources (Durieux, 1973; UNEDIC, Nov. 1973 supp.; Parodi, 1971) makes it clear that manual workers, especially the least qualified, and white-collar workers were those most at risk of unemployment, for the percentage in those categories as a percentage of the unemployed at any moment of time exceeded their percentage in the total population. For example, according to INSEE, the percentage of the unemployed classified as workers in March 1971 was 48 per cent, while roughly at the same time they constituted only 38 per cent (36 per cent excluding foremen) of the total active population. Similarly, white-collar workers in 1971 represented 19 per cent of the unemployed and only 15 per cent of the total active population. The reverse was true at the other end of the social hierarchy. *Cadres moyens* represented in 1971 8 per cent of the unemployed and 10 per cent of the population and *cadres supérieurs* and liberal professions represented 3 per cent of the unemployed but 5 per cent of the population. In short, the higher the qualification and social position, the lesser were the chances of unemployment. The same pattern is apparent when considering the proportion of each category of the unemployed—lowest among *cadres supérieurs* and highest among manual workers. Less than 1 per cent of *patrons* were unemployed in March 1972 and 1 per cent of *cadres supérieurs* and liberal professions, but 2 per cent lower *cadres*, white-collar and manual workers and 3 per cent of service personnel, a category including many manual workers, were without jobs.

Rates of unemployment varied considerably over the period since 1945 following the periods of economic boom and stagnation. The absolute figures have to be interpreted with caution as different methods of assessment give different results; for example, in 1968 the census gave a PDRE of 436,000 persons but the INSEE employment inquiry only gave 350,000 (Durieux, 1973: 38). They do, however, give an order of magnitude. In 1968 there were probably another 306,000 persons who constituted the PMDRE (*before* May 1968). By 1972 the PDRE (INSEE figures) alone had risen to 470,000 at least, and the figures subsequently rose rapidly, reaching approximately one million in September 1975. (This is taking into account the *apparent* rise due to more workers registering with employment exchanges as the rewards, particularly monetary, of so doing became greater and the network of agencies grew.) The figures also varied during the year and have been corrected for seasonal variations.

The *rates* of unemployment varied but the *structure* of it changed little over the last ten years until 1975. There was little increase in the proportion of young people (under twenty-five years of age) unemployed in spite of the influx of new generations to the labour market. One change, however, did occur, demonstrating another aspect of inequality by sex; the proportion of women among the unemployed increased, so that women constituted *half* the PDRE although they were still only *one third* of the labour force and, of course, they composed the major part of the PMDRE. The crisis first strengthened the trend for women (Eymard-Duvernay, 1974), but by mid-1975 the greatest proportion of the unemployed were men, *ouvriers* in particular (Revoil: 1975). Manual workers represented about 50 per cent of the

1975 unemployed, the same proportion as in 1963, as their numbers, both employed and unemployed, continued to increase proportionately in the period of boom,[9] at least until 1968. In keeping with the increase in their total numbers, the proportion of unemployed white-collar workers increased steadily over the ten years 1965 to 1975. Moreover, there is some evidence that much unemployment was caused by the very conditions of the boom, involving mergers and closures of establishments, both medium and small, and the number of the unemployed, made jobless through redundancy, had been steadily increasing throughout the 1960s (Durieux: 1973: 41). In the slump there seems little reason to suppose this much changed.

It is useful to see not only *who* is most liable to unemployment, but also to see for *how long*. Age was crucial, the older one was the harder it was to be re-employed and here it was less the manual workers than the *cadres* who were hardest hit. It also varied by sex: women again came off worst. Unemployment on average, even before the 1970s crisis, lasted several months. The average period registered among ASSEDIC beneficiaries in 1970–1 was 114 days (four months) for men but 146 days (five months) for women, and in 1971–2 similarly, for men 119 days and for women 152 days. The average age for both sexes was in the mid-thirties but it was the over-fifties who were hardest hit. The higher the qualifications and the higher the age the longer unemployment tended to be, unemployed *cadres* over 50 being those most at risk and for longest. The ASSEDIC, however, tended to have as clients the most qualified and the longest unemployed. This, as an ASSEDIC study in 1970 itself showed, was because information on rights was unequally distributed in the population; when they registered with the unemployment exchange, 54 per cent of the unemployed had never heard of the ASSEDIC, 2 per cent confused them with another body, and 33 per cent had heard of them but did not know what they did. Many people did not apply for ASSEDIC payments, as they were unaware of their rights and thought they were not eligible (68 per cent); a further 10 per cent had no documents. Ignorance of eligibility was

---

[9] The chances of unemployment and its length varied considerably by region, and it was not always the regions of declining industries which were most affected. In the north, for instance where the textile workers were mostly women, the growth of the tertiary sector compensated the other loss. Regional variation may be due both to the seasonal nature of much activity in the area and also the lack of a solid development base. Unemployment in certain industries, for example, steel in the east of France, hit hard whole communities and had far-reaching consequences as housing, shopping, and leisure facilities often belonged to the firm—for instance, de Wendel in Lorraine.

clearly linked to low education and thus to profession and, therefore, ASSEDIC figures underestimated unemployment among manual and the less skilled white-collar workers. Also, ASSEDIC insurance only covered approximately 40 per cent of the total unemployed,[10] the rest receiving only State aid or no benefits at all, and it seems likely that the remainder were the least informed and probably least qualified. Not all the poorer groups, such as farm workers (until January 1974), seasonal workers, and many immigrant workers were even covered, and these same categories were those least likely to register as unemployed with the ANPE (employment exchanges), so the true extent of unemployment among the poorer sections of the population tended to be underestimated in virtually all public figures. In 1973 with 400,000 unemployed 'officially' (PDRE) (and another 400,000 also 'marginally unemployed') and those not registered for various reasons, it seems likely that unemployment was a major and increasing cause of poverty in France in the late 1960s and 1970s, in spite of Government salary maintenance provisions. Not only were there many unemployed but unemployment benefits were on the whole, low; in 1973 the *average* daily payment by the ASSEDIC in France was 15 f. 34, which meant an *average* of 460 f. per month. This is a percentage of former salary and includes the higher paid. The State contributed a flat rate of 8 f. 90 per day for a bachelor and 17 f. for a man with two children—or 265—70 f. and 510 f. per month respectively. Further, since according to ASSEDIC calculations (personal interview, UNEDIC) only approximately 50 per cent of the salaried unemployed were eligible for both State and ASSEDIC aid, the income levels of many of the unemployed were desperately low. They were still low even when a person was eligible for both. It was also possible to apply for supplementary benefits from Aide Sociale and other sources, but it is not clear how many either applied or received such aid among the unemployed. Further, with inflation leading to rises in nominal income, many poor families became excluded from means-tested benefits. An OECD economist in 1975 estimated the income ceiling for receipt of Aide Sociale benefits to be approximately six years in arrears (personal communication).

Housing, holidays, consumer goods

The over-all increase in the standard of living of the French population between 1945 and 1975 can be seen in spending on consumer goods. In particular, the increase in ownership of consumer durables, from

[10] This figure refers to the period before the emergency decisions made in 1974 and 1975 in the face of massive loss of employment.

television sets and washing-machines to cars, was spectacular, and the
new 'affluence' and willingness to spend on 'non-necessities' formed a
constant theme of newspaper headlines and the subject of many books.
It was particularly noticed because of the alleged French 'innate'
aversion to mass production and insistence on artisan-type quality.
This aversion has been shown by many observers to be a myth, and
their insistent portrayal of increased consumption has tended to obscure
the fact that not all French households were able to participate in the
consumer boom to an equal extent. Moreover, and more important, it
obscures the fact that the increase in spending tended to be on consumer goods, while administrative and other rigidities on the one hand
and laxity in relation to speculation on the other meant that some of
the basic conditions of life were not well met. Hospital services remained
grossly inadequate, and schools were overcrowded and under-staffed in
many areas. Consideration of one fundamental aspect of living—housing—
and one aspect of the so-called 'leisure' society—holidays—may show
the limitations on their enjoyment by many families, even in the late
1960s and early 1970s.

Housing

Housing in France for two decades after 1945 was a chronic problem
for many groups in the society and an acute one for its lower-paid
members. A good part of the French housing stock was destroyed during
the Second World War and much that remained was old, in many areas
built before 1870, and inadequate. The wave of migration from country
to towns, and especially to cities, aggravated the shortage, made even
worse by the dramatic increase in marriage- and birth-rates throughout
the period: not only were more families having children but they were
having more of them. Building, slow to restart after the war because of
Government priority to heavy basic industries, long remained principally artisanal in organization and retained slow, traditional construction
methods. In the private sector there was much expensive speculative
building and the public sector was grossly inadequate. To meet demand
around 400,000 to 500,000 housing units needed to be built annually
in the 1950s and 1960s, but the realized figure was far lower. The crisis
was so acute until the mid-1960s, that even middle-class households
were affected, and many young married middle-class couples were
forced to live with their parents. Where this was not possible, in poorer
families, the only alternative was often the hotel and furnished rooms
with the kinds of sordid conditions vividly described by Andrée Michel
(c. 1956) for areas of Paris and by observers in the provinces in cities

such as Rouen and Vienne (Quoist: 1952) for large sections of the manual working class. Labbens (1969) showed that by the mid-1960s these conditions had by no means disappeared in central areas of Paris, but suggested that the extreme conditions were by then more limited in extent to the very low paid, the old, and in particular to immigrant workers. However, one should remember that one worker in eight earned less than 1,000 f. per month in 1972, and a far greater proportion, one third, earned less than 1,200 f.—not enough to pay the high rents of even 'social' housing in some cases.

The great shortage of dwellings began to ease somewhat in later years with increases in the building of new units, and the modernization of some of the old, but there were far from sufficient numbers of new units and even 'officially' recognized overcrowding concerned in 1970 around three million dwellings, of which more than one million were 'grossly' overcrowded (Dutailly, 1973: 61). One in five dwellings was overcrowded in 1970. Very many more were without some or all of the elements of 'comfort'—running water, W.C.s, bathrooms, and central heating. In 1968, while 90 per cent of main dwellings had running water (as against 58 per cent in 1954), barely half, only 52 per cent, had an inside lavatory, even fewer, 48 per cent, a bath or shower (10 per cent in 1954), and a third, 35 per cent, central heating. In all only two-fifths, 41 per cent, of the total housing stock of main dwellings had all these elements (Triballat-Seligman, 1969: 898). The least well-equipped areas in 1970 were the rural ones (only 8 per cent in 1970 had all basic amenities), but cities did not rate high either—a maximum of one-third of urban dwellings had these amenities in 1970. Only 20 per cent of Parisian dwellings were properly equipped, and 20–30 per cent in other cities at the same date. There were also great variations by region—60 per cent of dwellings in the tourist and wealthy areas of Provence—Côte d'Azur had all elements of 'comfort', but only 28 per cent in the industrial *Nord*. On the whole, the east and south were better off than the north and west.

The most striking differences, however, concerned the housing conditions available to members of the different social classes, for 'comfort', too, was unequally distributed.

The distinctive conditions of the different classes and particularly of the manual working class are here apparent. Whereas in 1968 47 per cent of farm workers and 44 per cent of manual workers lived in overcrowded conditions, only 14 per cent of liberal professional and executive families did so. More than a third of white-collar workers and almost a third of farmers also lived in overcrowded dwellings, while only 23 per

TABLE 3.11.
Conditions of housing by socio-profession category, 1968

Socio-professional Category	Total households (thousands)	% living in 'all comfort' dwellings	% in living in overcrowded dwellings
Patrons of industry and commerce	1,281	53	23
Cadres supérieurs and lib. professions	799	87	14
Cadres moyens	1,168	71	25
White-collar workers	1,184	53	36
Manual workers	4,412	42	44
Service personnel	388	34	50
Artists, police etc.	308	63	29
Farmers	1,266	16	31
Farm workers	303	17	47
Inactive	4,669	27	24
Total households	15,778	6,525 41%	4,985 32%

Source: Adapted from Triballat-Seligman, 1969: 901.

cent of the *patrons* of industry and commerce were in like case, and this in spite of the fact that the top social categories had larger numbers of children than white-collar workers and supervisory grades. Further, 87 per cent of executive and liberal professional households possessed all the elements of 'comfort', but only 16 per cent of those of farmers, 27 per cent of the retired, and 44 per cent of manual workers (although here the *patrons* did not do very well either). Over the period 1962–8 the number of persons per household for all categories of the population fell slightly but that of worker, *ouvrier*, households increased. Whether one was owner or tenant had a bearing on the conditions under which one was housed: just under 50 per cent of French households owned or were buying dwellings (1972), and they enjoyed more room and a greater comfort than their tenant colleagues.

The housing market in France generally improved over the ten to fifteen years after 1960, with more and better-equipped dwellings becoming available for buying and renting, and the housing shortage was officially declared by the mid-1960s to be no longer 'acute' However, not everyone had equal access to such housing. The provision of low-cost housing did not by any means keep pace with that of high-cost units. Official policy towards urban renewal and expansion meant, as

Le Monde of 7 March 1973 (p. 21) pointed out, with figures as proof, that 'in fourteen years the building of expensive flats . . . increased twice as fast as that of HLM., *habitations à loyer modéré*, social housing, to buy or to rent.' Over the period 1958–72, HLM construction grew by only 70 per cent for new projects and 85 per cent for completions, whereas the building of free market, expensive housing increased four-fold for new projects and more than five-fold for completions. *Le Monde* pointed out that the building of low cost housing for rent corresponded to the needs of many social groups—young married couples, old people, and immigrant workers, as well as persons on low incomes, of whom there were many, and concluded that in France as that time 'housing appears more as a sub-product of growth than the result of a choice made by the society.' Only later did the Government begin to be concerned by the depopulation of city centres such as Paris, with the resulting isolation of each social group in its own sectors and suburbs, for there was frequently little social mix in new housing projects.

Population growth, urbanization, and then the push from the city centre to the suburbs, together with the free market in land prices, meant ever-increasing housing costs. *Le Monde* (27 November 1973, p. 19) quoted a study by a property journal showing that the average price of a small four-roomed flat in the nearer Paris suburbs had risen from 135,000 f. in 1967 to 215,000 f. (approximately £21,000) in 1973, an increase in 60 per cent in six years. In order to buy it under the most usual conditions a man would have have to find a down pay-ment of 40,500 f. in 1967, of 64,500 f. (approximately £6,000) in 1973, and his repayments, 933 f. per month in 1967, had become 1,914 f. by 1973, a rise of 105 per cent over the period of five years. When we remember the income figures for the same period, it is evident that such prices were beyond the reach of the great majority. Dutailly showed that HLM buildings constituted only 12 per cent of total dwellings, and pointed out that the housing allowance most benefited families purchasing rather than renting accommodation (1973: 62).

The 'very poor', rather than the 'less well-off', benefited very little from the administrative measures designed to help with basic problems such as housing. Maurice Parodi, in a report (no date) prepared for an OECD. seminar on low income groups in the late 1960s, drew attention to the fact that one of the major sources of poverty in France was low incomes coupled with large families, and that the number of children belonging to a couple was a major determinant of whether or not the family was re-housed or even received a housing allowance. Parodi states (ibid.: 15) that the main beneficiaries of the improved housing were the middle and the upper-middle classes.

The housing deficit in 1963 was estimated at 1,828,000 units, indicating a need to build at least 500,000 units per year, including 170,000 low-rent flats. In fact the building figures remained far lower, and low-rent flats represented less than a quarter of dwellings constructed. Moreover, in spite of the fact that the law stipulated that most low-cost housing should go to persons with limited means, the upper income limit was fixed quite high. Out of every hundred low-cost dwelling units the housing board could reserve eighty for persons nominated by the co-investors in the scheme, and for whom *no* upper income limit applied, ten went to candidates chosen by the Board 'in the public interest', and, of the ten others, one went to a doctor, one to a dentist, and eight to families with three children whose incomes were below the ceiling. 'In these circumstances', Parodi concludes, 'the main beneficiaries of low-rent accommodation schemes are the liberal professions and middle executives, while low-income households are relegated to the slums, furnished lodgings, or the grey zones' (ibid.: 16). In another study Parodi pointed out that there were three times fewer low-income families in HLM. dwellings than in the total population (1971: 222).

The situation was exacerbated by the payment of housing allowances only to families occupying a minimum number of rooms equipped with minimum amenities. By a strict administrative rule no more than 5 per cent of the accommodation in low-rent schemes could be of five-room flats so that, as Sauvy notes,

a large family is refused a flat in a low rent block because there are not enough of these flats and is also refused a small flat because it would not be granted an allowance. Paradoxically, the arrival of a child is a tragedy for a family on the list for low-rent accommodation. The family admittedly becomes a more deserving case but, at the same time, ceases to be eligible for the welfare arrangements designed to ease matters. (quoted in Parodi, 1971: 16)

Such families were forced into slum accommodation for which they often had to pay relatively high rents.

The very poor, often living in hotels, furnished rooms, and 'transit' buildings were by no means only foreign workers, although those born abroad probably constituted almost the totality of the population of the worst accommodation in shanty towns and cellars. In the mid-1960s Labbens, studying two sectors of the eighteenth *arrondissement* in Paris, found that approximately half of the families on the 'active' files of the social services, mainly living in hotels and furnished rooms, had been born in France—in one sector 50 per cent of the couples (both spouses) and in the other 42 per cent were born in France itself, mostly, but not all, in the provinces. These families were those of low-income workers, some, for example, working full-time for the Paris urban transport company, RATP, and remained very poor in spite of the fact that approximately half the married women with children worked.

These studies, therefore, underline once again that where certain essential conditions of life such as housing were concerned the fast economic growth of the post-war period by no means eliminated class differences, and type and 'comfort' of housing still constituted indications of distinctive class positions and life-styles.

'Use of the products of growth': consumer goods and holidays

An advanced industrial capitalist society comes to involve mass consumption, particularly of household equipment (television, washing machines etc.), cars, and holidays and other leisure activies. These expenses increase proportionately with a higher standard of living, while those on clothing and food (especially the latter) decline as a proportion of total budget. As with other activities the various groups in the population participate differentially in the acquisition of the different 'goods' available, and in particular of holidays and 'cultural' activies. Consumption of the latter especially varies grossly by social category and 'under'- or 'over'-consumption of cultural facilities has important consequences for other aspects of life and life-chances, such as the success of children in education. The 'culturally deprived' at home do less well at school, thus increasing their deprivation and limiting their life-chances.

Budget and houshold equipment

Increased affluence showed first in the purchase of consumer durables, and only later in spending on health (helped by social insurance) and leisure activities. By early 1968, 69 per cent of households owned a refrigerator and 50 per cent a vacuum cleaner. In 1969, 55 per cent had at least one car (14 per cent in 1950). By 1968 61 per cent had TV (including colour sets), 90 per cent a radio, 36 per cent record-players and tape-recorders (Niaudet, 1969: 1139 ff.). By 1972 average consumption spending per household was 34,000 f. per year (around £3,000).

The over-all spending range was narrower between socio-professional groups than was the range of income because of the time-lag in consumption of certain groups and the 'glutted' consumption of others, but also because of the greater propensity to save among those with higher incomes. Calculations for the period 1956–63 showed little variation in consumption patterns by social class over time (1956–63), and gave some information on the differences (Pagé, in Darras, 1966: 106 ff.). The smallest variation by social group concerned food spending which was in the ratio 1:1·5 in 1963 between unskilled workers and *cadres supérieurs* and liberal professions. The disparities were much more marked in domains such as 'transport and telecommunications' and 'culture and leisure', being in the region of 1:6 in the groups considered.

The stability of this disparity by class in spending on cultural and leisure activities of all kinds, including holidays, seems particularly important because of its effects on the next generation and hence its role in maintaining social and economic differentials over time. Basic consumer durables gradually spread very widely through the different strata of the population, but this was less true of holidays and other leisure activies, which continued to vary both quantitatively and qualitatively. This is important, for, while there are doubtless differences of quality between cars and television sets, the social significance of these is negligible in relation to the importance of the qualitative differences in the consumption of leisure activities of all kinds. This is particularly true of cultural activities, the consumption article where 'quality' is supreme, and where consumption depends not only on financial means but on the possession of 'taste' and the capacity to 'appreciate' the 'things of the mind and spirit'.

Holidays

Holidays are a break from routine and a chance to see new horizons, geographical, cultural, and social. Departures on vacation increased fast in the late 1950s and early 1960s, but still in 1969 involved only 45 per cent of the population according to the minimal INSEE definition of holidays as 'being away from one's main residence for at least four consecutive days for non-professional and non-health reasons', while nearly 44 per cent went in 1964. Examining the trend, Le Roux (1970) concluded that 'the development of holidays has been slower than foreseen'. By 1972, 46 per cent of the population could take holidays, but this means that more than half, 54 per cent, could not do so. Holiday-taking was linked to factors such as place of residence, those living in large cities were most likely to leave, with Paris well in advance (83 per cent), but, as with other activities, holiday-taking varied most with income and profession. In 1969, only 9 per cent of farmers and farm workers went on holiday; within the non-agricultural groups,

43 per cent of manual workers took some vacation but 88 per cent of members of the liberal professions and *cadres supérieurs* did so, a rate double that of the manual workers. Further, the *patrons* of industry and commerce and the *cadres supérieurs* and *moyens* were the only ones to have increased their proportion going away on holiday; all the others *showed stability or even decreases* between 1964 and 1969 (Le Roux, 1970: 12).

For many people, as one might expect, financial difficulties were an important factor in the decision to stay at home. An IFOP study in 1972 found that of those who did not go at all one third did not go for financial reasons (half of those with large families), and another third because they could not leave their work—the latter were principally farmers, who represented, with other rural dwellers, three times more of the non-leavers than of the leavers (quoted in *Le Monde*, 5 August 1972: 7). Not all holidays involve exposure to new experiences. In 1969 36·5 per cent of holiday-makers went to stay with friends and relatives, probably essentially a return of city-dwellers to rural relatives; 15 per cent went camping and only 7 per cent to a hotel, 13 per cent to a second home, and 20 per cent to rented accommodation. While one cannot assume directly that those who went to hotels and rented accommodation automatically went further or to new places there is perhaps *a priori* a good chance that they did so.

Leisure and culture

Holidays, travelling, are one means of opening horizons on the world. More accessible is the television. Television audience surveys in France, as in Britain, in the 1960s showed differential viewing of documentaries, variety shows, and so on by social category, and the more demanding programmes had very clearly socially defined audiences. The same was true of newspaper and magazine reading, as was shown by various community studies, both recent and less recent (e.g. Bernot and Blancard: 1953). Access to books varied similarly in relation to both quantity and context. An INSEE survey carried out in 1967 reported that 61 per cent of *cadres supérieurs* declared that they had read a book within the last eight days, as did 41 per cent of *cadres moyens* and 31 per cent members of independent professions, whereas 56–8 per cent of rural workers declared they never read, as did 43 per cent of manual workers. These figures showed a very limited opening on the whole via the written word for between one-third and one-half of the French employed population.[11]

[11] The same was true to a large extent where social intercourse was concerned:

One does not necessarily only read about or view what is going on elsewhere in a society; one can also participate, whether in sporting or cultural activities. Here, too, membership and, above all, active participation, tended to be distributed differentially among the social groups. The same INSEE study, 1967, showed that less than one-fifth of low-income group families belonged to an association whereas nearly half of the better off (earning more than 50,000 f. per year) families did so. Active participation was closely linked to education and professional activity: 38 per cent of those active had no diplomas, whereas 54 per cent had university education. As only a tiny percentage of the population had been to university and the great majority had few or no qualifications, the 'rate' of active participation would seem to have been 'the reverse of the nation'. Where leadership of organizations and associations was involved, the correlation with class origins was even clearer (Lemel and Paradeise, 1974: 41 ff.). In 1972 Pitrou summed the situation up by suggesting that

the higher the socio-economic status the more the 'public' or social aspect of leisure activities increases, as though one needed to attain a certain degree of ease and confidence in oneself and ones associates (*familiers*) to participate in collective leisure activities and even more to play an active role in them. The *cadres* interviewed in our study presented a specific image of their main leisure activities; whether talking of the cinema, friends invited or visited, outings, walks, sport, holidays, and even belonging to clubs and leisure associations, they always distinguished themselves from the other groups . . . On the other hand, among the *cadres* domestic activities such as listening to the radio or watching television are much less in evidence . . . It is not enough to see there a reflection of financial inequalities; the principal cause is a better insertion in the activities where they feel at ease, perhaps because they often initiate or lead them . . . (Pitrou, 1972: 77).

Official figures, given above in considerable detail so as to serve as a reference for readers interested in any particular aspect, overwhelmingly show the continued clustering of access to material rewards over the thirty year period beginning in 1945. The picture may seem a depressing one and in sharp contrast to the dynamism and economic renewal of

manual workers, in factories at least, had little opportunity for verbal communication and discussion, and with farm workers, they comprised the group who invited and were invited least to private gatherings of friends and family (INSEE, 1973b: 40 ff.).

France emphasized by writers such as Ardagh (1968). Undoubtedly there was a sense of renewal, of forward movement, and a real, and in many cases dramatic, increase in living standards during the period. But too much emphasis has perhaps been laid by observers on the positive 'achievements' of the French economy and the beneficent rule of the technocrats. The limits of each began to be apparent in the 1960s and to infiltrate public consciousness, as the events of 1968 showed. Too much emphasis on the 'positive' side of the changes transformed those changes into an ideology which needed exposure as such. The emphasis needed to be reversed, to redress the balance. This is evident from the official statistics of the period. Some professional changes meant some material improvements; for agricultural workers, and probably many small farmers, entrance to the manual working class meant an immediate improvement in income and in social protection from risks such as ill-health, but there it stopped. Such movement did not (especially for farmers) mean social promotion in the sense of increased status, nor, necessarily, an acceptance of a new value-system. Their position in terms of the opportunity structure changed little and possibilities for future movement were almost non-existent. Their access to rewards, both material and symbolic, then became that associated with the manual working class. Whichever aspect of the social structure, the economic system, or the distribution of rewards is considered, it becomes obvious that the patterned nature of inequality between members of the society occupying different places in the production process, the relative positions of members of each class, remained virtually unchanged.

4. PROFESSIONAL CHANGE
AND SOCIAL INHERITANCE

Analysis of the opportunity structure in society through an examination of social and professional mobility emphasizes the individual, for it is individuals, and their immediate families, rather than wider groups, who are socially mobile. Rates of social mobility, whether measured in relation to movements in the course of a career or to changes over two or more generations, do, however, provide indications of the over-all rigidity of a social structure. The degree of inheritance either of the precise occupations or occupational positions of their fathers by sons and daughters suggests the limitations on the possibilities open to individuals as members of different social groups, and, even more important, suggests the degree of closure of the different social groups and the nature of the intermediate class as one of transition, a *classe charnière*.

In the early part of our period, discussion of social mobility in relation to France, as elsewhere, was entangled in the debate among observers, largely not French, about the 'convergence' of industrial societies, assumed to have important characteristics and an inner momentum in common. Thus, Lipset and Rogoff (1954) demolished the 'myth' that America was then a land of more equal opportunity than Europe, not by showing that in America opportunity was less equal than was commonly supposed, but by purporting to demonstrate that in European countries it was, mostly, more equal. In France itself, it has been suggested that the political aspects of this debate discouraged French sociologists from carrying out studies of social mobility. For this or other reasons, studies of this kind in France throughout the thirty years covered here were undertaken not by sociologists but by demographers and by the national statistical agency, INSEE, as part of studies of qualifications and job recruitment in the French population.

The analysis of mobility data is always difficult, for the concept itself not only has a number of dimensions, but also, even more important, is particularly linked to the notion of the class structure underlying the number and the arrangement of the categories used. The relationship between profession and social status and, therefore, between professional and social mobility, remains problematic. Most French studies have, although not always explicitly, assumed that professional mobility is the best indicator of changes of status and hence of social mobility. The many thousand 'raw' professional names used in occupational censuses are regrouped by INSEE into nine categories, partly on the basis of 'function', partly on status (whether self-employed or employing and in which sector of the economy), and partly on 'social rank', although no large-scale study of occupational prestige has been carried out in France.

Social and occupational mobility

Social mobility in the present analysis essentially concerns movement between three major groups for, although many aspects of life-chances cluster round the manual—non-manual division of occupations, there is important heterogeneity within the non-manual sections, and the studies made suggest both the existence and the persistence of three major groups in terms of mobility chances.

Discussing one of the early post-war studies, Brésard defines social mobility rather generally as 'the modifications to the social situation of a person in relation to his milieu of origin' (1950: 16). To this Bertaux adds that many observers consider it to be the 'movement of individuals from one social category to another, either in the course of their professional life or in comparison with their milieu of origin' (1970: 37), thus including both intra-generational and inter-generational movements. French studies of inter-generational social mobility have usually taken the father's profession at a point in mid-career, around the end of the education of his children, the son's[1] quite early in his career. Clearly, when using large samples, it is difficult to match exactly the points at which 'measurements' are taken, and there is often considerable variation. Moreover, the significance of posts held at given ages varies by type of profession and by social class; at age twenty-five years a manual worker could have ten or more years of professional life behind him, while a manager would be only just beginning his. The same problem holds in the use of profession held by father at the birth of children, manual worker parents generally being younger than middle-class ones. On the other hand, it is also the case that once a particular kind of occupation has been chosen at the end of formal education, the studies show relatively little movement out from that occupational category. If one is primarily concerned with intra-generational mobility, with changes of post or with particular professions followed, one needs to look carefully at the whole of a working life—which has not been done on any scale in France—but if, on the other hand, one is primarily concerned with changes of category over the generations, for example from manual to non-manual or routine non-manual to higher administrative, then evidence gathered even relatively early in given careers may

[1]   Daughters are, as usual, largely excluded.

be useful, in spite of important limitations to the whole 'transversal' method of collecting mobility data. In France, of course, as in other countries, consideration of the occupational structure, the actual jobs available, and the changes made to the structure over time is important. Because of the complexity of information and the variety of analyses to which data on professional and social mobility are subject, the following discussion is limited to aspects particularly relevant to an analysis of the social effects of economic growth relating to the social and class structure: who moves? where to? and within which sectors?

Inter-generational mobility

All French studies show the overwhelming predominance of professional heredity over the generations, particularly of occupational position but also of occupation itself, in spite of economic changes creating modifications to the occupation structure. Occupational immobility suggests the degree of social rigidity.

Three major studies were carried out in France between 1945 and 1970 and each shows a strikingly similar picture.

The 1940s: the INED study

The first large-scale enquiry was conducted by the Institut National d'Études Démographiques (INED) in November 1948, and directed by Alain Girard and Marcel Brésard. The results were published in the early 1950s by the INED journal, *Population* (1950 and 1951). The study covered 3,076 employed men aged from eighteen to fifty years and was reckoned, by covering their families over several generations, to provide information on over 22,000 people. Particularly interested in the relationship between family size and social mobility, the authors examined professions exercised by their subjects, their subjects' fathers, maternal and paternal grandparents, and fathers-in-law. The categories used, it will be noted, were not the same as those used by INSEE, in particular in the separation of state employees from others.

Table 4.1 shows the very considerable tendency towards professional stability over several generations among the employed male population at the beginning of our period, a tendency reinforced by marriage within the same professional and social group 'with the exception of Category 1, state employees, of executives and of farm workers, everyone marries more within their own milieu than into all the others' (ibid.: 341). The use of the INED study by Natalie Rogoff, in Paris at the time, as a basis for the papers she and Seymour Lipset published, which emphasized the similarities between France and America, has been severely criticized by Daniel Bertaux who, reworking the data, found that the original INED sample, although satisfactory for the purposes INED intended, was biased so as to under-represent the working class (*classe ouvrière*), including only 20 per cent instead of 35 per cent. When this is corrected, working-class upward mobility appears proportionately smaller while downward mobility from the upper classes becomes greater. For example, only 26 per cent of the sons of 'manual' fathers acquired 'non-manual' jobs as against the 35 per cent quoted by Rogoff, while 28 per cent of the sons of 'non-manual' fathers (including artisans etc.) took manual posts, as against the 18 per cent given by Rogoff (Bertaux, 1969: 421–2).

TABLE 4.1.

Professional stability over three generations: percentages

Professions of persons interviewed	Professional Origins %			
	Fathers	Paternal grandfathers	Maternal grandfathers	Fathers in-law
Farmers (owner-occupiers)	83	77·5	73	74
Small businessmen and artisans	54	36	28	36
Workers and unskilled workers*	48	35	34·5	40
Farm workers	37	31	30	29
Industrialists and liberal professions	32	16	15	28
State administrators** II and white-collar workers	31	11	9	29·5
State administrators I and management***	17	10	45	22

Ouvriers et manoeuvres   ** *Fonctionnaires*   *** *Cadres*
Source: Adapted from tables in Brésard, 1950: 540–1.

The 1960s: the first INSEE study

The next major study of social mobility in France did not take place until 1963–4, although INSEE did carry out a study of employment in 1953, some of whose results could be used to study mobility. The results of the 1964 INSEE study are particularly significant here, for they describe the effects, or lack of effects, of the first major wave of economic growth. The study, including over 25,000 interviews, used a representative sample based on the population registered in the 1962 Census, but limited to persons aged between fifteen and sixty five years on

1 January 1963 and inactive persons aged between fifteen and fifty five years at the same date, excluding young men in military service and the unemployed. The study, *La Formation et Qualification Professionnelle des Français,* essentially covered changes in the professional situation of French people in the middle years of our period, between 1959 and 1964. Where upward or downward social mobility, as opposed to horizontal professional mobility, was concerned, the *milieu d'origine* was measured by the socio-professional category of the father at the time when the son finished full-time education, and did not take account of either maternal origins or the situation of grandparents, etc. The mobility measured is therefore fairly specific to one point of time.

Data gathered cover father's occupation and son's position at three stages: the end of education, the beginning of career, and the situation at the time of the study. In-career mobility data were gained by the examination of professional changes at the beginning and end of a five-year period, and constitute two 'photographs'. As the population is limited to cover a fifty-one years' age-span, it may be assumed to be fairly representative of trends in the period. The study gathered information on both inter- and intra-generational movements.

In terms of the analysis of the rigidity or flexibility of a social structure, the degree of professional and social inheritance over the generations is particularly significant, and we take that first. Table 4.2 gives an over-all impression of the inter-generational mobility of the period.

TABLE 4.2.

Men born after 1918, active in 1959 and 1964: percentages

Fathers \ Sons	2	3	4	5	6	0	1	7	8	Total
2 Owners in industry and commerce	28	9	11	9	35	1	1	2	3	100
3 Higher executives and liberal professions	7	41	23	10	9	3	0·6	–	6	100
4 Middle personnel	4·5	17	36	11	21	2	2	–	7	100
5 Employees	7	8	18	15	43·5	1	–	1	6	100
6 Workers	5	2	8·5	8	71	0·9	0·7	0·5	3	100
0 Farmers	5	1·5	3	6	33	41	7	1	3	100
1 Farm workers	4	0·7	2	5	60	3	21	0·7	3	100
7 Service personnel	5	6	9	18	51	–	3·5	1	6	100
8 Others	5·5	7	13	11	46	1	–	–	16	100

Source: Adapted from Praderie *et al.,* 1967. 11.

The overriding impression is not of social mobility at all, but of considerable social immobility. In nearly every category there was a greater tendency for sons to enter their fathers' profession than any other. The major exceptions to this were farm workers' sons, who were nearly three times more likely to become workers in industry than to remain in agriculture in the sons' generation, and the sons of *patrons* of industry and commerce. This was clearly due to fundamental changes in the industry in the first case and to the heterogeneity (social and professional) of the category in the second. However, there was, of course, some movement in all categories.

The table has two particularly important features. First, the tendency for sons of all categories, with the one exception of that of senior executives and the liberal professions, to enter the ranks of the working class, the *classe ouvrière*, when they changed class. Not only was that the most frequent receiving category, but it was virtually always more frequent than all the other categories put together. Secondly, movements were very short; where sons did not enter their fathers' professional category and where they did not become workers, they were likely to be found most in categories adjacent to that of their fathers. Thus, for example, the greatest proportions of sons of employees were found to be employees (the same), workers (below), or middle-grade personnel (*cadres moyens*) in the category above. The groups *not* showing this trend were those that were either isolated, not receiving any entrants (agriculture), or heterogeneous, for instance owners of industry and commerce, who comprised quite considerable numbers of persons close to or from the working class. This remains true even if the period since the Second World War is taken alone, as Table 4.3 shows. Overall, few of these changes, therefore, involved changes of class in terms of the three class grouping.

TABLE 4.3.

Socio-professional category of sons born since 1945: percentages

	2	3	4	5	6	0	1	7
Same category as father	20	33	40	17	74	42	35	–
Next most frequent category	6/44	4/28	6/24	6/63	5/10	6/32	6/47	6/56

Source: Adapted from Praderie *et al.* 1967: 6. The figures underlined refer to the INSEE category code numbers.

These movements, short and principally into the working class, remained most frequent, a situation one might not expect given the job increases in the white-collar sectors. In fact some categories were becoming increasingly 'closed'. Thus, for instance, the percentage of 'sons' entering the working class, the category of their fathers, was actually greater for the 'younger sons' than for all the generations of sons counted together. While in order to have an exact picture, one would need more information on the ages of those concerned—and it should be remembered that these were young men at the beginning of their careers—such a situation runs counter to much popular belief.

The 1970 study

In 1970 INSEE replicated its 1964 study. The sample, stratified by socio-professional category, covered nearly 40,000 persons aged between sixteen and sixty years in 1970, drawn from households recorded in the 1968 census. The study covered job movements between 1965 and 1970, both 'horizontal' and 'vertical', the latter involving changes in 'socio-professional' category and, therefore, probably some social mobility, both intra- and inter-generational.

Table 4.4 shows that mobility had not increased. As Thélot himself points out, comparison of the two periods, 1959—64 and 1965—70, confirms the predominance of immobility over mobility, particularly at the top and bottom of the social scale, with sons of *cadres supérieurs* and members of the liberal professions and manual workers moving little. This is particularly true in the latter case where nearly two-thirds

TABLE 4.4.
Socio-professional categories of fathers and sons: percentages

Fathers \ Sons[†]	2	3	4	5	6	0	1	7	8
2. *Patrons,* industry and commerce*	28	11	13	9	33	2	1	2	2
3. Lib profs., *cadres sups.*	7	42	24	7	14	2	0	1	3
4. Middle management	5	21	32	11	25	0·5	0	2	4
5. White-collar workers	8	10	18	15	42	1	1	2	3
6. Manual workers	6	3	11	9	64	1	1	2	3
0. Farmers	7	2	4	5	35	39	6	1	2
1. Farm workers	8	1	4	6	56	7	16	1	2
7. Service personnel	8	4	18	12	50	1	2	3	3
8. Others	10·5	11	20	10	33	1	3	1	11

* Artisans seem to be included here.
  † Sons' occupation at the time of the study; fathers' is that exercised at the end of sons' education.
Source: Adapted from Thélot, 1973a, 62–3.

of the sons of workers were themselves workers, in spite of the greatly increased educational opportunities of the period since 1945. Moreover, one should underline that where sons did not remain in the same category as their fathers, they continued overwhelmingly to enter the working class. Thus, one-third of the sons of *patrons* (almost certainly *patrons* with the smallest businesses) and independents, 25 per cent of middle executives' sons, 42 per cent of those of white-collar workers, 35 per cent of farmers', 56 per cent of farm workers', 50 per cent of service personnel's, and 33 per cent of sons of 'others' became manual workers. This suggests that where mobility did occur it was frequently *downward*.

In terms of the rigidity of the social structure and of access to important social roles, it is important to emphasize that the 1970 study also showed, again as in the earlier period, that the 'distance' travelled by the socially mobile tended to be short. Where upward movement occurred it was, as before, mostly into the immediately higher category—middle to higher management and white-collar employment to middle executive. An exception, a very small one, was formed by workers' sons going slightly more frequently into middle management than white-collar jobs. The same was true of *downward* movement, from the senior level of management and the liberal professions, where 24 per cent of sons moved into the *cadre moyen* level, but this was almost certainly due, as Thélot says, to the narrowed possibilities for young people with high level diplomas of entering *cadre supérieur* positions at once, and probably simply shows a slight change in career structure.

The role of the education system appears paramount. Discussing this, Thélot shows how, at the one extreme, even the lowest-level Certificat d'Études Primaires (CEP, now abolished) served to distinguish its possessors from those with no diplomas at all and, at the other, that 63 per cent of those with a diploma equivalent to, or higher than, the *licence* entered professional life at a higher level.

Social and professional movement 1965–70

Two major points emerge from the 1970 study which are relevant both to inter- and intra-generational mobility, but in particular perhaps to the latter and which shed considerable light on the nature of the social structure in a period of economic change. The first is that there was generally much greater labour mobility between 1965 and 1970 than between 1959 and 1964: 30 per cent of those active in 1965 and 1970 worked in different establishments in 1970 than in 1965, as against 20 per cent in 1964. Because job movements are fairly clearly determined by job offers on the labour market, the increase in professional mobility was largely due to the restructuring of the apparatus of production in France after 1963–4 (Thélot, 1973b: 3 and 11 ff.). Analysed in terms of exchanges between sectors of production, these movements formed a system whose structure was very little affected by the increase in movement.

Equally important was the *stability* of the type of movement possible over a longish period–1959–70, almost a complete generation–in spite of radical economic changes. The increase in horizontal professional mobility did not change the type of changes made between sectors, and increased job movement did not affect the kind and possibilities of *social* mobility in the course of a career. Most movement remained at the bottom of the scale and within the working class. Where change did occur, however, it is important to examine the 'routes' taken. Table 4.5 gives some indication of paths followed where movement did occur.

TABLE 4.5.

Categories entered by 100 men changing category

Socio-professional category	a.	b.	c.	d.	e.	f.	g.	h.	i.	j.	k.	l.	m.	misc.	Total
a. Foremen		14							31	10				45	100
b. Skilled workers	20		22	5	9				13	11		5		15	100
c. Semi-skilled	6	47		10	10					7				20	100
d. Unskilled			47		7		8							12	100
e. Office workers		8	14	9					10		26	12		21	100
f. Shop workers			17								20		15	48	100
g. Farmers		9	31	22				21						18	100
h. Farm		8	24	27		30								11	100

i. technicians; j. artisans; k. *cadres moyens*, 1. *cadres supérieurs*, m. small shopkeepers.
Source: Greatly adapted from Thélot, 1973b: 24.

It is clear once again that the overwhelming amount of movement took place *within* the working class, rather than from that class outwards. Both intra- and inter-class mobility showed important links between certain professions. Some are obvious–farm workers to farmers, shop assistants to shop-keepers, but some are less evident, for instance those between foremen and technicians. Under the 'miscellaneous' heading the figures remaining show the extent, too, of apparently 'chance' movements, high for foremen and shop workers, low for unskilled labourers and farm workers. Some of this movement must be into the shop assistant category, which otherwise appears as having no entrants.

Not all members of the working class were equally likely to be mobile. The 1970 study confirmed the differential chances of in-career movement out of the working class according to original place within the class—in general, those higher in the class had the most chance of movement out. Over the two periods considered, approximately the same *proportions* moved out of the class, but in the second period more men left to set up independently. This aspect of the occupational structure, therefore, apparently did not disappear with the changing economic structure and concentration of firms into larger enterprises.[2]

Professional and social mobility involved risk taking. Most social mobility occurred through changing the place of work, through passage on the labour market, but this also involved greater risks; mobility could be down as well as up. Staying in the same firm offered fewer chances of promotion, but it also involved fewer risks. The risks involved were distributed differentially by occupation—skilled workers and middle administrative *cadres* ran most. In the former case the market for particular skills was probably limited, and in the latter lack of nationally recognized diplomas meant dependence on promotion through length of service. Passage on the labour market was by no means always voluntary—40 per cent of those seeking work in March 1970, when the INSEE study was done, had been laid off from their old job, and the percentage later rose. The importance of the labour market in mobility underlines once again the dependence of high social mobility in capitalist societies on a boom economy.

Professional changes: intra-generational mobility

INSEE counted as 'professional changes' all movements, whether of job level or type of change of firm, which meant a professional reclassification, the latter including about three-quarters of all movements, but only a small number of these involved 'social' mobility in terms of the nine point INSEE scale.

Description of mobility, both professional and social, is complicated in France by the fact that there continued to be a relatively low proportion of the working population who were salaried, leaving greater numbers than in England, for instance, of independent persons, mostly farmers, artisans, and small businessmen both industrial and commercial.

---

[2] Much of this movement is only apparent however. See below, p. 92–3.

Social mobility, therefore, often involved changes of status (*statut*), which essentially meant a change from independent to salaried and vice versa,[3] as well as changes within the salaried sector by socio-professional category. The latter constitute the movements most frequently discussed by sociologists in Britain; in France not only must the two sections be discussed separately, they must also be considered in relation to each other, for the routes for mobility are important. For example, the route for the manual working class seems to the linked more to the *artisanat* than to career mobility in the sense of promotion from the shop floor.

Change of status

First, changes of status, *statut*. The numerically and sociologically most important of such movements over the period 1945–75 were those between the salaried sector and the *indépendant* or even employing categories. Most of the persons moving from the privately employed to the self-employed sectors did so as artisans, or small shopkeepers and businessmen. Usually they were self-employed but some also became employers of labour. One's *statut* as a private or public employee also had a particular importance in France, for public employees (*fonctionnaires*) had many advantages in terms of job security, pensions, etc.

Between 1959 and 1964 quite important numbers of people changed status in a 'downward' direction: roughly 13 per cent of men and 11 per cent of women *indépendants* became salaried and 7 per cent men and 12 per cent women employers did so. This is the translation into individual careers of the changes in the economic structure of the period. As one would expect, fewer managed to make the reverse change; only 6 per cent of men privately employed and 5 per cent of women, and respectively 8 per cent and 4 per cent employed in the public sector had become self-employed or employers. Overall, 3 per cent of all privately employed persons were involved in such movements. In spite of this tiny proportion, Praderie and Passagez concluded that 'it seems that salaried status constitutes a kind of staging post from which certain types of artisan occupations recruit members, occupations which still exercise a considerable attraction in France' (1966, 40).

In an article based on the INSEE data, Jacqueline Frisch adds greater precision to the analysis of this movement. Most of the changes of status, independent and salaried, affected manual workers, but Frisch

---

[3]   Included among those changing status are persons classed as 'family help', *aide familiale*, frequently employed as part of the family in a family business. Movements of these people account for much of the movement registered.

(1966) points out that it was the upper levels of manual workers, foremen and skilled men, who were most likely to try to become independent, a finding which confirmed that of Andrieux and Lignon. Their
study of industrial workers in a Lyon suburb revealed the prevalence of
the wish to be self-employed, 'se mettre à son compte' (1960). Frisch
showed that 65,000 workers (*ouvriers*) and foremen (*contre-maîtres*)
became artisans, and 46,000 artisans joined or re-joined the salaried
sector. According to these figures the movement towards autonomy
was greater than the reverse flow. Some of both sets of movements, she
suggests, were related to changes in the life-cycle: first young men
worked for others; and then in their thirties or forties they managed to
become independent; as they got older manual dexterity declined, and
in their fifties and sixties they returned again to working for wages.

Life-cycle changes may explain the cyclical nature of some of the
movement, but it does not explain why it affected the skilled workers
and foremen more than other categories. Frisch suggests that these
were the workers who, from the over-all mobility figures, appeared the
least frequently promoted and the most often demoted, *déqualifié*, if
they remained in wage-earning jobs. They were most exposed to career-
blockage and regression, and thus had important 'negative' reasons for
taking their chance alone. But there seem also to have been positive
reasons, related to the image of work learned when young. Thus, Frisch
suggests, it seems that the ideal image of a piece of work finished and
the feeling of powerlessness to achieve that in industrial work were not
felt by the unskilled workers, who had never known it, so much as
by the skilled, who had been taught its value by their teachers in technical colleges and apprenticeship centres and therefore felt most their
situation of dependence. Foremen were not in quite the same position,
and were fairly satisfied with the promotions gained, but this satis-
faction concerned the past and as it was well-known that a foreman's
post was often the end of a manual career, so that little could be hoped
from the future; the alternatives were to resign oneself to the situation,
or leave (1966, 508—511). Workers frequently tried to leave, and
Andrieux and Lignon found that many were not resigned to the depriv-
ations of industrial factory work, even after many years.

In addition to the workers and foremen discussed above, 28,000
persons during the same period became small shop-keepers (*petits
commerçants*). The reverse movement only affected half this number.

Changes within the salaried sector

In relation to intra-generational mobility, professional changes in the course of a lifetime, Table 4.2 shows considerable amount of mobility at all levels of the society, but particularly in two sectors. Movement occurred most in the ranks of middle-grade administrative personnel and white-collar workers in both offices and commerce, and even more among semi-skilled and unskilled workers.

TABLE 4.6.
Changes in socio-professional category, 1959–1964

Socio-Professional Category (men) 1959	Proportion becoming 'independent' %	Rate of upward mobility %	Rate of downward mobility %
Engineers*	0·4	4	2
Higher administrative executives	1	5	4
Technicians	0·5	7	3
Middle-grade administrative personnel	2	9	3
Office employees**	1	11	3
Commercial employees	6	7	9
Foremen	4	5	4
Skilled workers	3	12	5
Semi-skilled workers	2	12	4
Unskilled workers	1	14	–

* *Ingénieurs*–a wider category than 'engineers', the title may be gained by examination or promotion. *Ingénieurs* graduating from the top Grandes Écoles in France have extremely high social status.

** Movements into this category are not included; nor are those employees becoming skilled workers (*ouvriers qualifiés*).
Source: Frisch, 1966: 504. The table is calculated from Annex IV, p. 144–5 of M. Praderie, *et al.*, 1966. The proportions relate to the totals for each category in 1959.

While it would need a study of entire careers to present a complete picture, the figures presented are nevertheless significant. They show a considerable amount of movement at certain levels of the hierarchy, especially 'commercial employees' and below, and concerning both changes in 'status' and upward and downward mobility, in the course of the five-year period. There was, particularly, a good deal of movement within the working class. In general, mobility increased as qualification level diminished, for 30 per cent of unskilled workers *manoeuvres*, changed category while only 15–16 per cent of foremen did so. Of all the changes made by the semi-skilled (*ouvriers spécialisés*) about half were into the ranks of the skilled, and another 20 per cent moved down to join the *manoeuvres* (Praderie and Passagez, 1969: 79). Much of this movement occurred when people changed firms, or where there were specific, and often short-term, demands for low-level skills, usually learned on the job. It seems unlikely that most such movements constituted very great changes for those who made them.

The middle sectors

Skilled workers and foremen had relatively low rates of mobility within the salaried sector and tended, when mobile, to move towards 'independence'. The middle sectors, however, were as heterogeneous as their name suggests.

The most mobile section of the middle 'classes' was composed of shop workers, *employés de commerce*. Between 1959 and 1964 11 per cent moved up, 9 per cent down, and 6 per cent towards independence. Many of the mobile were employees who, little by little, brought the business (as well as women who married the boss), but much 'promotion' seems to have been due to the development of longer commercial hierarchies in some sectors, due the the increased size of enterprises, and changes of rank for such people as commercial representatives (Frisch, 1966: 505). Some, undoubtedly, also become *cadres* by length of service (Praderie and Passagez, 1966: 83). Office workers, middle administrative personnel, and technicians were all fairly mobile, largely because the changing economic structure led to the expansion of these categories in the active population. In 1959, for example, there was one technician for every seven workers, and numbers of technicians continued to increase.

How much mobility?

The limits of the transversal approach

Recently sociologists have begun to be aware that the 'statistical mass' or 'transversal' approach to the study of mobility, which takes groups of individuals at two (or more) points of time and analyses professional and social mobility in terms of those points of time, as done by INSEE, tends to overestimate social mobility by misunderstanding certain professional changes. In an important article published in 1974 Bertaux re-analysed the 1967 INSEE data presented above and introduced the concept of 'counter-mobility' developed by Roger Girod in Geneva and emphasised the necessity of separating social 'belonging' (*appartenance sociale*) from the profession exercised at any given moment. This is the case of the sons of artisans who work as manual labourers for a certain period before succeeding their fathers at the head of an enterprise; 'the social relation which linked him (the son) to his father (inheritance) already existed before his birth, and only needed to be realized in an education, a vision of the world, a life; this relation has never been broken. There has therefore been no social mobility, only professional mobility' (Bertaux, 1974: 329). On the contrary, there has been a rein-forcement of the position of the son inside his group of origin (Girod, 1971).

By not considering this important 'counter-mobility', the usual interpretations of INSEE data greatly overestimate the amount of social mobility between manual or farm workers and artisans or other 'independent' categories. For example, data from 1959 and 1964 taken alone suggest that one in five, or even one in four, farm workers could achieve the status of 'independent' in the course of their working life; but in fact 93 per cent of those making the apparent change were in fact 'counter-mobile', for they were the sons of farmers whose places they were inheriting. Contrary to appearances, it seems that in fact passage from farm worker to owner-farmer was virtually impossible in the French countryside after 1945 (ibid.: 339).

More important perhaps, is the overestimation of movements between the manual working class (*ouvriers*) and independent professions as seen in the 'promotion' of skilled workers who 'became' artisans or small shop-keepers, of semi-skilled workers (O.S.), who 'moved' to artisan roles, and shop workers who 'became' small shop-keepers. Of the persons involved in such changes between 1959 and 1964, 39 per cent were the sons of 'independents', *patrons* or *cadres supérieurs*, and were therefore 'counter-mobile' and not socially mobile. Thus Praderie was over-optimistic when he stated that 16 per cent of shop workers became shop-keepers—the true figure was nearer zero per cent (ibid., 343). The only real changes were made by skilled workers who became artisans or small shop-keepers, especially in sectors such as the building trades. Thus, of all those who apparently changed status, 43 per cent only were truly the sons of salaried persons, while 40 per cent were the sons of *patrons* and 17 per cent the sons of farmers, most of whom had had active family aid, (ibid., 345). The same analysis applied to the different categories of the salaried population shows similar results, whether we consider movements from worker to non-manual positions or between the different levels of the non-manual hierarchy. In particular, the 'technical' route for mobility which could be open to skilled manual workers was limited to movement to the level of technician.

Re-analysis of the INSEE data using the biographical rather than the 'transversal' method shows a society even more rigidly structured than the tables above would suggest. 'Counter-mobility' accounted for more than half of the mobility found (ibid.: 354) where changes of 'status' were concerned.

Structural and net mobility

In a general sense, the insertion of individuals into economic roles is the result of the meeting of two populations; that of potential workers, and that of available posts. To the extent to which in any given society these two populations, persons and posts, do not coincide, the differences between them inevitably lead to movements by persons from certain social origins into other social categories. These movements taken together constitute *structural social mobility*. Once the effects of this have been subtracted from the over-all figures, there remains a certain circulation, *net social mobility*. The latter, unlike the former, is exclusively composed of *exchanges* between categories (Bertaux, 1970: 38). Movements constituting net social mobility affected only very small numbers in French society.

Structural mobility results from economic and technological changes, and the policies associated with them, and from a factor underlined long ago by Lipset and Rogoff, differential fertility among the various social classes. The political aspect associated with technological changes is here important, especially as it affects the timing of the 'pure' results.[4] Where differential fertility was concerned in France, Bourdieu and Darbel show that even with the great increase in the birth rate after the Second World War, the differences between classes remained the same. The number of children per family first decreased as one climbed the social scale and reached a minimum with the *classe moyenne*, and then increased as one approached the top of the scale (in Darras, 1966: 136–7). Precisely those persons in the most rapidly expanding occupational sectors had fewest children, whereas those already at the top of the social hierarchy had most.[5]

---

[4] Thus, for instance, the great agricultural 'exodus' could 'technically' have taken place much earlier in France than it did under a different agricultural policy.

[5] Differential fertility analysis often forms part of mobility studies, and it is relevant here to analyse the changes in family fertility behaviour among couples formed before and after the Second World War. Léry (1971) shows that couples formed between 1920 and 1934 had, after ten years of marriage, only 1·8 children on average, while couples formed after 1940 had after the same period of time 2·3 children. The increase in fertility was not uniform over class (nor within each class by socio-professional category) and geographical area, but was general to all in some degree. It is noticeable that *cadres supérieurs* and members of the liberal professions increased the size of their families most, while farmers did so least. Calot and Deville (1971), using data gathered from a family study covering 240 000 women in 1962, show that among manual workers there was considerable variation and that the level of fecundity varied inversely with the level of job

In order to measure the importance of structural mobility in France revealed by the INSEE studies, Bertaux constructed a model, a mobility 'ladder', based both on the kinds of posts available and sociological data on the family and on educational and social mechanisms acting in France to distribute persons in different roles. The model refutes the notion of direct movement from declining sectors into newly created higher-level posts elsewhere in the economy, and shows instead that in the mid-1960s

the differences between the working population and posts available mean that for every eleven posts 'lost', two are those of agricultural workers, two farmers, two small businesses. The eleven 'created' are one *cadre supérieur*, two *cadres moyens*, two *employés*, six workers. The result is that two sons of farm-workers become factory and other workers, of seven farmers' sons, five become workers, and two employees, one son of a small business man becomes an employee and the other a worker. In total, that means eight new workers and three new employees, which allows two sons of skilled workers to become technicians (or *cadres moyens*) and one employee son to become a *cadre supérieur* unless that post has been filled by the children of industrialists or bigger *commerçants*. This is the result of fundamental social mechanisms which tend towards social immobility or at best limit movements. The adjustment of the rising generation of the new population structures is done by 'cascades of small movements' (Bertaux, 1970, 42)

Once structural mobility is subtracted from total mobility there emerges a picture of net mobility. In relation to the total society the three major classes maintain very similar proportions over the generations, although they were subject to considerable and important internal modifications. Bertaux suggests that the *classes dirigeantes* comprised 7 per cent of the population, the *classes moyennes* 30 per cent, and the *classes populaires* 63 per cent. Using INSEE figures, he concludes that around 5 per cent of the population were upwardly mobile because of

---

qualification. Thus, the foremen (*contre-maîtres*) had fewest children, then came qualified workers, and lastly unskilled workers and miners, who had most children. Several groups had about two children per family; the liberal professions and *cadres supérieurs* (2·01), *patrons* of industry and commerce (1·94), and white-collar workers (*employés*) (1·93). Of all the social groups, lowest family size was found amongst *cadres moyens*, technicans, primary school teachers, and middle administrative personnel, those who constituted the mobile middle classes. Later data suggested the same trend (*Informations Sociales*, 1973). Low fertility of the middle classes, coupled to an increase of middle-class jobs on the labour market, meant possibilities of upward mobility for members of the more numerous working class.

structural mobility over the post-war years until 1965. The diagrams in
Fig. 4.1 pinpoint the differing possibilities of mobility.

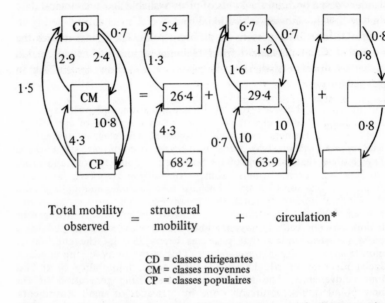

$$\frac{\text{Total mobility}}{\text{observed}} = \frac{\text{structural}}{\text{mobility}} + \text{circulation*}$$

CD = classes dirigeantes
CM = classes moyennes
CP = classes populaires

*This is in two parts to show the difference between perfectly symmetrical
movement and long upward movements balanced by two short downward ones.
Source: Bertaux, 1970: 43.

Fig. 4.1. Structural and net mobility

Bertaux suggests that the rate of upward mobility due to structural
causes was around 50 per cent; net upward mobility was 14 per cent
and downward also 14 per cent (since by defintiion it constitutes a
circulation).

The chances for mobility shown here were clearly not evenly distributed between social classes, and show the links and divisions amongst
them. The links between the *classes dirigeantes* and the *classes moyennes*
are there, and the transitional nature of the latter may be seen by their
links with the *classes populaires*. The *classes moyennes* provided almost
half of the personnel of the upper classes, and the *classes populaires*
provided one-third of the *classes moyennes*. Half of middle-class sons
remained in middle-class occupations; another 40 per cent became
workers, but 10 per cent rose. Three-quarters of the son of the *classes
populaires* remained there and nearly the whole of the last quarter went
to the middle class; only 2·2 per cent acquired top status thus confirming the radical separation in terms of personnel between the top and

To obtain an index of opportunity, this movement must be considered in relation to the size of the classes concerned. The comparison makes it clear that although the middle class and upper class contributed equally to the recruitment of the latter, the fact that the middle class comprised five times as many people meant that a son from that class had five times fewer chances of reaching the upper class than had a 'son' of the upper class of remaining there. The same was true for the middle class, considered in relation to the *classes populaires*. The latter were twice as numerous as the former, and thus, in spite of the fact that half the middle class sons moved down to the *classes populaires*, in practice middle-class sons were twice as likely to remain where they were than to move down (Bertaux, 1969: 475).

The rigid and limited nature of the opportunity structure is even more evident when the population is broken down into smaller categories. Working-class professional heredity was very great; 74 per cent of working class sons began professional life as *ouvriers*. Within the higher social levels there was more variety. The children of *cadres supérieurs* and members of liberal professions moved little (62 per cent were in the same category), and the sons of independent industrialists (*patrons de l'industrie*), who inherited family business, moved even less. The sons of *ingénieurs* were much less socially stable. *Ingénieurs* were more heterogenous in origin, a much bigger proportion acquiring their position by promotion, instead of by direct entry, than was the case, for example, with teachers or, *a fortiori*, the members of the liberal professions. *Cadres moyens* children moved most, but even there 54 per cent of the sons remained in the same professions as their fathers. Where the means of entry to a profession were more flexible, one found a wider variety of social origins, and hence of career patterns, both for parents and their sons and daughters (Praderie *et al.*, 1967: 8–17). The role of education is again crucial, facilitating social mobility for some but in blocking it for others.

There were also important differences in career patterns of members of different groups, even among those who had been socially mobile, and even mobile to the same degree: of the sons of farmers and small businessmen who had been upwardly socially mobile, the vast majority became *cadres administratifs supérieurs*, but the sons of businessmen mostly became *ingénieurs*, (Praderie *et al.*, 1976: 14).

'Real' and 'perfect' mobility

The most common scheme of reference for analysing the 'amount' of mobility and the 'rigidity' of a society is that of hypothetical 'perfect mobility'. Under such a system an individual would be allocated an economic role and the associated social position entirely without reference to his social origins as measured by the socio-professional category of his father. The difference found between a perfect mobility situation and the real one is shown in Table 4.7. The relatively close links between the upper and middle classes remain salient, since between them the amount of mobility was higher than in a situation of 'perfect' mobility, and the lower classes remained relatively isolated. The exchanges between lower and middle classes and between lower and upper classes were respectively inferior (1·6 times) and much inferior (4 to 5 times) than predicted under perfect mobility. Although the category 'worker' (*ouvrier*) contained persons of all social origins except *ingénieurs* and the liberal professions, and although virtually all groups at all levels of the system sent about 10 per cent of their sons into the working classes, the exchanges between the top and the bottom categories were fewer than under perfect mobility. Immobility here appears proportionately greater the finer are the gradations used; and the smaller the categories considered, the faster was the drop in relative numbers of 'departures' to other categories (Bertaux, 1970: 46).

TABLE 4.7.
'Real' and 'perfect' mobility

Perfect Mobility					Real situation of met mobility			
Social origins \ sons' position	CD	CM	CP	Total pop.	Social origins \ sons' position	CD	CM	CP
CD	0·4	1·6	8·5	5·4	CD	6·2	1·5	0·2
CM	1·8	7·8	16·8	26·4	CM	2·8	1·6	0·6
CP	4·5	20·0	43·6	68·2	CP	0·3	0·6	1·2
	6·7	29·4	63·9	100				

CD = *classes dirigeantes*   CM = *classes moyennes*   CP = *classes populaires*
Source: Bertaux, 1970: 44.

These findings about France in the period after 1945 may be compared to those about other countries. Fox and Miller, in an article on intra-country variations in occupational stratification and mobility, calculated the chances of sons of various classes of acceding to élite status in Great Britain, the United States, the Netherlands, and Japan at a similar time. Using a three-class division (élite, middle class, and working class, the latter being further divided into skilled, semi-skilled, and unskilled) they found that, in Great Britain, middle-class sons had almost three times the possibilities of skilled manual sons of entering the élite, six times those of the semi-skilled, and nine times the chances of unskilled sons. Even more important, the son of an élite father had five times the chances of a middle class son of becoming a member of the élite himself. In the U.S.A. middle-class sons had greater chances of entering the élite than they had in Britain but, perhaps at first sight suprisingly, it was in the United States that 'the ability of sons of élite fathers to inherit their fathers' status is greatest' (1967: 579). Such detailed percentages have not been calculated for France except to show that a son of the middle classes had five times fewer chances of joining the élite than had a son of the élite of remaining there. All the evidence suggests that the chances must have been distributed in a very similar way, and, perhaps because of the greater importance of specific educational qualifications in France, that the chances there in fact diverged even more widely between strata, at least as far as access to the élite was concerned.[6]

Whichever way one measures the phenomenon the conclusion for France remains the same; throughout the thirty years of economic expansion between 1945 and 1975, there remained a greater tendency towards immobility within each level of the social and class structure than towards movement. In terms of personnel recruitment, top and middle groups were linked, as were middle and bottom groups, but top and bottom groups remained almost completely isolated from each other.

[6] Fox and Miller found, however, that patterns of mobility differed in different parts of the class structure, and that inheritance and accessibility were different dimensions of similar phenomena. The French data outlined above undoubtedly support that suggestion, and it may not always be very illuminating to try to compare over-all mobility rates in such a way.

5. SCHOOL AND CLASS

The persistence of social immobility, particularly in relation to the inheritance of occupational and class positions, suggests an inflexible social and class structure involving certain basic divisions, and associated with those divisions a number of social institutions which exercise important constraints on the social and sociological possibilities open to individuals in given parts of that structure. Certain social institutions both made this immobility probable and acted to justify and legitimate it. The occupational order, based on the system of production, in any society, largely determines which roles are 'socially' available but other mechanisms, less directly linked to the economic system, act to direct particular individuals into those roles.

The most important of these social institutions in France was the education system; the systematic nature of class opportunities throughout the period considered was very clearly seen in the equally systematic nature of the selection process in education, such that in the different schools at each level of the *cursus* there corresponded in social terms a different 'public'. This correspondence suggests the role of the formally free and obligatory education system in the reproduction of social inequality in French society and its analysis involves discussion of the acquisition and use of *cultural* capital and the way in which in this case, too, capital attracts capital.

The ideal of education

The philosopher and revolutionary, Condorcet, wrote in 1792 that, 'to offer education should enable all men to develop their full potential'; he believed that one could, by this means, 'establish among citizens a *de facto* equality and also make real the political equality recognized by the law; this must be the first goal of national education and . . . it is a duty of justice for the public authorities.' One hundred and sixty-six years later in the Constitution of 1958 (the Fifth Republic) the French nation 'guarantees the equal access of children and adults to instruction, vocational training, and culture', and states that 'the organization of state education, which is free and non-denominational is a duty of the State' (Ambassade de France, 1971: 3). The ideals remained very much the same in 1970 as in 1790, and were enshrined in the official ideology of the State.

The reality, however, was different. Through the selection process it operated and the close links between diplomas held and job opportunities available, the education system remained after 1945 one of the main mechanisms which contributed to the continuance of low social mobility. It was also the education system which, by its verdicts on the gifts and hence the merits of individuals, justified the allocation of those individuals to their social and economic roles and by doing so legitimated the selection process. The functions of the education system linked it very closely to the class system and the structure of class relations. The more 'perfectly' it could operate, that is to say, the more children it touched, the more it contributed to the maintenance of inequality, while at the same time masking the reality of inequality of opportunity in France. This summarizes the view of most French sociologists of education, which were developed from studies of the school system after 1945.

Selection, advancement and elimination

Education in France after 1945 played a crucial role in élite recruitment and in the maintenance of élite positions. An education system is, Durkheim pointed out more than half a century ago, a social institution, and must be studied in its social context both past and present, for historical study of education systems shows that they depend on such social factors as religion, political organization, the degree of scientific development, the state, and the stage of industrialization, to which should be added the nature of the class system and the type of social mobility permitted. Different education systems allow for and deal with problems such as manpower expansion, curricular change, student motivation and choice, and the expansion of different education branches and levels in different ways and societies allow educational diplomas a different weight in occupational role allocation. These in turn seem to depend very considerably on the structure of class relations and the legitimating ideology in the society concerned, as well as the recognized ways of access to élite positions.

In 1960 Ralph Turner proposed a model for examining such problems. He intended the model to highlight the difference between the U.S.A. and Great Britain, which he took as his ideal types, but in many respects France fits it more closely even than Great Britain. Turner suggested a distinction between *contest mobility*, dominant in the U.S.A., and *sponsored mobility*, found in Britain. Context mobility, a system in which élite status is the prize in an open context and taken by the aspirants' own efforts, all aspirants being kept together as long as possible during the race, is compared to sponsored mobility, where élite recruits are 'sponsored' by the established élite or their agents who judge the candidate to have the qualities they wish to see in fellow members, élite status being given on the basis of some criterion of merit.

Such a controlled selection process claims to sort individuals each to the appropriate niche. Candidates' credentials serve to identify members of the élite to each other; ideal ones are special skills requiring trained discrimination for their recognition, such as intellectual, literary, or artistic excellence. Under this system, selection must proceed from an early age, as such skills must be taught over a long period. Education concentrates on 'culture', and inculcates the high evaluation of culture, while the teaching of the non-élite tends to be half-hearted, maximum resources being concentrated on 'those who can benefit most from them'. Such a system, Turner suggests, is mostly likely to exist in a society where élites are small in number and closely interlinked among themselves, with basic agreement amongst members of what constitutes the basis of élite status. Both the emphasis on the possesion of culture and a synthesizing mind, requiring early selection and long training, and a small number of interlinked élites characterized French society and appeared in the education system. The importance of selection, far from decreasing, became increasingly important after 1945 because of the tremendous growth in over-all numbers in all parts of the education system (see Table 5.1).

Secondary school studies

Sociologists in France in the 1950s and the early 1960s were especially concerned to analyse the social origins of the pupils in the then greatly expanding secondary section of the education system. In this perspective, Girard in 1948 found that it took at least two generations for a peasant farmer's or industrial worker's children to move to professions requiring secondary education; there were no unskilled industrial workers or farm labourers among the grandfathers of the children he studied. Ten years later Christiane Peyre (1959) found that although there had been an increase in the proportion of working-class children in *lycée sixième* (first-form) classes after the war, in the mid-to-late 1950s the proportion stabilized at about 12 per cent. In other words the great increase in *lycée* numbers was due not to working-class children's admission but to far greater use of the secondary school system by children of members of the *patronat* and the liberal professions, with some increase also in the numbers from white-collar homes. Thus, and this is important for the later theory, the upper classes

TABLE 5.1.
The growth of education

Year	Total Population (millions)	BR increase over DR	Numbers in primary education	Numbers in secondary education	Numbers in higher education (Univs)	% population aged 0–19	Education Budget as % total budget
1801	27,350						
1850	35,783	+ 72,600				38·5	
1900	38,962	+ 82,600				34·3	
1920	39,210	+ 84,600	(1924) 3,748,000	(1925) 243,500	49,900		
1930	41,835	+ 31,800	4,545,000	243,100	78,700		
1940	40,503	− 77,800	(1939) 5,255,000	(1939) 425,100	(1939) 79,000		
1945		− 78,000	4,535,000	462,800	123,000		
1950	42,777	(1946–5) + 322,900	4,460,000	563,000	139,600	29·5	
1955	47,558	+ 275,500	5,517,000	750,000	157,000		7·21
1960	48,600*	+ 295,000	6,153,000	1,207,000	210,900	31·8	9·63
1965			6,407,000	2,008,000	367,000		12·4
					(1968) 616,000		16·98 (1968)
1970	50,500*		6,245,000**	3,549,250††	680,000		17·4
							19·4

BR = birth-rate   DR = death-rate

* Figures approximate   ** Ministry figures, State schools only

†† of which 2,308,000 are in the lower secondary cycle. Ministry figures, State schools only.

Source: Dupeux, 1964; Prost, 1968; Ambassade de France: *Education in France*, and *Population in France*; London, late 1960s.

in the society began early to use the expanded facilities of the education system. The socially selective nature of the system was apparent in all the studies made and continued throughout the 1960s.

The emphasis of most studies of the secondary school was essentially on the family in relation to the school, and not the school as a social system with a role, both avowed and hidden, in relation to the rest of the society. Such studies provide us with excellent data on the former aspect of the problem and form the basis of the development of the theory concerning the latter.

Examining the links between school and family, Girard and his colleagues at INED undertook a remarkable study of a cohort of 20,000 school children arriving at the end of primary schooling in 1961–2 and entering the *sixième* classes of the secondary schools. These children were followed throughout their secondary education so that the influences on their 'choices' could be determined. Table 5.2 shows the situation by class origin of the children at the 'end' of primary education in 1963.

TABLE 5.2.
The percentage of children in different types of school at age of entry to the sixième*

Profession of father	Without Profession	Farm Workers	Farmers	Manual Workers	Artisans Indpendents	Employees (White-collar Workers)	Lib. Prof.	Higher exec. Business Civ. Service
Type of school								
remaining in primary schools	54	61	56	57	32	31	10	6
CEG**	23	21	24	29	34	34	23	19
Lycées	14	11	16	16	32	33	67	75
Total in *sixième* classes	37	32	40	45	66	67	90	94

* the first classes in secondary schools   ** Collèges d'Enseignement Général
Source: Girard, Bastide and Pourcher, 1963: 31.

A series of articles based on INED studies of education were published in *Population* during the 1960s. They have recently been republished in a volume entitled Population et l'enseignement, I.N.E.D., Presses universitaires de France, Paris, 1971.

Here the social selection is clear; most working-class children remained in primary education but even those in secondary school did not go to the better ones. Thus, the children of the *classe populaire* were to be found overwhelmingly in CEG., with very few in *lycées*. The middle sectors were virtually equally distributed and the higher ones in reverse order, the *lycée* predominating by far. The INED studies confirmed Peyre's findings, showing that all categories had increased their entry to secondary education by about twenty percentage points, thereby raising the lowest proportions to about 30–40 per cent (workers, farmers) but making entry to *sixième* classes a virtual certainty for children of the top three groups at 93–4 per cent of the age group.

Selection by 'ability' thus greatly favoured certain social groups in the early 1960s and meant that most working-class children did not receive any secondary education at all. The Berthoin Reform of 1959 introduced the principle of two 'cycles' of common education in the CEG and the *lycées*, and created the new Collèges d'Enseignement Secondaire (CES, the French 'comprehensive' equivalent) while raising the school-leaving age to sixteen years, to come into force in 1967. Theoretically, children were to be able to switch easily from one kind of school to another, including the reorganized technical education establishments, the Collèges d'Enseignement Technique (CET). In practice very little movement was possible, and although 'physical' movement between schools was no longer necessary, as the CES came to cater for all children in 'general' education,[1] the *lycées* having become preparatory institutions for the *baccalauréat*, there remained much separation in fact within the schools between children of different streams, and 'choice' of section and subject remain crucial to the *cursus* as it was before.

From the end of the second year in secondary school a series of important educational choices had to be made, although theoretically not final ones, between a variety of types of class and school. Within the schools there were 'cycles' of longer or shorter duration which constituted routes, *filières*, leading to different academic goals and hence occupational possibilities. The 'transition' classes, in particular, led outwards to the productive process at a very early age as children could still be released from the obligation of following full-time education at fourteen years of age if their employer declared them as in *pré-apprentissage*, pre-apprenticeship. The probabilities of children making certain types of choices in relation to the social origins in the

[1] Some physical separation also remained in the early 1970s, the transition classes' being frequently outside the main buildings (Warck and Wagner, 1973).

mid-1960s have been calculated by Baudelot and Establet. The probabilities are calculated using the number of children in *quatrième* classes, aged from twelve to sixteen years, from a given social class divided by the total number of children of that age from that social class.

TABLE 5.3.

Probability of educational choice at the level of quatrième*
by socio-professional origins*

Socio-professional category	4e classical	4e modern 1	4e modern 2	practical	CET
lib. profs., high. execs.	0·312	0·231	0·199	0·051	0·097
cadres moyens and white-collars	0·150	0·182	0·287	0·054	0·203
patrons, ind. and com.	0·131	0·146	0·257	0·040	0·145
workers	0·050	0·090	0·202	0·079	0·259
farmers	0·049	0·064	0·199	0·032	0·103
farm workers	0·037	0·061	0·251	0·087	0·193

* *quatrièmes* are the third year classes in secondary schools.
Source: Baudelot and Establet, 1971: 76.

Clear divisions are apparent in the table; *cadres supérieurs*' children 'opted' overwhelmingly for the classical and *moderne* 1 sections, while working-class and farm children were essentially diverted towards the *moderne* 2 section, the transition classes (practical) and the Collèges d'Enseignement Technique (CET). Choices made by the children of white-collar workers were much more dispersed, as were those of the *patronat*, both socially very heterogeneous categories. The reasons for the systematic nature of choices at the top and bottom of the scale and the 'mixed' nature of the middle categories will become clear below.

Selection for higher education

Higher education was the area where selection processes reached their apogee and where one may see the relationship between these processes and social class most clearly.

Over-all numbers of students in higher education began increasing fast in France after 1945. In 1936 there were approximately 74,000 students; in 1945, 130,000; by 1960 there were 210,000, reaching 367,000 by 1965, and increasing in 1970 to 489,000 and 680,000 in 1971. In the 1950s it was the higher echelons of the education system which were increasing proportionately the fastest as the economy changed, and a degree became necessary for a wider range of occupation.[2] This may be seen as a first indication of the use made of the education system by the bourgeoisie to maintain their position in a changing society. However, although by 1959 France recruited 2 per cent more of the eligible age-group into the universities than did England or Germany, only the same proportion, or a lower one, graduated, as only one student in three managed to get a degree.

The first major study of the class origins of university students appeared in 1964 when Bourdieu and Passeron published *Les Héritiers,* followed by *Les Étudiants et leurs études.* In 1962 Raymond Aron remarked that the representation of different social classes in the Universities was the reverse image of their representation in the nation, and the INSEE and BUS[3] figures used by Bourdieu and Passeron showed clearly the truth of this.

TABLE 5.4.

The social origins of university students, 1961–2

Socio-professional category	Millions in active population	Thousands students	% age-group of 20 years in universities
Agricultural workers	0·8	1	0·7
Industrial workers	7	14	1
Domestic servants	1	2	2
Farmers	3	12	4
Employees	2	17	9·5
Owners (industry, commerce artisans)	2	37·5	16
Lower executives	1·5	38	30
Liberal professions Higher executives	0·7	60	58·5
Without profession	?	15	?
Other	0·6	16	?
Industrialists	0·08	8	?

Source: Adapted from Bourdieu and Passeron, 1964a: 14–15.

Strikingly 'over-represented' were the offspring of members of the liberal professions and higher executives—only 760,000 in the active population but providing 60,400 students, 58·5 per cent of their twenty-year olds. Equally strikingly under-represented were the children

---

[2] At this period, too, it was clearly the sons of the upper classes who were accounting for the increase in numbers. See Aron, 1962. 260 81. Also 'Combien d'Etudiants?', *Le Figaro,* 3 April 1964.

[3] Bureau Universitaire de Statistiques.

of agricultural workers, whose numbers actually dropped between 1951 and 1961, although this could partly be due to their drastic decline in the active population. During the same period, workers' children increased their representation from 1·9 per cent to 5·5 per cent of the total number of students, an increase which did nothing to change the image of the University as the reverse of the nation.

The hierarchy of social classes in the wider society was faithfully mirrored in the hierarchy of educational establishments; the higher the level of a 'school', the greater were the chances of the children of the higher social classes to be there, to each school and type of school corresponding a particular public. The summit of the academic hierarchy was formed by the *École Normale Supérieure* (Rue d'Ulm) and the *École Polytechnique*. In spite of the reputedly 'democratic' nature of these schools, particularly the ENS, in 1961–2, 51 per cent and 57 per cent respectively of the students were the sons of fathers in the liberal professions or in higher executive positions, 15 per cent the sons of middle- and lower-grade executives, and only 1 per cent in each came from any section of agriculture and 3 per cent and 2 per cent from industrial workers' families. Similarly, the social origins of students

TABLE 5.5.
Social origins of faculty students and candidates and students of the top Grandes Écoles, *late 1960s/ percentages*

Socio-prof. category	Fac. sci.	Fac. letters	*Taupe**	*Khâgne*	Polytech.	Ulm sci.	Ulm letters
Farm wks.	3	3	0·5	3	0·4	2	0·6
Farmers	6	5	0·5	2	2	2	–
Manual wks.	15	15	4	4	4	2·5	5
White coll.	9·5	10	6·5	4	5	6	8
Artisans	5	5	2	1	1	2	1
Shopkeepers Midd. Exec.	8	9	5	3	4	3	2
Primary School tchrs	5	5	3	6	6	3	5
Higher Exec.	95	11	21	30)	26	21	30·5
Industrialists	2	3	6	2)	26	21	30·5
Engineers	8	6	15	5	20	14·5	6
Lib Profs.	8·5	9	8	10	10	14	10
Secondary & higher techrs	4·5	5	5	15	10	18	19

* *Taupe* are the classes in which one prepares for Polytechnique and similar. *Khâgne* for Ulm (the *École Normale Supérieure*).
Source: Bourdieu *et al.*, 1970, Annexe I.

varied systematically by faculty and by preparatory class for each *Grande École* (see Table 5.5).[4]

Not only where the admitted sudents at the highest schools largely drawn from the upper classes but they were from systematically higher origins than their unsuccessful colleagues in *taupe* and *khâgne*. It will be useful to compare these figures with those of faculty students by discipline over time and to compare these figures with those referring to students in other *Grandes Écoles* not mentioned above.

The differences in the social origins of students between faculties which were evident in 1960 remained almost constant in 1967 according to a study carried out by the Ministry of Education in the late 1960s ('Les étudiants en France', No. 3677, La Documentation Française, Paris, 1969: 13). Medicine and pharmacy continued to recruit most students from the highest social strata. This in medicine in 1966–7, 41% of students were the children of senior managers, 15% those of industrial and commercial *patrons*, and 14% were from middle managerial families (34%, 17%, and 12% in 1960–1). In pharmacy the proportions were respectively 43%, 19%, and 12% (42%, 24%, and 13% in 1960–1). Law came a close third with respectively 30%, 16%, and 14% such students in 1966–7. At the other end of the scale, in 1966–7 these faculties still recruited only between 3% and 9% of students from white-collar, manual, and farm families as opposed to between 2% and 9% in 1960–1; and this in spite of a doubling of overall student numbers over the period concerned.

From Tables 5.5 and 5.6 one is obliged to note the most complete immobility of the social structure of the student population throughout the 1960s. The proportion of students from each social class changed very little in spite of the increased representation of children from all social groups in the secondary education system, and indeed the increase in the numbers in the different groups in the whole population (although this might not yet show for the highest echelons of the system). Moreover, in terms of the social and economic value of the diplomas gained, the drop in attendance by students from the bourgeoisie in the faculties which had effectively the fewest outlets on the job market for their graduates was significant. They moved away

---

[4] The 'open-entry' (to baccalauréat-holders) universities are not the most prestigious institutions of higher education, that place being held by the selective entry Grandes Écoles, especially the major engineering schools and the École Nationale d'Administration.

TABLE 5.6.

Social origins of students in Grandes Écoles, late 1960s: percentages

Socio-Prof. Category	INSEAD	Polytec.	Mines (Paris)	Centrale	ENA	HEC	Ulm lettres	Ulm Sci.	ESCP	ESSEC
*Patrons** and *Cadres Sups.*	59·5 ⎫	24 ⎫	28 ⎫	30 ⎫	19 ⎫	38 ⎫	25 ⎫	16 ⎫	13 ⎫	6 ⎫
Liberal Profs	13 ⎬ 72·5	10 ⎬ 37	8 ⎬ 37	5 ⎬ 36·5	17·5 ⎬ 45·5	8 ⎬ 53	10 ⎬ 38	14 ⎬ 35	28 ⎬ 41	25·5 ⎬ 31
Senior civil Servs.	⎭	3 ⎭	1 ⎭	1·5 ⎭	9 ⎭	7 ⎭	3 ⎭	5 ⎭	12 ⎭	12 ⎭
Ingénieurs	13·5 ⎫	20 ⎫	13·5 ⎫	13 ⎫	6 ⎫	11 ⎫	5·5 ⎫	14·5 ⎫	12 ⎫	16 ⎫
Teachers	⎬	15 ⎬ 46	8 ⎬ 41·5	11 ⎬ 39	11 ⎬ 30	5 ⎬ 29	25 ⎬ 42·5	21 ⎬ 46	5 ⎬ 27	4 ⎬ 39
Middle Execs.	⎭	11 ⎭	20 ⎭	15 ⎭	13 ⎭	13 ⎭	12 ⎭	11 ⎭	10 ⎭	19 ⎭
Artisans/Shopkeepers	5	5	6	8	8	13	4	6	8	9
White-coll. workers	2	5	4	6	7	2	8	6	6	4
Manual Workers	2	4	5	4	4	1	5	2·5	2	2
Farmers and Farm wks.	4	2	6	5	6	2	3	3	2	3
Other	–	1	1	–	–	–	–	–	–	–

* Industriels

Sources: For INSEAD, Marceau, 1975. The other figures are from a study by the Centre de Sociologie Européenne, 1967, and the ESCP and ESSEC data are from Ministère de l'Education Nationale, Service de Statistique, 1971.

School Names: ENA Ecole Nationale d'Administration HEC Ecole des Hautes Etudes Commerciales Ulm Ecole Normale Supérieure (Rue d'Ulm) ESCP Ecole Supérieure de Commerce de Paris ESSEC Ecole Supérieure des Sciences Economiques et Commerciales (Catholic Faculty, Paris).

from letters and science faculties which were precisely those where the proportions of working-class children (and girls) were highest and growing the most.

The problems of arts graduates were not limited to France, but the science faculty graduates in France had special difficulties as the best science-based jobs went to alumni of the *Grandes Écoles* which retained the structure of their public almost intact; at the level, there were rarely 'too many' graduates.

School and class

In France, as in other countries, selection of children for different forms of education was formally determined by academic criteria, but the systematic selection by origins was such that at every level of the *cursus* children from humbler backgrounds were eliminated or eliminated themselves to a much greater degree than those from more privileged homes. If, at the lowest echelons of the system, the numbers of children in school represented proportionately each social group in its proportions in the active population, at all the highest levels the situation was the reverse; from being a majority working-class children became a tiny minority only. The inequality in relation to educational opportunity manifest here survived every reform undertaken after 1945.

Taking passage through the school system as a *cursus* it is evident that at each stage factors operated to push children from lower social origins, and girls of all social backgrounds, into certain kinds of studies. The possibilities of choice of study or job became more and more limited with each decision a child made. If he (or she) 'chose' a CET at eleven or twelve years he or she was relegated to manual work. If he 'chose' a CEG he was not able to go into the classics sections, he lacked certain kinds of teaching and stool little chance of obtaining a *baccalauréat*, and all that which the '*bac*' could lead to.[5] If he went to a *lycée* and chose certain 'modern' sections, those without Lation, some prestigious university courses, such as philosophy, would be impossible to follow and he was relatively unlikely to enter even the low-prestige arts or science faculties. He would also have no chance of entering the special lycées giving access to the *Grandes Écoles*. Only the classical and some

---

[5]   After the introduction of CES into most areas of France from 1968, the implications of choice of type of school were transferred into those pertaining to the choice of certain sections within the CES. In the late 1960s and the 1970s the importance of Latin studies to one's future career possibilities was replaced largely by success in mathematics.

modern sections of the *lycées* left the way open for a maximum period.

The first explanations of why most working-class children moved into the sections of the general and technical educational institutions (as well as outside the system first) which led the most directly out into the production process, and therefore to the least skilled jobs, essentially involved examination of the individual child in relation to the school and its teachers and in relation to the family of origin. Many studies of this parallelled those in Britain and the U.S.A. Thus Girard was first led to the conclusion that size of family was important as he found (1951) that only working-class and farm children from *small* families had any chance of reaching secondary education, a fact he put down either to the initial drive for social ascension in such families or to the selection of *lycée* pupils not for their intellectual abilities but according to the financial possibilities of their parents. Refining the analysis on the basis of their cohort study in the 1960s, Girard and his colleagues suggested that 'social origin' was more precisely the factor, 'the cultural level of the parents' which affected their wishes for their children's education. For example, a majority of rural families and very many urban working-class ones wanted their children to leave school as early as possible, whereas, of course, higher up the social scale the reverse was true. In particular, when it came to the choice of whether the child should enter secondary school or not, the institution of the family itself actively operated against entry for working-class children. 'Where there exist equal aptitudes and school success [in the child] the cultural atmosphere of the family and its level of aspiration favour children from higher social origins in relation to those from other social milieux. This factor of injustice seems linked to the institution of the family itself' (1964: 473). This 'cultural factor' seemed to operate both because aspirations depended on what was possible for the children, but also on how well parents understood the mechanisms of job selection, the minimum qualifications required for a given career, and how these were to be obtained. In the same vein Clerc, too, concluded that there existed a 'massive accord between the wishes of the families and the orientations chosen' (1964: 657). Three families out of ten had never envisaged putting their child in a *lycée*, many indeed could neither name nor place the nearest one.

Other studies emphasized the inter-relationship between teacher and family in the 'choice' of orientation of the children. For example, in a study of attitudes to children's choices many teachers, when asked whether they oriented their pupils as they did their own children and what they did when a child was clever but from a humble home, felt unable to reply or replied (the majority) that they wished to see the brigher children go further in education but that *they hesitated to push them* (my emphasis), fearing that the parents could not support the children long enough, but also fearing to cut the children off from their social origins while they were having difficulty integrating themselves into a new milieu (Berger and Benjamin, 1964). More recent evidence shows that teachers continued to orient working-class pupils into the CEG (where they still existed), rather than *lycées*, and into the more technical schools rather than the general ones. Even in the late 1960s, Grignon and his colleagues found in a village in the Sarthe that the teachers felt that, 'in the present social and school conditions our pupils are handicapped (*démunis*) at the start. We have become extremely modest and have pushed [our pupils] relatively little into *sixième* classes' (Grignon, 1968).[6]

---

[6] There also existed geographical variations in school provision. The 'external' difficulties faced by working-class children in relation to the school were often very great and the 'physical' problems of schools in different areas tended to hit working-class children hardest. All State schools were still 'free, secular, and obligatory', but the quality of teachers, and above all of facilities, varied enormously between town and country and from region to region. Many school buildings were old and in the cities very many classes grossly overcrowded, while in the country small, one-class, all-age, schools vegetated. In many areas there was a shortage of teachers as the Government did not foresee the permanence of the higher birth-rate. France's nursery schools were very good at their best, but many remained overcrowded and in any case scarcely existed in the countryside, (Duparc, 1971). The poor conditions in primary schools in the Seine *département* of Paris, in 1959 took considerable toll on the capabilities of staff and children alike (Berger and Benjamin, 1974) and Vincent (1967) has described the similar conditions of teachers in secondary schools. Moreover, the regions varied much among themselves in the educational opportunities they offered. Secondary schools were not evenly distributed and in rural areas CEG rather than CES predominated. For every child in secondary school in 1962 with parents in the lowest professional group there were ten with parents in the highest; but the number of secondary school places offered relative to the local population varied by 1:3 between *communes*, 1:2 between *départements*, and 1:5 between regions (Darbel, 1967: 140–1), although later there was certainly improvement in the worst areas. Most of the preparatory classes for the *Grande Écoles* like the *Grandes Écoles* themselves, were situated in Paris, which also had a heavy preponderance of those classes which actually allowed entry to the top schools, as opposed to the formal provisions for preparing the *concours*, and indeed the capital stood out as best supplied with all kinds of schools. There were thus 'physical' or geographical lacunae creating inequality in the very provision of school facilities. To this must be added the poor housing conditions, the overcrowding of many working-class family homes in particular, to which attention was drawn in an earlier chapter. 'Geographical' and social disadvantages, therefore, to a large extent overlapped; indeed, Darbel (1967) was led to conclude, that many apparently geographical differences were in fact class differences.

School and society

In the face of the persistence of massive inequalities in educational opportunity, relatively simple explanations in terms of individual families came to seem inadequate. Explanations were developed which emphasized a much more systematic relationship between the school system and the whole social structure, and in particular the role of the school in the reproduction and maintenance of the class structure.

These wider explanations first emphasized the importance of 'cultural capital' in relation to school success. On the individual level this is expressed through 'language' seen as the medium through which social differences are expressed and which, because of the similarity between school language and 'home' language, in France, as elsewhere, favoured children from middle- and particularly upper-class homes. Translating this into societal terms, language was part of a wider cultural heritage whose importance the school disguised by refusing to recognize it. The school, says Bourdieu, had the important role of transforming cultural differences into 'natural' differences; the concept of the gift, *le don*, seen as an innate talent that one either has or has not, was built into the French system of education and used to justify the selectivity by class that characterized it. A social heritage was transformed into a 'natural' gift. To underline the ideological nature of the notion of 'gift', Bourdieu shows that academic success rates which were usually explained as due to unequal individual gifts could be explained sociologically without reference to ability.[7] Cultural privileges were, he says, usually perceived at their crudest in specific aid by relations, help in school work, extra teaching or greater educational information, but in fact each family transmitted, directly or indirectly, to its children a certain cultural capital and ethos, a system of implicit and deeply entrenched values which defined attitudes to scholastic institutions. The amount of cultural capital available differed by social class and was responsible for the initial inequality of children in the face of the education 'test' and, through that inequality, for the unequal success rates. Cultural knowledge is acquired only slowly, over generations, so that differences linked to the length of time of access to culture continued to separate apparently equal individuals.

---

[7] Bourdieu found that he could predict the levels of success of groups of university students without in any way looking at their 'innate capacity but by using the cultural level of father, mother, paternal and maternal grandparents, and place of residence during secondary and higher education, as well as factors such as section of secondary education, type of school, etc.

The *savoir-faire*, the acquisition of certain tastes, and especially 'good taste', were the most important parts of the cultural heritage because usually put down to 'a gift', and therefore thought of a innate and not taught at school. Language is crucial because it provides tools for thought, a vocabulary, but also a syntax which provides a system of categories used to decode and manipulate both logical and æsthetic codes, and which depends directly on the complexity of the structure of the language initially spoken in the family circle. As all these factors are transmitted by cultural osmosis rather than formal training, they help to reinforce the favoured classes' conviction that they owe all their success to their natural aptitudes rather than to a long and continuous apprenticeship.

Further, 'parental wishes' must be interpreted carefully for 'wishes' reflected the reality of their children's chances as much as guiding it. Parents' 'wishes' took account constantly of the failures and half-successes of the children in their neighbourhood and of such factors as the advice of the *instituteur*, in effect 'taking reality for their desires'. Thus, to say of classical studies in a *lycée*, 'Such things are not for us' ('Ce n'est pas pour nous') means more than 'we could not afford it' ('Nous n'avons pas les moyens'). 'Such things are not for us' expresses both an impossibility and a forbidden act.

Passage through the school converted the cultural heritage into a school past (*passé scolaire*). In this process of conversion, in order to favour the favoured and disfavour the disfavoured it was necessary and sufficient for the school to ignore in the content of the education transmitted, in the methods and techniques of its transmission and the criteria of judgement used, the cultural inequalities existing between children of different social classes. By treating the pupils as equal in rights and duties, the French school system sanctioned the initial inequalities in culture: the formal equality inherent in teaching methods served as a mask for, and justification of, indifference towards the real inequalities of the children. By seeking to 'awaken' gifts, assumed to exist regardless of culture, teachers could in fact only address themselves to children who happened to have a heritage conforming to the demands of the school, that is to say, a bourgeois culture. The value of this culture which all were assumed to possess, was high throughout education. To its value in itself was added, by the school and the society, the additional value of it 'coming naturally'—children who attempted to acquire it 'scholastically' were despised. Receiving nothing which was educationally useful but good intentions from their families, the children of the *classes moyennes* were obliged to seek all and receive all from school, but were, by that token, also liable to be reproached by the school for excessive zeal. 'It is an aristocratic culture and especially an aristocratic relationship to that culture which is both transmitted and demanded by the education system.' The end result of such a system is that the latent functions given to the school are to reorganize 'the cult of a culture which can be proposed to all because it is in fact reserved to the members of the classes whose culture it is. The hierarchy of intellectual values gives the prestigious manipulator of words and ideas superiority over the humble servants of techniques; this is the logic peculiar to a system which has the objective function of conserving the values on which the social system is based' (ibid.: 339). The only way to overcome this would have been for the school to undertake general and systematic acculturation and that it did not do.

In sum, by conferring a 'neutral' sanction to socially acquired attitudes, by treating them as 'gifts' or merits, the school system 'transforms inequalities of fact into inequalities of right, economic and social differences into *distinctions of quality*, and legitimizes the transmission of the cultural heritage. Through this, education exercises a mystifying function' (ibid.: 342). The 'ideology of the gift', the key to both the school system and the social system, contributed to enclosing members of the disadvantaged classes in the destiny assigned to them by society by bringing them to perceive as natural lack of aptitude a factor which was an effect of an inferior social position, and by persuading them that they owed their social destiny, more and more linked to their scholastic one, to their individual nature, to their lack of gifts. The success of the few who escaped the collective destiny gave an appearance of legitimacy to educational selection and lent credence to the myth of the *école libératrice* in the minds of those it had eliminated, by making them believe that success is due to work and gifts. Moreover, those whom education had in fact 'liberated', *instituteurs* and *professeurs*, put their faith in the *école libératrice* objectively to work in the service of the *école conservatrice*, the latter owing to the former some of its powers of conservation. In this way Bourdieu concludes that the education system gave cultural inequalities a sanction formally compatible with democratic ideals and justified these inequalities, thereby legitimizing the *status quo* and protecting the privileged.[8]

---

[8]　Such an education system, says Bourdieu, can function properly only as long as it can recruit and select suitable pupils, that is, those who come equipped with suitable cultural capital. It is condemned to crisis, experienced as a 'lowering of standards', when such pupils are no longer available. For it to withstand the crisis fundamental changes would be necessary. In France, the democratization of

Education, society, and individual success

Looking less here at the ideological role of the education system than its role in social mobility or immobility, Raymond Boudon in *L'Inégalité des chances* (1973), basing himself on national statistics from France, Britain, and the U.S.A., suggested that relative disparities of chances of access to different levels of the school systems in these countries, as between children of different social classes, were *declining* towards the end of our period. But, says Boudon, this did not have any effect on the over-all amount of social mobility. The statistics show that educational level, while linked to it, nevertheless overall is *not* a good indicator of the economic level or social status (in sum, *social position*) of an individual or family. The reason for this, roughly speaking, is that each individual child makes a calculation of the costs and risk attached to any educational decision and as he reaches higher so he, in common with all the other children of his age, raises the over-all educational level attained by his age group which in itself means that employers demand higher educational qualifications. The result is that each entrant to the labour market, in spite of having a higher educational level than his father, finds that his job opportunities are not greatly different. Thus, an increase in educational opportunities for culturally (and economically and socially) deprived children, far from being a means of increasing chances of social mobility in the society, has precisely the opposite effect. Such an increase simply heightens the competition, which means that at each level cultural capital will have to be supplemented by economic and social capital (the terms are Bourdieu's, not Boudon's). The only solution would seem to be fundamental changes in the socio-economic structure of the society and these did not occur in any of the countries considered.

Grignon and Passeron apply a sociologically more detailed analysis when they examine the way in which social forces operate against children from humbler backgrounds. They suggest that at each stage of education both parents and children settle for what can 'reasonably' be hoped for, and what is 'reasonable' depends on the experience of those around them. The subjective estimation of chances made in this way become part of the objective reality of the group. Between 1961–2 and 1965–6 only at the extremes of the social scale were chances of

---

sixième entry and the creation of Collèges d'Enseignement Secondaire could have provided such radical changes, but did not do so because the new part of the system conformed, in its internal hierarchies and divisions, to the logic of the entire system.

access to higher studies modified. For workers' children the chances of access doubled but remained very small, while for the sons and daughters of businessmen access became virtually certain at around 86 per cent. The rise from 1·5 to 3·9 per hundred in the probability of such access for working-class adolescents did not reach the point at which it was expected that they would continue their studies; in other words, it was not enough to change their own and their parents' image of higher education which remained 'improbable' and 'unreasonable'. Grignon and Passeron concluded that 'the general rise in objective opportunities of access to higher education . . . has not therefore led to the democratization of university recruitment: for the working classes the probability of access is still low enough to be regarded as nil, while it is becoming sufficiently high in the case of the upper classes as to heighten their privileges, having become almost a certainty.' (1970: 77—80.)

Furthermore, the important question remains of whether the economic structure changes before the school system (and with that individual choices and employers' demands) or vice versa. For Boudon the school system would seem in certain senses primordial because he seems to believe that it is an over-supply of diplomas which forces up employers' demands, whereas it may be, as Darbel (1975) points out, that the economic structure changes first and employers' demands are dependent on that. The example Darbel gives is that of *cadres supérieurs*. For instance, he emphasizes that although younger *cadres supérieurs* hold more or higher educational qualifications, the same or similar jobs were held at an earlier period by men without such qualifications. The jobs were created by economic needs and changes—the later hiring of men with high-level qualifications may well be more of social origin than due to economic necessity (1975: 112). Moreover, there is also evidence that in the newer industries in France, promotion was more open to those who did not hold high-level diplomas because there did not exist appropriate ones—as an industry became more established so its recruitment policies referred more to scholastic achievements. Information on the job market is a crucial part of what Bourdieu, Boltanski, and de St. Martin (1972) have called 'reconversion strategies'. These strategies, undertaken by younger members of the privileged fractions of the dominant strata, frequently involved the acquisition of 'rare' diplomas, such as those supplied by business schools, when the labour market changes. An important part of the nature of the cultural heritage in France was perhaps precisely this information, which allowed certain children and young people always to be ahead of the rest in that they could match rare skills to the demands of the labour market.

The problem is not perhaps that there is 'over-education', in the sense used by Boudon, so that the general level is raised too high, but rather the low possibility for working-class children to acquire particular marketable diplomas. The change of emphasis is important to the argument.

Primary–professional and secondary–superior

In the mid 1960s Bourdieu and his colleagues brought together a number of findings on inequality in relation to education, and began the transformation of the emphasis away from the individual and family towards the more general role played by education in the maintenance of social inequality. In the later 1960s work undertaken from a Marxist viewpoint carried the argument further and, by a re-analysis of government statistics on education, suggested that there existed not one education 'system' in France but two. The two major proponents of this view, Christian Baudelot and Roger Establet, concentrate particularly on the secondary sections of the school system as they operated after the Berthoin reform of 1959. Analysing especially the passage from the last year of primary school, CM2,[9] to the first year of secondary school, they show how this choice was the beginning of a radical separation of children onto two educational routes, the primary-professional (PP) and the secondary-superior (SS), which corresponded objectively to the division in the productive process between the working class and the bourgeoisie, and which led directly to the recruitment of young members of the two halves of the productive process. Because, say Baudelot and Establet, the school is a sub-system of society, it is effectively dominated by the dominant form of social relations outside. As there existed in the society a third 'class', the petty bourgeoisie, dominated by its relationships with the others, so there existed in the school system an apparent third role between the PP and the SS, but this too was entirely dominated by the others and, therefore, had no 'real' existence as a separate route but only as a shorter version of the SS.

Rejecting the framework of analysis which concentrates on the various factors influencing differential success within the school system, Baudelot and Establet address themselves directly to understanding the meaning of the clear division into PP and SS, which appears from the

[9] *Cours moyen deux.*

official statistics once reworked. In their view, it is essential to look at the divisions and distinctions which operated within the school system and which created the basic division into élite and mass. One of the major dividing mechanisms was the insistence on certain 'norms', such as age, in each class, which in fact only applied to a small number of children. At six years and six months a child 'must' know how to read, but in fact one in three children at the end of their first primary year were unable to do so and had to repeat the year. This kind of situation continued throughout the system, in such a way that three-quarters of school children repeated at least one year: allocation to type of school depended less on the school results obtained but the age at which it was obtained. On this basis children were segregated at entry to *sixième* classes roughly by thirds: 34·6 per cent went into the most 'academic' *sixième* classes, the *classique* and *moderne 1*; 30·3 per cent went into the *moderne 2*; and 35·1 per cent either went into transition classes or out of the school system altogether.[10] Significantly, within these thirds, 70 per cent of all ten-year-olds went into the first two sections, as did 50 per cent of all eleven-year-olds but only 23 per cent of all twelve-year-olds, who in absolute terms were nearly as numerous as the eleven-year-olds (257,860 as against 331,484) and far more numerous than the ten-year-olds (of whom there were only 58,863). *No* children over twelve years of age went into those classes. Inversely, the transition classes took only 2·4 per cent of ten-year-olds and 7 per cent of all eleven-year-olds, but 19 per cent of twelve-year-olds went there (with another 21 per cent of that age group staying in primary classes or leaving the system). Age at each level was highly correlated with social origins and with 'good' or 'bad' scholastic results: 'good' results were a function of age but the 'norm' of age for each class was an evaluative and not a statistical one. The construction of the 'norm' in this way was a means of showing up 'backwardness' and was basic to the division at school into the 'good' and the 'bad', and from there respectively into the streams SS or PP.

The division began in the primary school, which research soon showed to be far from the unitary education believed in by many and solemnly declared as the only place of equality within French education by Langevin and Wallon when presenting their plan for reform in the late 1940s. On the contrary, Chiland in France and Malmquist in Sweden, have shown the importance for the whole school career of even the first year of primary school, the *cours préparatoire* (CP). In Chiland's small sample, at the end of the CP 86 per cent of the children from the higher

---

[10] The data refer to the years 1966–7.

social classes had good reading and writing results while 63 per cent of working-class children had poor or even 'zero' (nil) results.

Moreover, while the IQ of the children in the CP followed a 'normal' distribution curve, the IQ of those same children five years later had become bi-modal, the weak having become weaker and the strong stronger, again in clear relationship to social origins.

The school, therefore, divided from the earliest years. The division in the *sixième* classes was simply a continuation. The same was true for the *quatrième* classes as shown in Table 5.3 above which demonstrates that the children of *cadres supérieurs* had chances six times greater to be in 'classical' sections than had the children of workers. 'In other words, the order of probabilities in *classique* and *moderne 1* is already that of the university, in *transition* the order is the exact reverse.' (Baudelot and Establet, 1971: 75). In *moderne 2*, on the other hand, the situation was less clear, an indication of the equivocal nature of that class. On the one hand, it served as a 'catching-up' class for the least 'good' sons (and daughters) of the upper classes and, on the other, as a means of 'promotion' for the 'best' children of working-class parents. If we add to the table showing the choices at *quatrième* level those children (300,000 in 1967) who were of the same age but outside the system, the two educational routes clearly emerge—the PP, including the *quatrième pratique*, the first year of CET, and children outside the system, and the SS, including *classique* and *moderne 1*. Comparing these two the opposition between the two social classes is very clear. Of the sons and daughters of workers, 548 as against 140 were in the PP system and of those of the bourgeoisie, the reverse—543 as against 148 were in the SS. A working-class child had 54 chances out of 100 to be in PP and only 14 to be in SS; a bourgeois son had 54 to be in SS and only 14 to be in PP. That is to say, the sons of the bourgeoisie had as much chance to be in SS as working-class ones to be in PP. The middle classes had no *specific* education—their chances of PP and SS were mixed. There was no third way, no social class which had the greatest chances to be in M2, although the 'average' children of the middle classes did go there most frequently.

Choice of option at *quatrième* level is the 'last' one where one sees the basic division PP—SS. The choices made at entry to the *seconde* are essentially within the same system, the SS, in the *lycées*, although here, too, not all the sections left the same 'length of educational route' ahead open. Theoretically, there were 'bridges' open from the practical *troisième*, which were the highest classes open after passage through 'non-normal' *sixième* classes, but in 1966–7 only 0·6 per cent managed to change to a *baccalauréat* class and 0·9 per cent to a *brevet* (BET) class, and only 6,500 children managed to go from the *sixième* to the *troisième* in the 'non-normal' sections, that is, transition ones. We can see, therefore, say Baudelot and Establet, how a child who did not enter a 'normal' *sixième* would never get to a *seconde* class. The same is true of the chances of children in the three 'normal' sections of passing from *troisième* to *seconde* classes; in 1966–7, 75 per cent of the *classique* and 79 per cent of the *moderne 1* classes in *lycées* went into 'normal' *seconde* classes (A & C–letters and maths), while only 24 per cent of *moderne 2* children did so. The majority of the latter (59 per cent) did not enter a *seconde* class at all.

Technical education

In France it has always been the best sections of the general education system which have led to the élite institutions of technical education, the engineering *Grandes Écoles*. In the 1960s, however, there was much emphasis in official circles on the creation of a new technical school system at lower levels, and it may be thought that this constituted a means of social mobility through education for children from the working class. It could, in theory, constitute a 'third' route.

Examination of the social origins of pupils in the different levels of the technical system suggests that it did not in fact do so. Overall the Collèges d'Enseignement Technique (CET), the lowest-grade state technical schools, had pupils from the lowest social origins, and even within the CET social origins varied systematically between the short and long full-time teaching cycles leading respectively to the Certificat d'Aptitude Professionel (CAP) and the various *brevets*. Pupils in the higher level technical *lycées* were on average of higher social origins and the same was true of the final rung of this part of the technical ladder, the Instituts Universitaires de Technologie (IUT).

Examining recruitment to the CET, Grignon (1971) notes that although the CET were at the bottom of the academic hierarchy, and were the places to which the other schools sent their 'worst' products, even they selected an élite. Thus, while pupils with poor academic records had little chance of entering or remaining in general secondary education they also had little chance of entering a CET. Academic criteria were dominant even over learning a manual trade and as entry to a CET became more competitive—there were far from enough places— so the academic level necessary at entry gradually was pushed higher and higher. Moreover, although the CET might seem to be the *école du peuple*, in fact the children from the least favoured social classes had fewer chances of entering a CET and of any apprenticeship at school, than had bourgeois children of entering the high schools of the general education system. For the sons and daughters of the *classes populaires*, who represented 70 per cent of all CET pupils, entry to a CET remained less probable than entry direct to the productive system or an 'on the job' apprenticeship. The probabilities only became the same for children from the higher levels of the working class and the lower levels of the *classes moyennes*. Further, as is the case in all the other types of school, the situation seemed to be constant over the generations, varying with the education of the parents—the higher the diploma of the father, the greater the chances of entry to a CET of the child.

The values of the general education system, with its emphasis on abstraction and ability to generalize, also dominated the curriculum and the attitudes of the teachers within even the low grades of the technical school structure. There existed in these schools a hierarchy among the trades taught, a grading based by the teachers on the 'intellectuality' and 'cleanliness' of the job and the ease with which one afterwards obtained a post. In relation to this too the social hierarchy predominated: the social origins of the students of mechanics and the electrical trades, for instance, were higher than those of their colleagues in boiler-making or the building trades. Teachers graded the pupils in the entry examination and oriented the 'good' ones towards the more skilled and better-paid trades. Pupils coming from the *lycées* and the CEG/CES, the 'failures' of the secondary schools, were oriented to the 'better' trades and never to the building ones, for instance (Grignon: 1971).

In the study referred to above, Baudelot and Establet point out that even within the technical system there was the same division into PP and SS as in the general system. The 'unity' and 'specificity' of the technical, they say, were purely ideological. The CET recruited, while nevertheless selecting, above all children from the working class, but once in a 'practical' *sixième* or *transition* class, entry to any institution higher than the CET became almost impossible, as did passage onwards from the CET to the higher secondary technical schools. For although on an organigram the technical and general education systems appeared to have a parallel existence—CET appearing as 'equivalent' to CEG and CES, *lycées techniques* 'equivalent' to *lycées*, with parallel teaching-training colleges, joining together at the summit in the *Grandes Écoles*—in practice this was not the case. Just as the curriculum in the technical schools was dominated by the ideology of the general education system, so access to technical education was dominated by 'success' in the general system at each level.

Each level of the technical system led directly out to production. At each stage the way was outward and not upward, as no stage had an upward path in its own right. Neither the professional sections of the CEG nor the third-year classes of the CET could normally lead to *seconde* classes in a technical *lycée* (only 5 per cent pupils made that change); the great mass of technical *lycée* pupils came from the general sections. No *troisième* section specifically trained for technical education and the 'technical' sections 'chose' from the general sections the less good pupils from *moderne* 1 and *moderne* 2 (almost none from *classique*). These children were not, however, mostly from the working classes, but were middle-class offspring who had been 'relegated' earlier on into the primary-professional route which passed through the CET and not through the general system. The same was true *a fortiori* for the higher technical sections, those preparing the *brevet de technicien.* Thus a person with a CAP could not enter for a *baccalauréat*, and a person with a technical *bac* could not enter the literary faculties but had to read sciences. The *brevets* led only to the IUT, which prepared students 'directly' for entry to professional life in supervisory technical functions in production ('Les Étudiants en France . . .', 1969: 8), and did not lead on to higher university diplomas and, even less, to the *Grandes Écoles.* Consequently the technical system was as divided as the general system into routes, PP and SS, and linked in the same way to the divisions in the productive process and the class system. Far from being a means of upward social mobility for working-class children, French technical education acted principally as a means of preventing further fall by children from middle- and upper-class homes.

This was even true of adult technical education and of the newer permanent education, *formation continue.* For instance, the Conservatoire National des Arts et Métiers (CNAM), which offers part-time classes leading to engineering diplomas, catered over our period more for the sons of the *classes moyennes* and the 'failed' sons of the bourgeoisie than for working-class sons in spite of the fact that possession of the *baccalauréat* is not required (Champagne, Grignon, 1969).

Return on investment in technical and general studies

The systematic relationship between social origins and the type of school attended was evident at every level and indicates the 'limits' to the possibilities for most people of social advancement through the use of the education system. Furthermore, in France at the time, the importance of diplomas was high both in job recruitment (see below,

TABLE 5.7.
Active population born in 1918 or later and diplomas held

Level of Diploma	Patrons ind./com.	Lib. profs. teachers engin's.	Admin. tech. com. exec.	White-collar	Manual workers	Service pers'l.	Farmers	Farm workers	Other	Total
Men										
I. No diploma	21	0·5	8	13	40	28	46	69	10	31
II. CEP	42·5	5	18	42·5	30	55·5	38	21	36	31
III. 2e education	6	9	20	15	1	2	1	–	7	6
IV. tech. ed.	27	17	40	28	29	14·5	15	9·5	31	28
V. higher ed.	2	68	14	2	–	–	–	–	15	5
Women										
I. No diploma	23	1	4	9	47	48	51	84	11·5	31
II. CEP	52	2	9	37	40	40	40	13·5	16	36
III. 2e education	7	7	47	13	1	–	2	–	37	9
IV. tech. ed.	17	11	28	39	12·5	10	7	2	27	21
V. higher ed.	1	79·5	11	1	–	1·5	–	–	8	3

Source. Salais, 1970: 51.

Chapter Six), frequently even at low levels, and as a component of job security and protection from 'dequalification' (Frisch, 1971). Thus, if advancement could not be gained through education, the possibility of gaining it from on-the-job promotion was also limited.

Table 5.7 first makes clear the low level of diplomas held by the vast majority of the population; in 1960 90 per cent of farm workers, 84 per cent of farmers, 83 per cent of service personnel, and 70 per cent of workers, had at best only the CEP and respectively 46 per cent, 69 per cent and 28 per cent and 40 per cent had *no diplomas at all*. It is important too to note here that this low level is not only true of the older generations but also of young people. An article in *Économie et Statistique* (1971: No. 20), based on 1968 census data, showed that nearly one third, 29 per cent, of young persons of under twenty-five years of age had at that time no diplomas at all, only 8·5 per cent fewer than in the total active population of over fourteen years of age. Among the young unemployed at the same time, two-fifths of the men and one-quarter of the women (all of those of less than twenty-five years) had no diploma. The education system even late in our period, therefore, failed totally to touch considerable numbers of young people in terms of giving them a diploma which they could use on the job market.

For those who had diplomas, the correlation at the top and the bottom of the scale between posts and diplomas held was high—there was less relation in the middle for, as usual, these were heterogeneous groups.

The lowest diplomas gave very little chance of social mobility and even of job security. The lowest discriminatory technical diploma in France was the CAP; Grignon's study (1971) showed that CAP holders had seven out of ten chances of remaining manual workers, although they did stand a better chance of being recognized as skilled and becoming foremen (1971: 17). The CAP was not scarce on the market and jobs were by no means 'guaranteed' to its holders in the way that the holder of an engineering diploma was 'guaranteed' an appropriate post; moreover, the 'title' was revocable. Such persons remained more subject to unemployment that did the holders of higher diplomas, and for newly created jobs existing CAP often became irrelevant and un-recognized. In fact, Grignon says, many small firms found it impossible to use rationally even the lowest-level CAP skills, and they complained that the CET gave the young workers 'airs'; further, with the constant creation of new diplomas, people holding the older ones often found that their level in the hierarchy had dropped. Employers, Grignon points out, tended to do well out of periods both of penury and over-production of certain qualifications—during the former, people without diplomas were paid less for doing the same work, while during the latter, competition for places tended to push down the value of the diploma. In particular, frequently CAP holders (especially women) were employed as unskilled workers and the 1970 INSEE study showed that this contributed a great deal to the job mobility they showed (Thélot,1973: 22).

The lot of people with somewhat higher technical diplomas was often similar. Persons with a *bac. technique* or a *brevet de technicien* got the appropriate technical jobs but, although their diplomas in this way contributed to their mobility, they often allowed no possibility of further rising. The 1964 INSEE study showed the technicians as a seldom promoted category, and those who were appointed to positions as *cadres moyens* usually came from the general education system rather than the technical one. Grignon's re-analysis of the INSEE data showed that in spite of the relative rarity of their diplomas, the holders of the technical qualifications, BEI or BEC, had less chance of rising to 'management' positions than holders of the *brevet d'enseignement général*, reported to have no outlets. While those who had the ordinary *bac* had four in ten chances of having a post in the *classes supérieures*, the theoretically equivalent technical qualifications gave only one or two. The same distribution appears at the higher levels, between holders of the *licence* and the higher technical diplomas. Graduates of the IUT, created specially to ensure suitable professional outlets, found that their diplomas were not recognized by the *conventions collectives* which in France regulated conditions of employment and promotion prospects.

Just as each level of the general education system remained linked to the class origins of its pupils, so, too, the technical system failed to provide a means of long-distance social mobility.

The whole of the education system, therefore, in France after 1945 remained in close relationship with the division of labour emanating from the productive process. At each level each part of the system selected differentially children of different social origins, and rapidly eliminated some from education altogether. At the same time, the ideology attached to 'equality of all' in access to the school legitimated the whole social system of the distribution not only of roles but of rewards, for educational success was equated to 'merit' and 'natural' superiority. The more the system expanded, the greater were the numbers touched by the action of the school, the more 'perfect' the role selection could seem. Only towards the end of the 1960s did the contradictions between official ideology in relation to equality of opportunity begin to seem blatant but, apart from the creation of new *filières*, education routes, in a vain attempt to link diplomas even more closely to the job market, few serious attempts at fundamental reform were made.

6. POWER AND ITS POSSESSORS

Power in a society is an attribute both of persons and of positions. If Poulantzas (1968) is right, political power is not a special case of economic power and vice versa, but both are aspects of a total structure and of active class relationships. This, however, remains an abstract formulation. On the empirical level, it is difficult to assess access to 'power' by a thorough-going analysis of decisions made and imposed by those in positions (institutionalized or not) of power, and indeed this is not necessarily the best approach (Lukes, 1971). However, by examining the social composition of, and recruitment to, institutionalized power positions, one may deduce at a secondary level, if not necessarily in whose interests the system works over time and overall, who at least has the greatest probability of access to positions which seem to carry most weight in the making of public decisions in the widest sense of the word. This is the approach taken here.

Recruitment to institutionalized political power positions, namely to power as Members of Parliament and to positions in the high civil service, and to economic power positions in business, particularly manufacturing industry, necessarily involves some consideration of the linkages between the different aspects of the institutions of power, whether personal or positional; an essential aspect of power is that it is cumulative, while also being apparently refractive.

Business

Cadres supérieurs

Positions of power in the everyday affairs of modern French enterprises, at least the larger ones, were dispersed and held by numbers of delegates, senior executives, *cadres supérieurs*.

It is not always easy to distinguish possibilities of access to high-level positions, for many studies look simply at *cadres* and do not divide them into *cadres supérieurs* and *cadres moyens*. However, in some ways this emphasizes the limitations on access, for taking all the *cadres* together shows patterns which other evidence suggests were accentuated when only the *cadres supérieurs* are considered. Moreover, although their numbers grew fast with the economic growth of the post-1945 years and the increase in size of enterprise, they remained a small part of the total active population (1–2 per cent in 1968), and possibilities of access to such positions necessarily remained limited. Most important perhaps, the social origins of *cadres* remained limited. Writing early in the period, 1955, Jacquin suggested that then *cadres* were from families rising socially over (at least) one generation. However, he adds:

the dispersion of the origins of the cadres should not create too many illusions . . . but means of access do exist. Of the two major ones, the first comes via the group of white-collar workers, technicians, and lower civil servants while the second via that of artisans and shopkeepers. The first group is most numerous in the fathers' generation where it outnumbers those of peasants and workers. The second, a very large group among the grandfathers, is a more important source of supply for recruitment to *cadre* positions and to members of the liberal and industrial professions.' (139)

More recent work by Maurice and his colleagues (1967) found that the fathers of 397 *ingénieurs* and *cadres* studied were distributed roughly by thirds; 31 per cent were from the *classes populaires*, 37 per cent from the *classes moyennes*, and 35 per cent from the *classes supérieures*. There was, therefore, room for social mobility even in these very modern enterprises. On the other hand, two qualifications are necessary. First, precisely because a modern industry was 'modern', there were fewer fully trained people available, and the school system had not operated upon recruitment to the industry to its full extent. Secondly, *cadres* of all levels were put together, and examining only *cadres supérieurs* in the metallurgical industry, on the whole, the familiar differences reappear; the higher the level of the post, the higher were the educational diplomas required to fill it. The social recruitment of the schools conferring such diplomas, indicates the higher social origin of the *cadres*. Table 6.1, referring to the metallurgical industry and carried out by that industry's own leaders, shows the pattern clearly. It illustrates the preference for high-level diplomas in recruitment to high-level posts in an industry whose leaders claim that it is 'still today and indeed more than yesterday an open profession' (UIMM, 1970: 36). The concentration of certain diploma-holders in certain positions is striking. Thus, Polytechnique ('X') graduates constitute only 2 per cent of the *cadre* and *ingénieur* labour force in the industry, but 36 per cent hold director (chief executive) posts, and a further 11 per cent the highest administrative posts. There is a clear hierarchy of diplomas for the top posts. Thus, while 36 per cent of Polytechnicien graduates in the industry hold director jobs, only 22 per cent of Centraliens and 18 per cent of Mines graduates do so. Nearly half the Polytechniciens are in the top two sets of posts but only 32 per cent Centraliens and 28 per cent Mines. Below these top schools the situation is even clearer, with only 11 per cent of alumni of the various Arts et Métiers Institutes being Directors, 3 per cent of those from the Faculties and 3 per cent of those promoted from the ranks, and respectively 5·5 per cent, 13 per cent, and 8 per cent for the top administrative positions. The contrast is evident.

TABLE 6.1.

Recruitment to cadre *posts by diploma, 1970*

Functions	Polytech. (2)	École des Mines (1)	Centrale Paris (3)	Arts et Metiers (7)	Faculties (3)	PST
Direction	36	18	22	11	3	3
Administration	11	10·5	10	5·5	13	8
Commercial	8	7	10	4	7	4·5
Technico-Commercial	7	6	10	5	9	4·5
Labs.–R & D	26	23	26	24	52	38
Production/Maintenance	3	22	13	34	5·5	22·5
Means/Control/Tests	6·5	10	6	13	7	15·5
Diverse	2	3	3	3	2·5	1
Total	100	100	100	100	100	100

Source: Table constructed from data given in Union des Industries métallurgiques et Minères, *Ingénieurs et Cadres,* 1970: 40–7. Figures in brackets are the percentages from these schools in *cadre* and *ingénieur* positions in the industry. PST = Promotion sociale du travail.

Referring to *cadre* recruitment as well as success in other fields, Girard concluded:

Birth into a favourable milieu is a very useful trampolin if not a completely indispensable one for high-level success. If privilege is abolished in law, French society has substituted for it a certain number of selective tests, examinations, and *concours* which presuppose study up to the highest level. The great majority of the 'personalities' observed, 85 per cent, have followed such study and have been able to do it because they belong to a milieu where that is the rule. (Girard, 1961: 103)

Ten years later, Benguigui and Monjardet (1970), writing about French *cadres* in the 1960s, could only come to the same conclusions, summarized in the following sentence: 'Those ruling business, the *cadres dirigeants,* are recruited from *ingénieurs* trained in the *Grandes Écoles*; the pupils of the *Grandes Écoles* spring from the ruling class' (1970: 101).

Business leaders: owners and 'assimilated'[1]

The most important power-holders, because they control the crucial elements of the economic system, are the owners of businesses themselves. To them may be added those who in joint-stock companies frequently hold effective power, the chief executives, PDG (Présidents Directeurs Généraux), and other top managers, *cadres dirigeants*, 'assimilated' to ownership positions (see Poulantzas, 1974).

An early study, carried out in the late 1950s by Delefortrie-Soubeyroux (1961), gives a picture which may be used for comparative purposes. The study, based on a sample of 5,000 *cadres dirigeants* (of whom 2,947 returned usable questionnaires) mentioned in yearbooks such as *Who's Who in France 1953–4*, showed that men who were themselves sons of leaders of industry (*dirigeants*) constituted 27 per cent of the sample and 41 per cent of all the known professions, (not all the respondents answered that question). Of all the professions attached to industry they formed 35 per cent of the sample and 52 per cent of the known professions. The other social origins were concentrated in the upper echelons of the society, for the industrial leaders were the sons of high civil servants, parliamentarians, diplomats, and members of the liberal professions. In short, the majority of the *dirigeants* studied in the mid-fifties came from the bourgeoisie.

A study of 2,000 'personalities' in the *Dictionnaire biographique français contemporain* (1954–6), supplemented by a sub-sample from four of the major *Grandes Écoles* and another from among Paris University professors, showed that (the origins of) the personalities observed were very limited. Their recruitment was by no means left to chance. Accession to (high) posts and even more to fame or 'success' was generally

---

[1] Although the social significance of the petty bourgeoisie is undeniable and small *patrons* in industry and commerce exercised power over their workmen, the area of their power tended to be greatly restricted. Moreover, while they did in some instances carry some influence in local politics (although even here it seems that members of the liberal professions were more likely to hold official positions such as mayor or *conseiller général*: see Longepierre, 1970), it seems reasonable to treat them as important parts of the local, but only minor parts of the national, power structure of principal concern here. Indeed, the very number of small businesses in France, in every sector and every region, precluded their *patrons* from forming a coherent group, except for defence when their interests were directly threatened, as in the Poujadist movement. Although in the last Government of President Pompidou, they had their own minister, Mr. Royer, and the industrialists had their voice in the PME, while the small shop-keepers had theirs in the CID-UNATI, their national-level political effectiveness was largely limited to that of prevention rather than positive action. Primarily, therefore, access to senior positions, in large-scale or otherwise nationally significant, industry, is discussed here.

only possible for men born in the highest groups on the social scale (1961: 91). Five per cent of the sample had fathers who were *cadres supérieurs*, 17 per cent *chefs d'entreprises*, 22 per cent in the liberal professions, and 23 per cent high civil servants. 'Such a distribution appears diametrically opposed to the professional distribution within the population as a whole' (Girard, 1961: 91) and 'more than 68 per cent of contemporary personalities are recruited from 5 per cent of the population, or 81 per cent from 15 per cent (ibid.: 93). Because success there depends more on special 'gifts' than on success in the institutions of education, widest recruitment was found among personalities in sports, politics, religion, arts, and letters. On the contrary, recruitment to the civil service, industry, and business, those for which family and education were important, was narrowest.

That the situation changed little in the 1960s was confirmed by a much later study. In the mid-1960s three teachers at the Institut Européen d'Administration des Affaires (INSEAD), carried out a study of the PDG of the 500 bigger French companies in 1966–7.

TABLE 6.2.
Social origins of the leaders of French industry, 1966–7: percentages

Professional Origins	Fathers	Grandfathers	Fathers-in-law
Head of Enterprises*	42	25·5	31
Liberal Professions	20	21	27
Executives**	15	7	13·5
Shopkeepers***	7·5	9	7
Civil Servants****	6	6	10
Working Classes†††	11	31	9

    * *Chefs d' entreprise.*
   ** *Cadres,* including civil servants in senior and middle-level posts.
  *** *Commerçants,* including both large and small.
**** *Fonctionnaires,* civil servants other than those above.
  ††† White-collar and manual workers, farmers and artisans.
Source: Hall and de Bettignies, 1968. 2–5.

As the authors themselves admit, nearly three out of four PDGs were sons of the 'upper- and upper-middle classes' (1968: 4). Only 10 per cent were born in the 'working-classes', including therein artisans and farmers, half of the total. Over 40 per cent of the PDG had fathers who were themselves business leaders and 50 per cent had grandfathers who belonged to the upper classes; indeed one-quarter of the grandfathers were also chief executives, so that one in four came from at least two generations of men at the top in the business world. The tendency to social closure was reinforced by marriage within similar social circles.

Comparing these findings with the situation in other European countries—Germany, Italy, Britain, Belgium, and the Netherlands—Hall and de Bettignies conclude that 'France appears to have the most rigid society of all the countries in our study. Over 85 per cent of [French] chief executives come from the upper social class and less than 3 per cent from the lower' (Hall *et al.*, 1969: 52). Interestingly, French PDG were also the oldest and the most highly educated in terms of diplomas held (ibid.: 53).

Other, later, studies confirmed the major conclusions of Hall and de Bettignies. Studying the PDG of the 300 and 100 biggest French firms in 1972, Bourdieu and his colleagues found the expected link between social origins and education, but also suggested the link between changes in recruitment of business élite to changes in the economic structure and the mode of ownership and control of enterprises.

The central administration of the state

Senior civil servants

Senior civil servants are both instruments and sources of power. In France, this duality is assured, not only by the particularities of recruitment to senior posts in the civil service, but also the personal, as opposed to positional, links between them and business through *pantouflage*—movement from a high civil service post to a similar one in industry and commerce.

Governmental instability under the Fourth Republic led many French observers to consider whether the country was really ruled by senior civil servants, rather than its elected representatives, and a good deal of the early work on the *hauts fonctionnaires* concentrated on that question. It seems highly likely that at least during that period the higher civil servants formed an important part of the policy-making area of government, a position probably strengthened under the Fifth Republic because of the Presidential nature of the regime and the deliberate bypassing, at least under de Gaulle, of deputies and senators. Indeed, since ministers did not have to be elected, some civil servants became ministers. In 1974, for instance, Giscard d'Estaing chose Simone Weil, then a highly competent magistrate in the Ministry of Justice, to be Minister of Public Health. Moreover, an accepted part of the promotion ladder for young and gifted civil servants was a period in the *cabinets ministériels*, the small groups of advisors around each minister. But such opportunities were not open to all.

The Grands Fonctionnaires The Civil Service contained many levels, with personnel recruited in different ways. Gournay (1964) estimated *hauts fonctionnaires* to number between 3,000 and 10,000 persons, depending on definition. The *grands fonctionnaires*, however, were numbered in hundreds rather than thousands, and occupied the top posts in the *grands corps*, the dominant sections in the different ministries, arranged in a hierarchy of power and prestige, and culminating in the controlling body within the Finance Ministry, the Inspecteurs des Finances.

After 1945 recruitment to the senior parts of the civil service was via a special school, the École Nationale d'Administration (ENA), created at the Liberation to try to ensure a wider social representation among members of the *grands corps*, to 'democratize access' to state administration.[2] Entry to ENA was through two different competitive examinations (*concours*), one for students and a minor one for members of the junior grades of the civil service.

Theoretically the *concours* were open to all students holding a higher diploma, but in practice to succeed it was virtually necessary to have studied the Section Administration Publique of the Insitut d'Études Politiques (IEP) in Paris, the ex-'Sciences Po', which was a major training ground for high public servants before 1939.

ENA First, then, recruitment to ENA. In 1951–2 Bottomore carried out a study on the social origins of students at ENA between 1945 and 1951, and compared them with those of candidates to the school. He found that candidates from the higher social origins had greater success rates than those of lower social origins—a phenomenon common to all the Grandes Écoles in the 1960s. Of the accepted students, 65 per cent came from the upper classes (23 per cent were sons of industrialists and members of the liberal professions, 42 per cent sons of senior civil servants and *cadres*), 28 per cent from the *classes moyennes* (11 per cent artisans and shop-keepers, 17 per cent lower civil servants and white-collar workers) and only 3 per cent from the working classes, all of whom were the sons of skilled workers, and 4 per cent from the farming community (1952: 169).

Democratization of public service through ENA was totally ineffective. Fifteen years later Bourdieu and his colleagues found almost

[2] *Polytechnique* graduates were also entitled to enter the senior ranks of the civil service but decreasing numbers of them did so. Suleiman (1974) has suggested that ENA reinforced previous recruitment patterns and by formalizing promotion through one school actually cut down possibilities for civil servants of lower social origins.

identical proportions—8 per cent from the *classe populaire*, nearly 30 per cent from the middle classes, and over 60 per cent from the upper classes (Bourdieu *et al.*, 1970).[3] There is even some evidence that recruitment from ENA to the *grands corps* increased the proportion from high social origins from 55 ·5 per cent to over 60 per cent (Darbel and Schnapper, 1972: 105), although it decreased professional heredity in the more limited sense, in that there were fewer sons of senior civil servants. The social origins of ENA students necessarily formed the social origins of an increasing part of those of members of the *grands corps* and the central administrations as the students moved on to fill these places.

The ministries and the different functions within them themselves formed a hierarchy and each ministry offered places according to the *rang de sortie*, the over-all position in the final examinations of the students. Thus, the Inspection des Finances offered places to the top few and so on down the list, while the diplomatic corps, the 'career', had sometimes—to its shame—'to go down almost to the middle' (Chazelle, 1968: 5). The technical ministries were nearer the lower end. The top students, thus, had a wide choice of career offers, the choice becoming progressively more and more limited as the *rang de sortie* went down. There is, moreover, reason to suppose that those who did best while at ENA, and who, therefore, went into the most prestigious ministries, were those from the higher social origins.

The order of prestige in the 1970s was the same as that before the war; by descending order, Inspection des Finances, Conseil d'État, Cour des Comptes, the Civil Administration Ministries, and, indeed, it may have been becoming more rigid (Darbel and Schnapper, 1972: 142). Once inside, chances of moving 'up' to another *corps* remained virtually non-existent and the hierarchy of prestige was reflected even in salaries (ibid.: 144). In their earlier book (1969), Darbel and Schnapper pointed out that

civil servants whose fathers belonged to the 'popular' classes, constitute 9·5 per cent of the 'external' services [i.e. not the central administration], 10 per cent of the central administration, and only 5·5 per cent of the *grands corps*, the *corps de contrôle*, and the technical *corps* . . . Civil servants from middle-class origins are mainly to be found in the central administration (39·5 per cent), external services (39·5 per cent), and 30 per cent in technical *corps*, 26 per cent in the *corps de contrôle*,

[3] The civil service *concours* was more 'democratic' in social origins than the student one—if only ENA entrants from the latter were considered the social origins would appear higher but it was very minor.

and 18 per cent in the *grands corps*. [On the other hand] civil servants from the upper classes constitute 76·5 per cent of the *grands corps*, 67·5 per cent of the *corps de contrôle*, 63·5 per cent of the technical *corps*, and only 50 per cent of the external services and 47·5 per cent of the Central Administration corps. (1969: 102)

As the same authors said earlier:

It is in the Social Ministries (14 per cent and Education (13·5 per cent) that the fraction of higher officials from working-class origins is highest; then in the technical (7 per cent) and controlling (*régaliens*) (6 per cent) . . . it is in the Ministry of Finance (5·5 per cent) and the services of the Prime Minister's office (2 per cent) that they are lowest. (ibid.: 95)

Working-class representation in all ministries remained extremely feeble, and that of the middle class only slightly less so. When they were present at all, these classes were mostly to be found in the less powerful Ministries and almost never in the services of the Prime Minister's offices. The same was true of opportunities to be even advisers to other Ministers (Darbel and Schnapper, 1969: 103).

L'Inspection des Finances   The first choice of the best graduates from ENA (and often from Polytechnique) was the Inspection des Finances, that small body of men who controlled the working of major sectors of the French economy, particularly the nationalized industries, and oversaw the working of ministries and other official organisms. They were *par excellence grands fonctionnaires* in all senses of the phrase. Constituting the most powerful body within the high civil service, they formed the major links between government and administration and the world of business. Because of their key position it is essential to examine membership of the Inspection.

Writing in 1953 Charles Brindillac remarked that of the forty crucial economic direction positions in the administration, thirty-five were occupied by members of the Inspection, and they were the most important in the State (1953: 864). In 1952 there were seventeen attached to the Pinay government and at the same time they controlled fifteen financial organisms, including the big banks. A further forty-five could be found running other public enterprises. Brindillac concludes:

Thus, it is that above 3,000 or 4,000 senior administrators who form the high *cadres* of the public service but who rarely rise to control the 'command levers', there emerges an oligarchy composed of men who have passed similar *concours*, after receiving the same training, and who are linked by the solidarity of the *corps*. (1953: 865)

What were the social origins of this group? Basing himself on the work of the American Jesse Pitts, Brindillac shows the pre-war preponderance of the aristocracy and *haute bourgeoisie*, followed by the *bonne bourgeoisie* and, far behind, the *moyenne* and *petite bourgeoisie*; the first two categories provided sixty out of the 112 Inspecteurs recruited between 1919 and 1939, while the last two groups only produced twenty. During the post-war period the predominance of the higher levels of the upper classes dropped in favour of an equalization of representation of all categories of the bourgeoisie (1953: 865). This, however, appears to have been the limit of 'democratization'.

In a study later in the 1950s Lalumière, confirming the narrow reruitment of the *Inspecteurs*, added that over the previous eighty-five years nearly half, approximately 40 per cent of the Inspecteurs had been Parisians, of whom two-thirds came from the 6th, 7th, 8th, and 16th *arrondissements* alone. Thirty-five per cent of the most powerful body in the Central Administration was recruited from 1 per cent of the French population. Important family traditions were involved in entry to the *Inspection*; the biggest contingent of fathers was that of *hauts fonctionnaires*. Between 1919 and 1954, thirty-five of the 260 *Inspecteurs* (13 per cent) joined their fathers there (Lalumière, 1959: 45). After 1947, two-thirds of the sixty-eight *Inspecteurs* recruited through ENA came from the highest social strata—the aristocracy, the *haute bourgeoisie* of industry and banking, and the liberal professions, senior civil servants, and *cadres*. There were no representatives of the working class (including farmers in that term), although there were 27 per cent from artisan and commercial families. The major beneficiaries of the creation of ENA were the children of the *petite bourgeoisie*—a reflection of the educational expansion throughout the 1950s and 1960s. Nevertheless, high-level business and administration family names frequently recurred, although this was less the case in the 1950s than it was before 1939. Members of the Inspection des Finances retained considerable links via their families of origin with major sectors of the economy and it was they who most often left public service to go into private or nationalized business.

Politics

Political leaders and quasi-leaders

The third 'Pillar of Power' is the most directly political. Who is it who makes, or at least has formal responsibility for, the central policy decisions, those embodied in laws? Whether the under-developed state of research in France on deputies and senators, their professional and social origins, and attachments to different sectors of the community, reflects the low level of importance accorded to Parliament by the Government is not clear, but there exist few major studies of the legislators as a group over the years of the post-war period.

On the other hand, much has been written on electors and on the electoral geography of the nation at each time of voting, showing, for instance, that voting alignments changed very little in France between the early 1900s and the late 1960s (except in exceptional times such as 1936, 1945, and 1968). Although the names and the number of the parties changed, political tendencies and the positions of electors on the political spectrum remained stable, only sliding occasionally slightly to the right or to the left and perhaps accepting for the time new alliances, as in the short-lived Rassemblement du Peuple Français started by de Gaulle in the late 1940s. Occasionally, threatened groups expressed anger in times of rapid economic change, creating movements such as Poujadism in the early 1950s. Links between social position, religious convictions, and voting behaviour remained important, and the left-wing parties were well entrenched in Paris, other industrial cities, and industrial regions and the south-west, while the right gathered most votes in the predominantly rural areas of Brittany and the east, with the centre having basic support in the Centre and prosperous rural areas and smaller towns and cities.

Deputies and senators 'represent' these interests in Parliament. Major studies of deputies were carried out by Mattei Dogan in the 1950s and early 1960s. Examining first the social and professional origins of deputies elected during the Third and Fourth Republics, and later extending his studies to include persons who stood as candidates but who were not elected, Dogan covered more than 4,000 deputies in the Third Republic. Some of these studies are available in English, and the data are presented here in greatly abridged form.

Changes of Parliamentary personnel were extremely slow, and would have been even slower if, during the period, 650 deputies had not died, 938 moved to the Senate, and 100 resigned. Although half the 4,300 deputies elected during the Third Republic ended their careers in electoral defeat (voting alignments were stable, but many were elected on margins of less than 10 per cent), many were elected for very long periods. Indeed, just under 500 deputies (one-ninth) had between them around 12,000 years of parliamentary time and sat in between five and twelve parliaments, each holding their seats twenty years at least, and often a quarter or   a third of a century or more. Excluding the extraordinary circumstances of the first and last two legislatures of the Third Republic, two-fifths of the deputies were elected between three and ten times (Dogan, 1961: 58). There were thus considerable opportunities for certain voices to be heard. Under the Fourth Republic (1945–58), itself a much shorter period, the duration of mandates was also very much shorter. However, nearly half of the deputies were elected between three and five times. Unfortunately, Dogan's study does not examine tenure of office under the Third Republic by party affiliation.

Representatives and represented

While deputies may have represented the different sections of the nation in terms of defending their interests, their socio-professional origins show the different strata unequally represented; indeed, the greater the proportion of a group in the total population, the smaller was its representation in the Chamber of deputies, and vice versa.

Table 6.3 reveals two important phenomena. First is the numerical importance of what Dogan calls the 'intellectual professions', teachers, journalists, doctors, and lawyers principally, with a few engineers, architects, and senior government officials. The teachers were concentrated in the communist and socialist parties, while the lawyers were concentrated in the radicals and moderates, although there were also a number on the socialist left. The reasons for the predominance of intellectuals included local importance (especially for teachers and doctors) and a less clear association with particular interests, enabling them to present themselves as representing either a wide variety of interests or no particular interests but those of the French 'people' and public well-being.

Only one-fifth of the deputies were from the working class, including in that the lowest levels of the civil service, and only 12 per cent were, before election, manual workers. Moreover, the latter were mainly constituted of union officials, often from the major unions, and had long since ceased to exercise manual professions. *Cadres*, shop-keepers, and industrialists together formed 10 per cent of the deputies, although their numerical importance in the total population was much smaller, but the striking fact, Dogan suggests, is that the Fourth Republic was the reign of the middle and lower-middle class. 'After the Republic of the Dukes came the Republic of notables, after the Republic of the upper-middle class there came . . . the reign of the middle and lower middle class' (1961: 74). The 'reigning' personnel became separated from the 'ruling' groups. There is some evidence that under the Fifth

TABLE 6.3.

Original occupation of deputies in metropolitan France 1945–58

Professions	CP	Socialists	MRP	Radicals	Mods. Indeps.	RPF & 'Gaullists'	Extreme Right and Poujad.	Unclassifiable	Total	%
Cadres	4	9	14	4	7	2	1	3	43	
Merchants & shopkeepers	1	2	15	5	6	6	29	–	64	16
Industrialists etc.	–	2	9	14	16	18	6	3	68	
Engineers and architects	4	5	11	8	9	8	–	9	54	
High public officials	3	4	9	8	6	7	1	4	42	
Lawyers	2	28	25	28	38	11	2	8	142	
Doctors/Pharms.	3	13	15	13	8	10	3	–	65	48
Journalists	5	19	17	12	6	2	1	2	64	
Professors, 2^e and higher	12	35	21	13	7	7	–	4	99	
Primary school teachers	29	32	1	3	–	–	1	1	66	
Farmers	29	10	29	11	40	12	–	5	136	12
Subordinate pub. oficials	7	15	5	3	1	–	–	–	31	
White-collar workers	37	16	19	2	–	–	–	1	71	21
Manual workers	99	11	21	–	1	1	–	–	133	
Army & eccles.	1	–	3	1	6	6	–	1	18	
Women, no profes.	11	1	2	–	1	1	–	–	16	3
Total	246	198	216	124	152	91	44	41	1112	100
% distribution	22	18	20	11	14	8	4	3	100%	

Source: Slightly adapted from Dogan, 1961: 67.
CP = Communist Party   MRP = Mouvement Républicain Populaire   RPF = Rassemblement du Peuple Français
The Socialists were composed ot the Section Française de l'Internationale Ouvrière (SFIO) and the Independent Socialists.

Republic there was no further enlargement of the social base, and with the decline of the Communist Party until elections in the 1970s there may even have been some narrowing. It would also be useful to know how length of Parliamentary service varied according to the social origins of deputies as well as according to their party affiliation.

More detailed information on candidates shows that chances of election as well as final representation were highly dependent on social origins: 'The most numerous social categories, which are also the least privileged of the nation, provide fewest candidates' (Dogan, 1961: 292). There were almost no women. The average of one elected for seven candidates hid important differential chances of election by socio-professional origins. 'List dosing' by many parties—that is, presenting candidates from different social groups to 'balance' its image—enlarged the apparent social base: right-wing parties put up workers, and all parties put up farmers (included on nine-tenths of all lists except in the Seine *département*), but placed them so low down on the lists as to have virtually no chance of election. Only the Communist party ensured some worker representation.

No workers were first or second on RPF lists, and only one worker was elected for the RPF, which gives some indications of the nature of the 'people' de Gaulle assembled in his party. Even within the working class, as was suggested above, not all sections were equally represented. 'The political potential of workers working in the very concentrated [i.e. very important] industries is greater than that of those belonging to medium-sized industries' (1961, 303). Of the forty-nine worker M.P.s, thirty-four came from big industries which only occupied one-third of all French workers, principally from four *départements*. For other categories the reverse was true: not only were they 'over-represented' among the candidates, but a far greater proportion were elected. For instance, one lawyer in thirty-nine was a candidate (one in fourteen if one considers only male lawyers), and constituted the proportion of one in eight deputies against one in seventeen candidates, although lawyers only formed half of one per cent of the electoral body.

Deputies and ministers

Although during the Fourth Republic Parliament carried considerable weight, cabinet ministers represented government power and at least initiated policy. Unexpectedly, in comparison with the Fifth Republic, there was considerable ministerial stability, even though the Governments nominally were unseated. Who had the greatest chances of becoming Ministers and thus of having most influence on policy is an important question.

Some deputies accumulated power; twenty-seven deputies had previously been in the top levels of the civil service, and at least sixteen of these had, before becoming deputies, spent long periods in ministerial cabinets, and so were well experienced in political decision-making and had a number of high-level contacts within the civil service, where they had held posts in the most important sections. Of these six had been in the Conseil d'État, two in the Cour des Comptes, five had been diplomats, three were Inspecteurs des Finances, three Inspecteurs Généraux in the Central Administration, three Préfets, and so on. A third of all senior civil servant candidates were elected and of these thirteen held ministerial posts. Similarly, one-third of the doctors and one-half of all the lawyers became ministers (before or after 1951). Thirty-eight barristers became ministers or secretaries of State. Amongst them, six became Présidents du Conseil, including such well-known figures as Paul Reynaud, Robert Schumann, Edgar Faure, and Pierre Mendès-France. Other lawyers became important party leaders, president of parliamentary groups, and indeed President of the Republic (Auriol and Coty). By contrast, only four shop-keepers and deputies and only six worker deputies, all communists, acquired ministerial functions. University teachers stood a better chance of becoming ministers—and they were from higher social origins—than did the lower-grade teachers.

It is evident, therefore, that access to the higher levels of political power remained open very unevenly to different social groups, at least in terms of direct representation. Possibilities of access to power remained as systematically patterned as did those within other parts of the opportunity structure.

Dogan's studies of the social and professional backgrounds of deputies and of the paths leading to the holding of political office were carried out in the 1950s. Later studies showed the situation to have remained virtually unchanged.

A major study was carried out by the Centre d'Étude de la Vie Politique Française Contemporaine of the Fondation Nationale des Sciences Politiques in 1969–70 on the social and professional origins of the deputies, and examined how and at what age they had first become interested in politics and the political paths (*filières*) which led them to stand for office and be elected. It showed systematic variations by party on almost all the dimensions in question, with parties on the left and right being most homogeneous and those in the middle, and particularly the composite Gaullist UDR, being most heterogeneous.

Many deputies came from families with strong political interests. More than half (56 per cent), had a father who carried out political functions, a quarter had a grandfather in politics. A fifth had another near relative, such as mother or uncle and 13 per cent had both a father and a grandfather who were active politically. Politicians thus tended to be drawn from political families, were political 'specialists'.

In the late 1960s, therefore, 79 per cent of the previous professions of the deputies placed them in the well-off sections of the population, with 11 per cent being industrialists, 28 per cent members of the liberal professions, 21 per cent *cadres supérieurs*, and 5 per cent shop-keepers (3 per cent large-scale merchants), while only 13 per cent came from lower on the social scale and had previously been manual or white-collar workers and technicians (5 per cent in all), or primary-school teachers, artisans, or *cadres moyens* (8 per cent).

A similar situation was shown by family origins: thus, 25 per cent of the Républicains Indépendants (RI) were from the dominant classes, while 13 per cent of the PDM,[4] 20 per cent of the Radicals, and only 4 per cent of the Socialists were so (and no Communists).

It is clear, then, that under the Fifth Republic there occurred little widening of the socio-professional basis for recruitment to elected political office; indeed there was some narrowing.

The proportion of persons in the Palais Bourbon belonging to the *catégories dirigeantes* has been growing; the increase is particularly clear when one compares the deputies of the present majority party (UDR and Républicains Indépendants) who were first elected under the Third and Fourth Republics, and those who have been elected since the beginning of the Fifth Republic. The progression can further be seen in comparison between those elected in the elections of 1967 and 1968. (Cayrol *et al.*, 1973: 43)

The party which subsequently produced the current President, Valéry Giscard d'Estaing, the Républicains Indépendants, in terms of the backgrounds of the deputies, represented the most traditional, Catholic (practising), Parisian fractions of the bourgeoisie and had close links with the highest levels of industry, banking, and commerce (Cayrol *et al.*, 1973: 27).

Only in the left-wing parties, especially the Communist Party, were worker deputies in the majority, and only there was there a majority of members with considerable numbers of men from humble social origins.

The social patterning of access to the upper levels of power also remained strong under the Fifth Republic. Ministers tended to be of higher social origins than the ensemble of parliamentary personnel. An

[4]   Progrès et Démocratie Moderne, a Centrist party.

American observer, E. Lewis, analysing the occupational and educational backgrounds of ministers between 1944 and 1967 shows that ministers throughout the period were a cross-section of the upper bourgeoisie; most were lawyers (58), civil servants (41), industrialists and directors of corporations (40), and teachers (34) (1970: 566). These four categories accounted for 63 per cent of all ministers after 1944 and 76 per cent of all ministers under de Gaulle. Adding doctors, engineers, and career officers to the above professions accounts for 86 per cent of all Gaullist ministers; industrial workers only accounted for 3 per cent and farm workers 4 per cent. Of ministers over the period, only 14 per cent (out of the 87 per cent known) had less than university education, and the ministers included twelve Polytechniciens, twelve Normaliens, and forty-three graduates of Sciences Politiques, graduates of the most prestigious and bourgeois Grandes Écoles (ibid.: 565).

Further information on the composition of the other elected body, the Senate (indirect election by electoral colleges), and the departmental administration (*conseils généraux*) would be useful; the Senate had the reputation of being more conservative than the Chamber of Deputies and of holding up legislation it disapproved. Unfortunately, such studies are few, as are those of local government, elections to *conseils municipaux*, and of mayors.

One short study on the Senate, however, does make the important point that

the stability of the electoral regime of the Senate has as a direct result the stability of its political colouring and its personal composition . . . The High Assembly is renewed by one-third every three years . . . and, therefore, is not subject to radical changes. Except in 1879, 1885, and 1909 the [electoral] colleges have always re-elected two-thirds of the previous members. (Le Reclus, 1969: 45)

As Le Reclus points out, senators must be more than forty years old and tend to be the 'enemies of abstract deductions and "adventures" in all domains, especially the financial and social.'

Under the Fifth Republic, the Senate was composed of men from the professions listed in Table 6.4.

The majority of senators were also the mayors of small *communes*, showing the representation of the people at that level as well. In both these political spheres, Senate and *communes*, there was an important 'over-representation' of members from the liberal professions and, particularly in the Senate, from rural areas.

Tremendous social inertia could be seen in the stability of election of the *conseillers généraux* (who formed the electoral colleges of the

TABLE 6.4.
Social origins of Senators

Profession	Percentage
Liberal professions	27 (of which 11 per cent are lawyers)
Farmers	23·5
Industrial/commercial professions	16
Cadres supérieurs (including senior civil servants)	13
Teachers	9 (4 per cent high-level)
White-collar workers/cadres moyens	8
Workers	3

Source: Le Reclus, 1969: 56.

Senate). Between 1945 and 1964 the number of conseillers généraux re-elected each time was never less than 65 per cent, and in 1964 more than one-third of them had been in power constantly since the Liberation, showing not only the entrenchment (enracinement) of the political class but also, through the apathy of the electors seen in massive abstentionism, the total incapacity of the system to select new élites (Longepierre, 1970: 9). Many conseillers généraux were also mayors, and as such the lowest level in the administrative hierarchy, spending at least as much time implementing government decisions as passing upwards the wishes of their electors.

The powers around the throne

Analysis of recruitment to positions of power in two of the major institutions of the State, the high civil service and the legislature, and to the major areas of the private economic sector, shows the limited origins of personnel, mainly from the Parisian bourgeoisie, either major or minor.

It is therefore important to assess the extent to which the personnel emanating from these major groups were linked together, thus joining groups within these power institutions, whether or not they were linked outside them. It has been argued that it is not sufficient to demonstrate similarity of social origins in order to prove that a 'ruling class' exists; some demonstration of common purpose is also required (Aron). Such demonstration would involve an analysis of major decisions, and some attempts have been made at this by French political scientists, although these have not been conclusive. Regardless of common purpose, certain sections of the population manifestly had and continued to have greater or lesser access to important decision-making posts. The most important of the mechanisms behind such limitation was the education system which selected young people at an early age but after that ceased to operate directly other forces, in part caused and in part justified by and justifying it, entered the arena.

Overlapping personnel

Powerful persons may be linked together through the overlapping of personnel, through their social contacts (reinforced through marriage in particular), and through the symbolic (cultural) factors encouraging the cohesion of the group. The separation is an artificial one—in reality all are aspects of the same phenomenon. Whether in politics, administration, or business, personal linkages tend towards the closure of the ruling groups.

Civil service and business In the late 1950s *pantouflage* from positions in the high civil service to top posts in industry and commerce became more and more common (Lalumière, 1959: 68). By the use of the *mise en disponibilité* and detachment, as many as 50 per cent, over the previous eighty years, of the Inspecteurs left the central administration after ten to twelve years' service, the rate varying somewhat with economic circumstances. It was especially those who had family links with the upper echelons of the private sector who moved, and the latest resignations seemed to confirm that trend, for twenty-nine of the thirty four leaving in the late 1950s were cited in the Bottin Mondain, the French equivalent of the Social Register (Lalumière, op. cit.). Family links meant rapid introduction to important posts in business life, and constituted the best of recommendations. Indeed, it is possible that certain Inspecteurs already had a place reserved for them in big firms before even going into the Civil Service, and their experience in the administration was simply their 'apprenticeship' for their private business career (ibid.: 76).

Such movements were into the most important and dynamic sectors of the economy and to the crucial nationalized industries, above all important merchant banks, metallurgy, chemicals, and cars. Directing the nation's most important financial organs, the Inspecteurs formed part of the 'capitalist oligarchy'. In great majority they joined boards of directors, and, although sometimes beginning as *cadres supérieurs* (especially those with no family connections), this was usually brief.

The internal coherence of the Inspecteurs as a group was assured by a number of factors. In the early days of a career similar backgrounds and similar education, if not the same graduation class (*promotion*) in the same school or *préparation*, were paramount factors of solidarity. At work, the group of *Inspecteurs* was fairly small, facilitating close contacts and identification, and within it even smaller groups and closer links were formed in the *tournées* (rounds) of the early career, where several inspectors toured the provinces to carry out financial controls on the different administrative organs and spent much time exclusively in each other's company (ibid.: 125–6).

The central administration's link with politics springs from its very function, but certain members were more closely involved than others. Many men from the highest social origins served in ministerial cabinets and became deputies or ministers themselves (Dogan 1961, and Cayrol *et al.*, 1973). Useful to business because they knew intimately both the central organization's rules and methods and, no less important, how to get around them, ex-civil servants, also held an important amount of social capital (*relations*) as they retained many contacts with persons still in office, in their own branch of central government and in many others. Further their previous education in one of the *écoles du pouvoir* (Polytechnique, HEC, ENA, etc.) forced links of camaraderie, both potential and actual, with member of the *promotion* who followed different career paths.

Business and politics   Important sections of business were well represented in terms of families of deputies under the Third Republic and the reign of the *grande bourgeoisie*. In the nineteenth and twentieth centuries, under the Third Republic, State and business were inextricably interlinked. Studies of the origin of the French *patronat* show the closeness of the business, banking, and political careers of the major figures of the nineteenth century—for example the Périer brothers, the Méquillet-Noblot family, and the de Wendel family, as well, of course, as such international families as the Rothschilds (in whose bank Georges Pompidou held high office before going into politics under General de Gaulle). Members of the de Wendel family, owners and managers of a giant metallurgical form, have always been attentive to their relations with the government, and were to be found in Parliament, as deputies and senators, throughout the nineteenth century and in the twentieth until the Second World War (Priouret, 1963: 24). According to Priouret, the family controlled the elections in their *département,* and Robert Schumann was 'their' deputy in *Meurthe-et-Moselle* from 1919 to 1936 inclusive. They were the counsellors of political leaders of the time and one de Wendel, a friend of Poincaré, was also *régent* of the Banque of France, whence he precipitated the financial crisis in 1926 that brought Poincaré back to power.

After the Liberation the French *patronat* reorganized. The American political sociologist Henry Ehrmann wrote that, after 1947, the CNPF (equivalent of the Confederation of British Industry) moved close to open support for de Gaulle's right-wing movement, the Rassemblement du Peuple Français. Because of the low electroal pull of big business, influence over the *rapporteurs* of the powerful standing committees seems to have been especially cultivated. The *rapporteurs*, suggests Ehrmann, seem to have had more faith in private sources of information than the Government ones (1957: 233), and he quotes Williams's conclusion that such committees soon became the 'institutional façade for the operation of pressure groups'. Business interests, however, were still directly represented. In a rather polemical work, *Les Français qui mènent le monde* (1955), Coston lists some of the business interest of the Fourth Republic's Ministers. From one cabinet alone fourteen ministers are listed with extensive business interests in almost all sectors of the French economy, banking, metallurgy, the electrical industry, agricultural implements, and oil, to which should be added many overseas interests, especially in the French colonies, such as mining and transport. Even under the socialist government of Pierre Mendès-France business interests were important, although not usually so open. Although there is little direct evidence, there is indirect evidence that under the Fifth Republic links between business and politics seen in direct representation increased.

Business and business   Business is the most dispersed and in some sense heterogeneous of all powerful groups. Recruitment studies showed the similar social origins of major business leaders and their passage through élite schools, creating strong relationships of camaraderie (cf. Kosciusko-Moriset, 1973, on Polytechniciens). Apparently distinct businesses were linked by holding companies and organized into 'groups'. The number of these concentrations from the mid-1950s onwards grew fast, with a consequent diminution in the number of leaders.

A study by J. Houssiaux on the 100 biggest French firms in 1952 showed 998 known financial links between them, of which 27 link firms within the group of 100 . . . Certain sectors are the field of an intense control activity: 150 financial links for one firm in the group in the glass industry, 45 links within the group of 100 for the 352 metal transformation companies, and financial links are further reinforced through the merchant banks. The accounts of the twelve big merchant banks show 677 links, of which 75 are between firms within the hundred . . . If to the financial links one adds the personal links, which permit a more or less direct control of the boards of directors (*Conseils d'Administration*), one discovers that the internal consistency of the group is greater by far . . . 975 Directors belonging to the firms in the group between them formed 3120 personal links between different companies, and there are 473 interlinkages within the group of 100. The average number of links per firm is therefore 31·2 and per director 4·73. As for the financial links, there are important differences between the sectors; mining and the glass industries are in the lead, with paper and the press last. With 1124 personal links, the 348 directors of the 35 firms in the metal transformation industry contribute greatly to the consistency and density of the network along whose channels circulate information, suggestions (*injonctions*), and commands. (Cuisenier in Darras, 1966: 377–8).

Examining *La Structure financière du capitalisme français* François Morin (1974) shows the powerful groupings which grew up throughout the 1960s, in particular alongside the traditional control of even many big businesses by single families. Half of the two hundred biggest French companies were still family controlled in the early 1970s and of the twenty biggest six were family controlled. The remainder, and many others of slightly lesser stature, were increasingly linked into groups of companies, often dominated by banking and finance houses. For example, 103 firms were linked together in Pechiney-Ugine-Kuhlman, 113 in CGE and, through the group, to banks such as Paribas (Banque de Paris et des Pays-Bas) in the CGE case. Within these groups, and between many of the groups, there existed important links in the form of overlapping directorates and especially links between the *grands fonctionnaires* and the major banking groups. For instance, examining the composition of the Conseils d'Administration of the companies Paribas and Suez (Compagnie Financière de Suez), Morin says,

'one cannot avoid noticing the dominant share held by ex-senior civil servants (*grands commis de l'État*). By *grands commis de l'État* we mean persons who, by virtue of their past (or present) duties, occupied for many years (or still occupy) posts of responsibility at the highest level in the state's administrative apparatus. This is particularly the case of the Inspecteurs des Finances, who by their training have access to the highest economic and financial responsibilities. (ibid.: 94–5)

he adds: 'in June 1974 there were five Inspecteurs des Finances in the Conseil d'Administration of Suez and six in Paribas' (ibid.: 95), where they held all the major *direction* posts.

Further, amongst a wider range of the major financial-industrial groups, personal links between members of the banking 'technocracy' were particularly strong, and there were links with the 'traditional' capital held by families such as de Wendel, Peugeot, de Dietrich, etc. (ibid.: 192).

Links, unions, and social surfaces

Marriage and family

Many of the studies on recruitment to power positions emphasized the role of links of family and affinal relationships through marriage in maintaining the social homogeneity of the important recruiting grounds of the nation's political, administrative, and economic élites. In a large-scale sociological study on the choice of a marriage partner, Girard, using a sample of 14,000 people drawn from the census of 1954 and, from them, a sub-sample of 1,646 couples who were interviewed, revealed overwhelming social and geographical homogamy (marriage within the same group). Nearly six-tenths of spouses lived in the same *commune*, seven-tenths in the same *canton*, eight-tenths in the same *arrondissement*, nine-tenths in the same *département* or region at the time of their marriage. Over time a slight drop in numbers in the same *commune* appeared, which represents the increasing mobility of the French, but the drop was still relatively small. The top social categories married geographically 'furthest away', but even there fully one-half of all marriages took place between persons from the same region—and some of those who lived in 'separate' administrative regions may in fact have lived virtually next door.

Social homogamy is similarly pronounced: Girard calculates it as being twice high as if the spouses were chosen independently of social origins, for over two-thirds of households were formed of spouses both from the same milieu or two adjacent milieux, whether measured by professions of spouses or those of fathers of spouses (and women did not raise themselves by marriage more than men). In all milieux the spouses always had more chances of having the same social origins than of having different ones. The highest social groups especially married into their own group, effectively limiting access to the group through marriage. At the lowest levels, too, there was little movement.

Social mixing (*brassages sociaux*) through marriage was greatest in the milieux of the petty bourgeoisie, *cadres moyens*, shop-keepers, and other small independent businessmen and craftsmen. Thus, all three factors in the analysis—education, socio-professional mobility, and marriage—appeared to be linked, and it is clear that they all formed part of the same system and all both reflected and acted on each other, social origins affecting access to education, which in turn was basic to profession exercised, and both of these acted to limit the choice of marriage partner.

Marriage had an extremely important role as a means of concentrating, maintaining, and expanding capital of all kinds—economic, cultural, and social. Dowries remained important to the transmission of economic capital; nearly half of the couples, studied by Girard, belonging to the liberal professions and the *cadres supérieurs* had dowries, either from both parents or the parents of the wife (especially), and of these 30 per cent had money or shares. Similarly, 43 per cent in these same categories had a marriage contract serving to maintain the patrimony of the spouses intact. Delphy (1969) found similar results for shop-keepers and my own research on a small sample of French upper-middle-class families has confirmed both the importance of social homogamy and the continuation of the practice of dowries (Marceau: 1974 and 1975). The latter research has also suggested the importance of the wives for their husband's social and economic position in terms of social as well as economic capital. The wives came from families usually well-established in the liberal professions, especially law and medicine, the Army and business, thus providing through their families important social contacts and relationships. Larger than average families continued to be the rule at the higher end of the French social scale, so that these relationships were numerous both at the level of the parents' generation—a large number of uncles—but also at the level of spouses' generation, where there were many brothers and many sisters to marry into similar milieux.

Marriage acts to limit access to the higher positions of power in French society. Numbers of power positions may, however, seem large, and there arises the problem of means of control of these posts by the milieux concerned. Perhaps the most important is the overlapping of personnel, the multitude of posts covered by the same persons, the number covered rising systematically with place in the social scale.

The 'fields of power'; multiple position-holding and social capital

Multiple post-holding was the centre of an important study by Luc Boltanski, of the Centre de Sociologie de l'Education. Taking as his point of reference the professors, all part-time, of the prestigious Institut d'Études Politiques (formerly École Libre des Sciences Politiques) in Paris, which principally recruits students from the Parisian bourgeoisie and prepares many of them for ENA and the higher ranks of the Civil Service as well as of business, Boltanski examines what he calls their positions in the different 'fields of power' (*champs de pouvoir*).

Taking a continuum from the 'intellectual pole' to the 'power pole', Boltanski analyses five fields of power: the academic field, the field of cultural diffusion (mass media, etc.), the administrative field, the economic field, and the political field. Each teacher at IEP possessed on average three positions, or nearly five if we include those held in the past, and many held six, seven, or eight, spreading across all the fields of power. This positional analysis allows one to describe the 'social surface' (*surface sociale*) held by powerful individuals; the 'social surface' being

that portion of social space which an individual is able to pass through (*parcourir*) and dominate by occupying *successively* the different social positions that he has the right to occupy *simultaneously*, the only condition being that he physically possess the gift of ubiquity which is socially conferred on him. (Boltanski, 1972: 9)

The size of the individual's 'social surface' depends as much on the dispersion as on the number of positions held.

Using this concept, Boltanski finds that the professors of IEP had very unequally distributed social surfaces. While some held only a small number of positions situated close together in the same field of power, others held a large number of very dispersed positions. The number of positions held regularly increased with the social origin of their holder— those with fathers who were manual or white-collar workers occupied on average 1·7 positions as against 2·8 for those whose fathers were shop-keepers, 3·6 for middle-level state administrator fathers, 4 for teacher or other intellectual professions, 4·4 for the liberal professions and *cadres supérieurs* (private sector), 5 for senior civil servants, magistrates, or officers, and 6·7 for fathers who were *patrons* of industry (ibid.: 11).

These differences are important, for they reveal not only the systematic and significant role played by social origins in access to power positions, even when small groups among the élite are considered, but also, and as a reflection of this, the importance of 'extra-professional' factors in the extension and holding of power positions. Thus Boltanski says:

To understand the social advantages which are the correlates of the possession of an extended social surface, one should remember that among the *ensemble* of the privileges which are the instrument and the product of power, there is none more important than the capital of social contacts (*relations*); by the intermediary of the network of contacts, familial or of friendship, are carried out an important number of transactions, which are objectively political or economic but which, not being carried out with money, are not perceived as such . . . for example, recommendations, exchanges of information, etc. Moreover, the occupation of a given position implies itself the possession of a certain capital of social relations, of prestige, of symbolic credit, legitimacy, and power. It follows that the social capital that an individual can mobilize depends not only on his family origins but also on the social surface that he can himself dominate (which is itself at least in most cases social capital accumulated by the family), which depends in its turn on the breadth of one's network of contacts, multiplied by the social surface controlled by each member of one's extended family, and, to a lesser extent, that of each of the members of the network of contacts. One could not explain the omnipresence of certain names, certain lineages, of certain individuals, able to control indirectly, at a distance, a far greater number of positions than that which they are able to occupy directly, nor the breadth of their power, without bringing into [the analysis] a multiplier of this kind. (ibid.: 10—11).

Further, Boltanski's analysis shows the five fields of power to be of unequal weight in the total power system and as giving unequal possibilities for a broad network of contracts and the holding of a multiplicity of power positions. The intellectual pole had fewest possibilities— academics remained within the academic field, especially those who taught letters rather than law. Maximum power was given to those belonging to the major state administrative bodies, once again, the Inspecteurs des Finances, who tended to hold positions in the administrative, political, and economic fields, sometimes even in the academic field.

The sample, drawn from professors at the Institut d'Études Politiques who were selected by the criteria of the school is a rather special one. However, the image that the school presented, and wished to present, of itself was one closely linked to the most important sectors of the society since it was preparing students to occupy élite positions in that society. Hence, it seems likely that the sample reflects the reality to a considerable extent in terms of the differential numbers and breadth of positions held by persons principally involved in one field of power rather than another, in other words that the hierarchy revealed was the 'real' or relevant one.

Such an analysis shows both the differential power of different fractions of the élites and overlapping and interaction in terms of possible roles and positions, and how a small number of persons can hold a large number of posts. This in effect limits access to such positions. Further, the fundamental interests of the system for the dominant class are summed up by Boltanski as follows:

[multi-positionality] permits, in conformity with the logic of magic by which the whole of a personality, individual or collective, resides in each of its parts, the division of the dominant class while at the same time maintaining its unity, as the existence of automomous fields of power is counterbalanced by the freedom of individuals . . . to circulate between positions and fields.

This is important for ideological reasons because

by favouring the import and export of persons between fields and thus the circulation of ways of speech (*langages*), manners, themes, and questions, [such circulation] leads to the production of *problématiques* common to the whole of the dominant class. Thereby, too, it contributes to the production of the class consciousness of the ruling class as a sentiment of familiarity and solidarity, which does not need to be raised to a verbal and explicit level to maintain the unity of the class, by containing within tolerance limits the different factional quarrels born of the objective diversity of material and symbolic interests. (ibid.: 33)

The symbolic representation of the interests of the class serves not only to permit group cohesion but also to 'recognize' and recruit the relevant personnel. In their analysis of the 'symbolic goods market' and its relationship to accepted 'culture' and cultural capital and the appropriate attitude towards it and use in interpersonal contacts, Bourdieu and his colleagues emphasize the expectation of social ease and cultural and intellectual 'excellence' and a 'cultivated' approach which must in all cases seem natural and in no way 'learned'.

At different levels of the educational system, the importance of symbolic means of differentiating almost 'identical' products becomes more and more important, perhaps being seen to culminate in the major written and oral examinations taken by candidates to ENA, which explicitly judged the general culture of a person but did so less by *what* he expressed, those sentiments being common to many, than by the *way* he expressed it and the ease and sophistication of his approach. As the ENA examiners themselves said, the 'first-day examination', the most general dissertation, is that which 'should be the expression of the personality of a young man or young woman' (quoted in Darbel, Schnapper: 1972: 99). This can be seen to favour students from upper-class Parisian backgrounds, as does to an even greater extent the oral test, which is designed to appreciate the 'moral and intellectual quality of a candidate' and to check that the future élite of the administration 'will not lack humour and be reduced to the *forts en thème*' (good essay writers), as expressed by the President of the ENA admission jury in 1969. Such qualities do not explicitly form part of school curricula at any level, and must be developed in homes where discussion and repartee are the norm and which are developed by contacts with those already in place, as essentially was the case with the students of IEP in Paris, who constituted more than two-thirds of the accepted students at ENA.

Such privileged relationships with, and access to, the most legitimate and general and yet at the same time most exclusive aspects of 'culture' continued to play their part throughout the career of many, and in particular of those in the senior levels of the civil service. Promotion juries were composed only of civil servants who chose to promote those most like themselves (Gournay, 1964: 224).

It is clear, then, that the dominant social groups in France throughout the period after 1945 remained linked together in a multiplicity of ways. Marriage, multiple position-holding, family links and the capital of relations, camaraderie based on common education and the values imparted by a bourgeois (and aristocratic)[5] upbringing, constant contacts made in and reinforced by everyday professional activity, linked together men powerful in the major institutions of the society. Business was linked to politics, administration to both. In all a network, more or less dense as one approaches the centre (geographical concentration in Paris was important here too), becoming sparser around the periphery, joined together men and women active in the most important spheres of life in the public and private sectors. These linkages, allied to the major mechanisms of educational selection and professional 'choice', continued to act to limit severely the possibilities of access to powerful positions by members born into any groups but those already in dominant positions.

    [5]   De Negroni (1974) has shown the customs by which members of the *grande bourgeoisie* and aristocracy maintained contact from early childhood to old age. At *goûters* (teas), school (private and Catholic), dances, weddings, and, for men, in business, political and leisure activities (sports clubs) members of the most important Parisian fractions of these groups, constantly met the same 'suitable' people.

7. SYSTEMS, STRUCTURES, AND IDEOLOGIES

Rewards and responsibilities, access to power positions, and opportunities for improved social status remained distributed in unequal and highly patterned ways throughout the period of economic growth between 1945 and 1975. Such a picture of patterned inequality suggests the existence in society of important conflicts of interest, potential or actual, and poses directly the question of why such inequalities persisted and why they took the form they did. The question is a fundamental one and can be approached on a number of levels and in a variety of ways.

It is important to distinguish between the 'reality' of society in the empirical sense used in earlier chapters to examine the distribution of income and other rewards, and the *representation* which a society makes of itself, of its nature, of its past, of its future. These constitute both the means by which divisions within a society can be camouflaged and 'explain' differences (especially hierarchies) and provide outlets for the 'legitimate' aspirations of the less privileged. In France the State had, of course, an important repressive side which should not be underestimated, evident, for example, in police response to street demonstrations of many kinds; but French society was based as much on the acquiescence (or resignation) of its members as on force.[1] Certain social mechanisms particularly contributed to the production and maintenance of this acquiescence, to a large extent because of the dominant ideologies they developed and transmitted.

Analysis of the Ideological State Apparatuses (Althusser's term (1970) for the ideological forces in both public and private sectors), while rather outside the theoretical framework used in this book, suggests which specific sectors and institutions of French society contributed most to acquiescence in the social and political structure.

Studies available refer more especially to the later parts of the period up to 1975. This is perhaps no accident, for the contradictions and problems associated with the French capitalist form of economic growth and its failure to solve basic problems of inequality and power were increasingly evident to sociologists and other observers. The failure

---

[1] This acquiescence should not be over-emphasized. It is evident that many strikes took place, some of which, as in May 1968 but also before, made radical political demands. Certainly, the role of the Army in political life was greater in France than in Britain.

of economic growth in itself to do anything to change patterns of inequality, or even to eliminate all forms of poverty, had been evident even before May 1968. The explosion of public consciousness apparent during the spring of 1968 represented increased and acute public discontent, but it wrought no basic structural damage. Evidence of the problems, and the existence and ultimate failure of the May movement, led observers to a renewed emphasis on ideology and the power of ideology as a legitimating mechanism in the society.

The role of each part of the system varied over time. For example, before the advent of mass ownership of television sets in the late 1950s and early 1960s, clearly that channel of the mass media was of marginal importance, but it gained constantly in social weight. When mass consumption of any goods became possible, the ideology of 'happiness' through consumption in particular gained ground and reflected attitudes towards a whole range of values and activities. With economic growth and the concentration of public attention onto new possibilities, not only for consumption, but also in terms of job promotions, for individuals and for their children, the ideology of social mobility was reinforced and made more salient, paradoxically allowing the school to play even more successfully its role in the conservation of the basic socio-economic divisions in the society and to justify them further. Education, indeed, played that role in a number of ways. Not only did it turn 'social' gifts into 'natural' ones, and use this as the basis for the positive selection (and negative elimination) of individuals for roles in the economic system; it also, through its teaching methods and curriculum, presented a certain image of French society, of the values underlying it and the arrangement of the various groups within it. In the books used in primary schools, for example, the daily experience of the mass of children did not appear; there was little reference to manual work and working conditions, none at all to those of families living in large blocks of flats, segregated in the one-class housing estates on the outer edges of cities. Rather the image emphasized remained that of the independent, petty bourgeois family secure in an individual house with its own area of freedom constituted by the private garden, however, small, and in which mother stayed at home to make cakes for tea (*quatre heures*, a now solidly entrenched French institution), an image also still much cultivated in 1975 by stories in the 'better' children's magazines such as *Pomme d'Api*. Most working-class children, particularly in urban areas, did not recognize themselves in such images, but seem nevertheless to have come to internalize the social values pertaining to them.

The same kind of images were frequently presented through the Catholic church and absorbed into the trio 'family-religion-nation'. Although the proportion of practising Catholics varied greatly by social class and geographical region, the influence of the church continued to be felt and was important in such matters as voting behaviour throughout the period, suggesting again the continued internalization of certain values. Perhaps, however, the representations a society makes of its entire political system are in some ways crucial, for the other parts of the system frequently define themselves, and are defined, in relation to the political system, and if the political system appears 'just' or as emanating from the 'will of the people' the resentment of many groups in the society appears to have less justification, for the means of changing the situation apparently exist.

The political system in France, of course, underwent some quite radical changes during the thirty years after 1945. The traumatic period of intense party politics, coupled with the death throes of an empire, followed by a period of calm dominated by the persona of de Gaulle, tended to breed a certain political apathy in relation to established institutional politics, but from the mid- to late-1960s political interest intensified. The analysis made here, however, refers to the more general aspects of a democratic parliamentary political system, of which a certain variety may be said to have existed in France through most of the period 1945–75, although becoming increasingly presidential towards the end.

Politics and the political and legal systems

The 'political system' in a society is closely linked to the social system and the system of class relations, and constitutes, in Touraine's words, the 'political scope' of those relations. It has a certain autonomy and specificity and a certain 'dominance' in the representations a society makes of itself and relationships within it, important both to the dominance of a certain class and the acquiescence in that domination by the dominated.

In general, Touraine suggests, class relations, taking on a political form, lead on the one hand to the opening of relations between political forces and on the other to the closure of class domination, transformed into the legitimate order, protected by the forces of order, and reinforced by all the mechanisms of social control. A government and its executive dispose of force, and maintain through force the frontier they trace between the legal and the illegal. Violence exists at all levels of the society, as it also does in the action of social classes in social movements, and within the framework of organizations. The particular form of violence at the political level is force, employed in the name of institutions or against them. Transformation onto the political level hardens social domination, closes it by seeking to render intangible its foundations and its continuity. Class relations, transformed into political relations, become *institutionalized* and thereby an essential element of the process of social change (Touraine, 1973). Class relations were largely expressed through institutionalized political mechanisms in France after 1945, but at certain important times, particularly at the height of the Algerian war, relations of force came into the open and forced a transformation of the political system of the country. Even once that system had been renewed and institutionalized into the Fifth Republic, its fragility remained apparent for some time, as could be seen, for instance, in the near succcess of the Generals involved in the putsch in Algiers in the spring of 1961.

A political system is always at once both reformist and repressive. In Touraine's view, contrary to frequent representations of it, a liberal regime, with an open political system, is a regime which is particularly dependent on class relations, for 'an open political system is the least autonomous. The more political forces can enter without constraint into the game of influences, the more the political system tends to "represent" faithfully social interests and, therefore, in the last analysis social classes' (1973: 225–6). He goes on to say that 'Political forces are at one and the same time the *agents of integration* and the political *representatives* of class actors, and to the extent that class relations are open, that social movements confront each other, classes or fractions of classes have their political *representatives*.' The system rejects, and places outside the law, all that is not compatible with the system of historical action and that which is threatening to the upper class. The ensemble of the mechanisms of social control is charged with the rejection of all that is unacceptable and with the greatest possible extension of the domain of the acceptable, so as to give a solid protection to the system of historical action and above all to the domination of a class (ibid.: 226–8).

This sytem, at once integrative and repressive, possesses its own agents, which do their best to invent for the system a determining role which it does not in reality possess. Its agents create a series of representations of it which are favourable to them; they present the legislator as the origin of all power and the political sphere as commanding the social. The system produces a rhetoric which provides a unity of content, at once factitious and important, to the practical discourse. A particular form of historical action and relations become known as 'civilization', the 'Renaissance', or 'industrial society'.

At the institutional level, the creators of the rhetoric are the jurists, who, striving to express the unity of the spirit of the law, speak of due procedure, of natural rights, of equality, of the protection of minorities. Their work gives coherence to the institutional structure and renders 'visible' certain lines of evolution.

The important thing, Touraine suggests, is to distinguish with the greatest possible clarity three realities which the work of the jurists tends to confuse— the ideology of the ruling class, which is also the dominant ideology, the institutional discourse, and the jurists' rhetoric. The ideology of the ruling class, or, more exactly, the combination of the ideology and the utopia of this class, tends to dominate the whole of the institutional system, so that one can speak of a bourgeois society. However, this dominance has two limitations. First, political discourse has not only a class content but also manifests the exigencies of the system of historical action, through which is also manifest the presence of the working classes. Secondly, this ideology is not entirely dominant, as the complexity of any social formation means that a dominant class, rising or falling, is never completely unified and never fails to ally itself with other social forces.

There exists, therefore, a considerable distance between the ideology of the ruling class and a complex institutional discourse. That discourse, sometimes more archaic than the dominant ideology, sometimes sensitive to the influence of social forces which transcribe the action of the working classes, always has a certain autonomy and internal exigencies so that *the rhetoric of the jurists is not the simple transposition of the ideology of the ruling class* (ibid.: 228–9, emphases in original.)

A number of different elements deserve greater emphasis here. Touraine's analysis suggests that the formal representation of the different classes in a society in a liberal political system gives an *illusion* of participation to them. In this it contributes to their acquiescence in the society. Secondly, the fact of the 'mixing' of the dominant ideology (its 'dilution') with that of other classes means that the class nature of the ideology is less directly perceptible and is therefore more acceptable. Thirdly, the operation of the legal system provides an important legitimating 'cover', as it constructs representations of the society which suggest, in the widest sense of the formula, that all are equal in the face of the law (itself once a revolutionary bourgeois concept), that the society is composed of different but for all crucial purposes 'identical' individuals. By the creation (the role of other intellectuals must also be important here) of 'unifying names for a particular social formation', and by opposing the dominant 'rule of law' to the 'savagery' of other systems, the lawyers impart a sense not only of unity but also of common purpose (exemplified, for instance, in the 'civilizing' mission of all the French by virtue of being French in relation to the natives of their colonies). This, unifying function, as well as the wider aspects of the repressive activities made possible by the law, and reported for instance by Denis Langlois (1971), shows the importance of the ideology of the law.

The political and legal systems in a society are important in part at least because they provide the organizational framework for the operation of the other systems, particularly ideological institutions.

Education

In France 'the ideological state apparatus which has been installed in the *dominant* position is the *educational ideological apparatus*' (Althusser, 1972: 258). The school-family couple has replaced the church-family couple. In examining the role of education in French society, it is necessary to regard the social hierarchy as paramount and see how it is served by the education system. The cultural reproduction function of education must not be divorced from its social reproduction function; symbolic relationships are crucial to the reproduction of relations of force, in other words, of class relations.

The sociology of education has its proper subject when it constitutes itself as the science of the relationships between cultural reproduction and social reproduction, that is to say, when it attempts to establish the contribution that the system of education brings to the reproduction of force and of the symbolic relationships between classes by contributing to the reproduction of the distribution of cultural capital between these classes. (Bourdieu, 1971: 45)

For this reason modern societies furnish the education system with multiple opportunities for exercising its power of transforming social advantages into scholastic advantages. Through its emphasis on 'gifts', *le don*, the school transformed social differences into 'natural' differences, and ensured their retransformation into social ones. This function was distinct from, but implicit in, the school's technical, information-giving functions. By delegating to the school system the power of selection to occupational and social roles, the privileged classes could appear to abdicate their power to a neutral institution and thus appear to renounce the more arbitrary privileges of the hereditary transmission of privileges. By its verdicts on the merits of different individuals, verdicts which in fact virtually never worked against the interests of the privileged classes, as shown in the figures of enrolment in university courses and the Grandes Écoles, the school system could, in the only way possible in a society proclaiming itself democratic, contribute to the reproduction of the established order. Moreover, far from being incompatible with the reproduction of existing class relations, the mobility of individuals that did occur through educational success contributed to its maintenance. This mobility guaranteed social stability through the controlled selection of a limited number of individuals who were themselves changed by the ascension process. In this way credibility was given to the ideology of social mobility, itself most perfectly expressed in the idea of the *'école liberatrice'* (Bourdieu, Passeron: 1970).[2]

The most characteristic and specific function of the education system is precisely to hide its true function of disguising the real state of class relations in a society. Bourdieu and Passeron emphasize that the school system, with the ideology that its relative autonomy as a sub-system engenders, is to bourgeois society in its present phase what other forms of legitimation of the social order and other forms of the hereditary transmission of privileges were to other social forms which differed from it in the specific types of class relations and antagonism existing and in the type of privileges transmitted' (ibid.: 252). In brief, it encourages people to remain in the places allotted to them by 'nature'. 'Not being able to invoke the rights of blood [or nature or ascetic virtues] . . . the bourgeois heir of today must call on the school's verdict which confirms both his gifts and his merits'. Thus, in a society such as France after 1945, where the attainment of social privilege depended more and more on the possession of diplomas, the school system provided a discreet means of transmitting what the bourgeoisie could no longer transmit directly and openly. In short, the school is the 'privileged instrument of bourgeois society which confers on the privileged the supreme privilege of not appearing privileged, and it manages all the more easily to convince the disinherited that they owe their scholastic destiny to their own lack of gifts or merits because in cultural matters absolute dispossession[3] excludes the consciousness of that dispossession' (1970: 253). Thus everyone is fitted into the social slot his 'gifts and talents'

---

[2] This may, of course, be overdone, and the bourgeois interest in subordinating education to the economy may come into conflict, as it did in the later years of the period considered, with the aspirations of the 'over-educated' who have been led through their education to expect the automatic recognition of their social claims (ibid.: 265).
[3] To which one may also often add even relative dispossession.

allow: the successful can feel they owe their success to their own efforts (and they largely did feel this, as Bourdieu and other have shown elsewhere), while the unsuccessful can console themselves with the thought that they had done their best but nature had not allowed them to go further. Against nature there is no redress; the inclusion of the society into the 'natural' order discourages attempts to change the social order.

The learning of what and how and who

What do children learn at school? They go varying distances in their studies, but . . . they learn to read, to write and to add . . . [and] elements of 'scientific' or 'literary' culture which are directly useful in the different jobs in production (one instruction for manual workers, another for technicians, a third for engineers, a final one for higher management, etc.). Thus they learn 'know-how'. But besides these techniques and knowledge—and in learning them—children at school also learn the 'rules' of good behaviour—the attitude that should be observed by every agent in the division of labour according to the job he is 'destined' for. These rules of morality are those of civic and professional conscience, which in reality are rules of respect for the socio-technical division of labour . . .' (Althusser, 1972: 245)

Examining the statistics concerning who in France went where within and between the different sections of the education system, sociologists such as Baudelot and Establet concluded, as we saw above, that there existed not one education system but two—the primary-professional and secondary-superior-, which corresponded very closely to the socio-professional origins of the pupils and led them to the productive roles for which they were 'destined', in exactly the way which reproduced the society.

Although their analysis refers to the whole education system, Baudelot and Establet were especially concerned to demonstrate the ideological and divisive role played by the earliest teaching of reading and writing within the primary school. While Bourdieu and Passeron emphasize the importance of the school language, seen as 'universal' but in fact the language of the middle and upper classes, which meant that working-class children were not in possession of the relevant 'code', Baudelot and Establet emphasize rather the distinction between oral and written language, the latter being, for working-class children, very similar to a foreign language. The 'scholastic' discourse to which the children were subject not only was contained within a 'foreign' mode of expression but did not refer to the things which formed their concrete daily experience:

the street, the blocks of flats, the exploited work of their parents, the fatigue, the unemployment, the overtime, the salary, about which they know, they cannot recognize in all these rustic houses with peaceful gardens which are the illustrations of their books for learning to read; the real life of their parents they cannot recognize in the reassuring image of a petit-bourgeois family with two children savouring, in the cool evening, the perfume of a newly opened rose. (Baudelot and Establet, 1971: 234)

More than a different 'code' is necessary for children to be able to appreciate such images, but the images nevertheless fulfil the role of inculcating certain ideals and of favouring certain ways of living above others. This apprenticeship functions in such a way that is is expected to reproduce a dual result useful to the dominant class: first it dis-courages, by depriving the children of the authorized procedures of speaking and writing, the expression of the real conditions of existence of the exploited classes and thereby of the claims which would result from them and, second, it imposes positively, with the usage of correct French, the expression of aspirations which conform to the demands of the dominant ideology. (ibid.: 235)

This is particularly noticeable in relation to work: ' "Work", "working", "worker", are almost completely absent from the vocabulary, while "carpenter", "farmer", "pastry-cook", are frequent' (ibid.: 238). But even there the work the latter do is presented in moralistic terms.

'Near the force the blacksmith will hammer the red-hot iron on the anvil. You will find it beautiful: perhaps one day you will be a black-smith!' 'John is an apprentice, the whole week one can hear him ham-mering beams and supports; he fixes them firmly; they will last a long time, the boss (*patron*) is pleased'. (ibid.' 239)

Or again the pairing of words is such as to render them harmless: 'Lunch and dinner. Tea and supper. Butcher and baker. Shoemaker and shoe-mender. Farm tenant and owner. Worker and boss (*ouvrier et patron*)' (ibid.: 165). This was in a book for immigrant workers, but was similar to those used in primary schools. Everything was made concrete rather than abstract, discouraging conceptualization.

The 'timing' of the teaching of subjects was also important. The organization of curricula was such that children who did not go far through the system were deprived of the culture which would be of most relevance and use to them, both by the timing of the introduction of the different subjects and the scholastic division of subjects into 'literature', 'history', etc., each of which was again divided into 'centuries', which, it was assumed, only made sense in time sequence and could therefore only be taught one after the other. One could teach mediaeval literature in the third form but modern writers had to wait until the fifth or sixth form, thus excluding the majority of children from any access to them at school. This was not, say Baudelot and Establet, as arbitrary as it seems:

whether it is a question of the history of the world, or that of France or of literature, the scenario is always the same; continuity is paramount; revolutions are just accidents and merely precipitate the time sequence; the French Revolution contains more events than the Regency but not many more than the century of Louis XIV. In every case ruptures are denied or absorbed; never are the rise and development of capitalism visible. (ibid.: 136–7)

Moreover,

For the less 'academically gifted' who find themselves in the transition classes there is no order and no linkage between themes. Each is separate. Indeed, no effort is made to *teach* the children but rather to occupy them until they can leave school. One wishes to 'ensure them some years of school happiness' in the words of a teacher in a *Centre de formation des maîtres de transition*. (ibid.: 138; my italics.)

Thus, Baudelot and Establet conclude, the two forms of education—primary-professional and secondary-superior—fulfilled their mission in diverse ways but in particular they had a common function;

By their different teaching methods, in particular, they tend to create two distinct ideological species; on the one hand the bourgeois unconscious of being one (with his different masks—cultivated man, élite, honest man, a wise, knowledgeable, or humanistic man, or artist); and on the other, the petty-bourgeois worker, individualistic and oriented towards either acceptance or towards individual upward movement. (ibid.: 168–9)

The Church

The education system, Althusser and others suggest, has, in modern industrial societies, largely superceded the Church as the main mechanism of social control through ideological attachment to a particular form of society and as the main legitimating mechanism for inequalities within it. The Church, however, still has, particularly in predominantly Catholic France perhaps, a role in the development of an ideology, which means that social and political questions are approached in one way rather than another and that radical social changes are rejected. The analysis of religion in this sense has not commanded much attention from French sociologists in recent years, but a few important papers give some indication of the dimensions of the role of the Church, in the political field particularly. It is, of course, well known that in France, even after 1945, many important political parties had an explicitly Christian viewpoint, such as the *Mouvement Républicain Populaire* (MRP.) in the Fourth Republic, and trade union confederations were for many years divided by the religious issue. The main competitor of the Confédération Générale du Travail (CGT) was the Confédération Française des Travailleurs Chrétiens (CFTC). The latter abandoned the Christian part of its name in the mid-1960s and became the CFDT (Confédération Française Démocratique du Travail), but a small CFTC survived. The role of the Church was by no means negligible in the field of public action.

The ideological role of the Catholic Church was to provide a framework upon which people built a certain world view. This view, which found political expression in voting behaviour, was essentially organized around the twin poles of religion and hostility to communism. It referred to an underlying system whose nucleus was the unit individual-family-culture. Perceived as a threat to this unit, communism in particular (and occasionally capitalism) was rejected.

Analysing this, Michelat and Simon (1968) describe a way of apprehending communism and of remaining fundamentally separate from it. While agreeing that 'there is something good' in the communist doctrine, many Catholics felt that to be already subsumed in Christianity ('Christ was the perfect communist'). Personally knowing a 'good' communist could not overcome the fundamental gap between the transcendent and materialist bases of the belief system, and the negative 'information' that Catholics received on communist countries made them suspect duplicity even among the 'good' communists whom they knew.

Within the Catholic belief system a number of basic oppositions appeared. The communist 'mass' against the Catholic 'person-family' was perhaps one of the most important. Deemed to be crucial to the individual, the family had a dual basis and function: founded on religious values, the family also had material elements which made it (and its independence) possible—family patrimony, land, individual houses, objects which were part of the family, handed down by its ancestors and which the family would then transmit to its descendants. To the value attached to the patrimony were linked the values of work (work makes the patrimony fruitful), because one must deserve what one has and the patrimony is made to be handed on: 'spiritual values, family values, freedom, personality are thus indissociables' and opposed to the 'massifying' effects of communism.

Person, family spiritual values were linked to the possession and transmission of private property; to be oneself, one had to be master of one's house, a 'freedom' seen as the essential of French society, of being 'French' as opposed to the 'foreign' communism. Communism might be good elsewhere but certainly not in France. The linkage of person, family, property, region, country, nation, seemed 'natural' and a 'birthright' which could only be changed by a slow evolution (as in nature—no rupture, no revolution).

The apotheosis of this value system appeared in attitudes to aspects of the political sphere. While elections were considered important, Government was the management of a 'natural' order, outside 'politics', and concerned simply with the 'common good', without dissension and conflict, just as a body in good health is silent. 'Politics', on the other hand, implied division—parties, sects, factions—believed useless and dangerous. To the Catholics questioned in the study political organizations were doubly dangerous because their justification was to be found in the realm of *ideas* and not of *people* whom one should like and serve. There was a profound and essential division—politics were divisory and incomprehensible because based on specific action and expressed in an 'intellectual' way. To the 'obvious' secular 'normality', internalized effectively, politics opposed the empty abstraction of 'programmes', of words against human daily experience.

'Nature' shows us inequality, which is 'normal', like differences of 'intelligence', and linked to the division of functions between command and execution: 'one always needs officers and soldiers' or, as mind (spirit, *esprit*) is superior to matter, those who command are the élite and owe their position to 'natural' gifts, received at birth. As each milieu 'needs' different things, so individuals will 'do' different things with what they have—some will save, some will waste, and they should have 'freedom' to do so. 'Progress' will take care of the worst points of the society: 'factories are now all "checked" by the social security', and anyway in France one lives better than in many places. Many of the worst things are essentially individual 'faults', such as alcoholism. Abuses of power are 'human', so changing the ruling personnel would change nothing: 'if one were a boss one would be like them, it's human.'

The role of the Christian ideology in making certain political choices more probable continued to be extremely important. Social analysis was contained within individual or 'human nature' terms and society seen as a 'natural' order in which the essential elements are person, family, private property, and spiritual values. In that order dissension is 'unnatural' and imperfect behaviour 'human'. All this, in the analysis of Michelat and Simon, was opposed to the analysis of the self-declared non-religious communists, who expressed attitudes organized in terms of class affiliation and of a boss-worker dichotomy in relation to unions and politics.

Religion in action

Religious beliefs seem to have been important to the acceptance of certain changes. In Brittany, for instance, the Jeunesse Agricole Catholique (JAC) participated actively in the search for solutions to agricultural problems caused by the capitalist industrialization of France since 1945. In the first phase of this development, characterized by the integration of each farm into the general productive process, the farmer became a 'domestic worker' doing the things capitalism does least well. Secondly, there occurred an increased specialization of production, and thirdly, there developed a new differentiation of farms on the basis of degree of accumulation of the means of production and mode of adaptation to the new conditions of production (Dulong, 1974).

Not all these changes could necessarily be construed as 'improvements'. All did, however, involve important 'innovating decisions' on the part of individual farmers. As the ecclesiastical organization (through the parish) was the dominant ideological apparatus linking the sections of the peasantry together and them all to the dominant class of 'notables', innovation, if it were to come, had to involve the Catholics, both individually and as organized groups.

The Catholic action movements constituted a powerful instrument for this operation of change of mentalities. They were not the only organisms to orchestrate a campaign in favour of innovating decisions by farmers. Structures explicitly destined for this work—the CETA etc.— were created by the State in the 1950s; the professional press, the farmers' unions, the Chambers of Agriculture participated in this vast movement which permitted the capitalist mode of production to overcome the ideological obstacle which was opposed to it. However, it seems that in this work the Catholic action movements were by far the most effective structure. If they were not the only path by which ideas of 'viability', 'modernization', 'adaptation to one's time' made their breakthrough to the peasantry in the west, they were the shortest path.[4] (Dulong, 1974: 87–8)

---

[4]   The Church's role in change may, however, develop beyond what can easily be maintained within the limits of the Church. Thus, members of the JAC rapidly found that there were aspects of the change programme which involved contradictions, and they came into conflict with the Church hierarchy which had always preached unity.

The information system

The press

'It's in the newspapers.' Here for many people is a measure of the 'truth' and 'objectivity' of a piece of news. Many analysts question the 'objectivity' of the news, but for numerous readers of newspapers and watchers of television it is extremely hard, if not impossible, to maintain sufficient distance not to accept most of what is presented as not only the 'truth' but also the 'whole truth'. Few are aware of the effects of technical, social, and political processes inherent in not only the collection and presentation of news but also in the particular 'private' (and public) ownership of newspapers and the organization of information.

Above all the role of the local newspaper would seem crucial in determining the views of its readers by the presentation of reassuring news and images. People are used to their newspaper—most people they know read it, it is almost part of the family. Having read it, people 'know' what is happening in their immediate environment and feel closer to the recognized élite of the region. But the kind of news the reader gets is essentially reassuring—marriages, births, banquets, ceremonies of all kinds, local sporting and cultural activities. The worst part is perhaps the road accidents. All are presented as the most important news of the area and, by the intimate nature of what is presented, the items of news appear as extensions of individual family life. The photographs are usually of families or of responsible citizens receiving their recompense for faithful service. The writers refer to 'our region', 'our mayor', 'our firemen', etc., giving the impression of essentially public services open equally to all.[5] The role of the local newspaper was perhaps particularly important in France because there existed few national daily newspapers and particularly few aimed at a mass audience (*France-soir* was the only exception), so that provincial, local, newspapers were the major or only source of daily news. Few readers and listeners have had the opportunity to acquire the necessary tools for anlysis; within the school system knowledge remains 'knowledge' and 'apart' and does not lead to any particular form of analysis or heightened consciousness. In France in the 1960s and 1970s,

[5] The analysis made of the local press in Liverpool by Harvey Cox and David Morgan (1973 and 1974) showed how rarely unemployment problems, for instance, were raised but how frequently the 'common good' of a particular area was represented as a reason for action and how an area was presented as an undifferentiated 'unity'. The same analysis could be made of the French provincial press but yet remains to be carried out in depth.

the mass media, particularly the press, contributed to the construction and maintenance of a world view that was 'natural' and 'anodyne' and relatively undifferentiated.

In particular the society was 'idealized' through the absence of any discourse on social classes or by a biased discourse.

How could one believe in the existence of classes, and of class struggle, since there exists *one* newspaper (in the provinces especially) where all can meet together to watch the spectacle of the event? By making itself the real support of an illusory common place, where all can meet without distinction of group etc., the newspaper disseminates the illusion of the real disappearance of classes. No more classes, only a cloud of individuals; no more history, only a mosaic of events; this is the daily message. (Geng, 1973: 13)

Of the many examples given by Geng, one is striking; an article on the metallurgical industry of Lorraine in *France-Soir* (13 November 1969), which essentially concerned the giant firm de Wendel and the people who worked in it. Having spent a Sunday with these men, the reporter described de Wendel himself: 'at the wheel of a blue Jaguar, a red-haired man, of austere appearance, tall. Leaving the car and entering his chateau at Hayange he leaves a discreet odour of Marigny. The last heir of the de Wendels smokes only French cigarettes.' Here is the picture of the *patron*, smart, elegant, essentially French. Geng compares the rosy terms used by the journalist—'Thus the sky which you see grey remains golden. A metallurgical worker earns on average 1,100 f. per month', which made no mention of the conditions of labour (nor of the hierarchy of salaries)—with the terms used to describe the metallurgical industry by the sociologist Pierre Belleville in *Une Nouvelle Classe ouvrière* (1963). Belleville notes: 'The conditions of work are extremely hard in all factories. Heat . . . noise, gasses, dust, danger, that of burns and that which results from the intense rhythm of the manipulation of heavy objects in an encumbered space, tasks which remain physically hard for a large number of workers, the rapid rhythm imposed by machines, these are the characteristics of work in metallurgy' (1963: 60, quoted in Geng, 1973: 41).

Insisting on the satisfactory level of wages the newspaper did not speak of the night work etc. necessary to obtain it. The only immigrant appearing was a Portuguese worker described returning to his lodging where he saw 'from his window, as does the heir of de Wendel from his,' the sky obscured by the slow-rising smoke of the blast furnaces. The writer finished his article by proclaiming that 'work is really a fête in Lorraine'.

Emphasizing the active social role played by ideology, Geng says:

Ideology is not the inert element wherein takes place the bilateral exchange of informative communication, but an active determinant producing the circulation, the picking-up, and the retention of news. Let us remind ourselves, however, that if, in relation to the production of news, ideology acts as the central operator controlling the programming of the exchanges, the great massified subject of enunciation, the sovereign script writer, ideology itself, is determined by basic forces, and is inscribed in its turn in the language, institutions, mentalities etc. (ibid.: 64)

Television

On television the spoken word is supported by the visual image, and the two together are perhaps a particularly powerful ideological tool.[6] Apart from the presentation of the 'news' as such, on French television as in other countries there were many hours of 'entertainment'. Examination of both the content and the form of one of the major parts of this entertainment, the serial (feuilleton), shows some of the ideological biases involved.

The serials, like children's books, largely ignored many important themes. Those which were treated were subject to considerable bias, largely through lack of analysis, remaining on the level of the 'obvious' (in the sense of both 'evident' and 'visible'), in both choice and treatment of subjects. 'Work' was a theme which only late in the 1960s became the subject of serials on French television (Piemme, 1974). Even then when 'professions' did appear they were essentially the 'independent' or 'liberal' ones—independent haulage agent, independent manager of a petrol station, or boat-owner/fisherman on one hand, lawyers and doctors on. the other. The choice of the independent profession was, like the choice of illustrations in school books mentioned earlier, not by chance. The only 'liberation', the only place where it is easy to transform man's battle with his work conditions into a personal struggle against the 'elements', into good and bad luck, is where he does, effectively, have a certain amount of room for manoeuvre.

In the serials professional problems were largely attributed to non-social forces. Although these problems were essentially linked to the financial structure of the surrounding society, on television they were attributed to 'bad luck' or the 'bad character' of competitors or employees, elements which are 'unforeseeable'. Success, on the other

---

[6] Governmental recognition of the importance of the control of this tool was particularly evident under de Gaulle.

hand, was attributed to hard work, to temerity in risk-taking, to 'professional conscience'. The difficult conditions of work with which many people had to cope were put down to the credit of the personal value of the person who did 'all' the work and who took on all the responsibility.

Among the themes the television series particularly devoted time to, one of the most important was the 'family', and a second concerned relations with the world outside and certain other ideologies. With regard to the second, the serial discussed, directly or indirectly, the threats which menaced the society, especially from left-wing or right-wing total-itarianism. An American director of Gallup Polls once remarked with pride that '70 per cent of all the messages circulating in the world at any one time are of American origin'. This also applied to serials, many of which were made in the U.S.A. and spoke more or less directly of American interests and activities, for example, in the spy stories referring to the 'red peril'. The 'white [Right] peril', as Piemme points out, was more individual and essentially conceived as a 'madman' from whom the society had to protect itself.

Finally, the serials presented the society as an extension of the family, and 'therefore' as solidary, with no essential conflicts of an internal kind. The social order seen in the serial was not only 'normal' but 'normative'.

The serial proposes a norm, but hides the fact that it is the serial proposing it. Better, producing by the structure of its discourse an effect of representation, it hides the norm's existence as a norm; it remains thus as a given factor which legitimizes the ideological use of the couple normal-abnormal. Firmly entrenched in common sense, this ideology of the normal and the abnormal recognized in the serial by the viewer supports the 'middle position' view: the middle is the reasonable point from which one can judge the unreason of the extremes and, at the same time, the obvious error of the extremes justifies the right of the middle to present itself as a judge. It is by this circularity that the serial constantly designates the rightness of its social order; it is precisely this circular game which the ideology already present in the spectator prohibits him for perceiving as such: thus the social order appears all the more legitimate the better it is linked to the ideology; it appears all the more 'true' the more it is 'false'. (ibid.: 39)

Family life

The difference between the 'reality' and common perceptions of the family is subjacent to the discussion in this section. The in-bred world of marriage, its role in the perpetuation of social homogamy among the different groups and their social divisions between themselves, allied to its role in the maintenance and expansion of all the forms of capital—economic, social, cultural—have been treated in the analysis of power above. The ideological role of the 'family' in France throughout the period after the war seems to have been of immense importance to the continuation of the acceptance by the less privileged members of a society of their position in it. The couple family-school may have replaced that of family-church, but the family half of the couple remained strong. The socialization role of the family in virtually every society is paramount, involving as it does a basic social cell to which children 'belong' and which dominates their earliest life and ideas. By a process of active teaching and more implicit inculcation it imposes a series of norms, of moral constraints on behaviour, of aspirations and expectations, and provides a way of 'understanding' the environment which essentially gives it a certain normative content, inducing at the limit guilt feelings in relation to 'revolt' or attempts to change either environment or the normative order. By its hierarchical nature, it tends to be the first, and thereby primary in the dual sense, experience the child has of authority, power, rules of behaviour, and punishments. Acceptance of these within the family makes easier acceptance of them when encountered in other institutions such as school or later in the organizations of the productive process. The school may be the one State ideological apparatus which has all children obligatorily for several hours a day most days of every week—the family has it not only as a child but also as an adult. It is of little wonder, therefore, that the State and its ideological apparatuses, including the law, devote so much time to the family.

Television serials, Piemme notes, concentrate attention on the family. One production in four was devoted directly to the family and its problems, and the other three made constant reference to the family unit, in contrast to the relative lack of attention given to work. The simple family model—father, mother, children—was presented as 'natural' and unalterable, always thought of in terms of paternity and maternity; the arrival of a child was never a problem, always uniting, never dividing. The family, almost always petty bourgeois, contained always the same distribution of roles—dominance of the father, active complementarity of the mother, intelligent liveliness of the children. The mother usually stayed at home, her role being essentially one of dependence even in her professional life: 'The more she is a wife (and mother) the more she is herself.'

Equally important, the family was always presented as a place of warm affective communication—things only went wrong through lack of love and especially through failure to discuss problems. Once these were restored the family was restored.

Thus structured, the family model and the ideological themes which are attached to it define the general framework of an ideology of self-fulfilment and development through interpersonal relationships. This fulfilment is obtained in the properly functioning family ... There are seldom serious problems to be faced—death, sickness, unemployment, political divisions are absent . . . but their absence is to be read as a positive advantage of the family modes. The family is an enclosure against which the outside world which could imperil it is powerless. (Piemme, 1974: 32—3)

In this way, the family was presented as of paramount importance to individual happiness and safety, for it constituted an inherent structure resulting from the innate needs of individuals, a part of the 'natural' 'order' not varying with historically changing social conditions and formations. Reference to *the* family, rather than to bourgeois or working-class nuclear or extended families, underlines the 'naturalness' and, therefore, unquestionable morality of a particular family form.

All discourse on the family implies the social order which surrounds and supports it, but some television serials explicitly made this relationship apparent by presenting the social order as a more complex variant of the family, suggesting that the social body formed a coherent and homogeneous whole in which the interests of each member were solidary with those of all the others. As all the members of a family are complementary, so the other members of the wider social whole have harmonious relations of complementarity amongst themselves. In the serials, the family is the simple cell; the society the whole body. Bosses and workers, small and large firms, farmers and urban dwellers are the very sign of a diversified but inextricably linked living organism. Diversity is only apparent since, in their fundamental elements, as seen in their existence in the family, all men and women are the same, with the same goal, to be happy, and the same fears (death, pain, betrayal) which make all equal. Discord can only be temporary. Here, then, the ideology broadcast by the television on the family joined that disseminated by the Church as the triplets—family, property, liberty.

The cultural system

If the couple family-school replaced family-religion as the dominant couple in French society the first couple remained inextricably linked to a third, culture-school, which in turn was an essential part of a fourth, culture-nature.

Culture, in the sense used here, may be subsumed as 'symbolic goods', which are linked to a symbolic understanding and justification of the social order. Symbolic goods may be appropriated and accumulated in the same way as material ones and equally be exchanged and transformed into other kinds of advantages, or one may exchange material goods for symbolic ones, as in the traditional hero of the folklore of industrial societies who, having made good in the material sphere, marries a penniless aristocrat. In these ways, in Bourdieu's words, 'culture' contributes to the dissimulation of relations of force in a society by transforming them into symbolic relationships.

'Culture' is not only a set of symbolic goods but also a picture of the world; it involves a hierarchy, which is normative as well as 'factual', and people who 'own' (or control in the sense of understanding in particular) most of the cultural goods have a moral worth denied to those who 'own' least. Their position is justified on all counts, and because such cultural attributes are seen as 'natural' attributes differential access to works of culture is not seen as problematic.

The reality of cultural inequalities in post-war France was undeniable and clearly linked to educational inequalities. In general terms, the more a cultural practice is abstract and intellectual and requires a long apprenticeship, the more inequalities in relation to it can perpetuate themselves from generation to generation and the more useful the practice is for social differentiation. The 'importance' or 'purity' of cultural practices, whether literary or artistic, is defined by a limited but influential set of people most 'in the know'. The sets of people concerned in each practice overlap considerably, gradually fading out and becoming more dispersed as one moves from the 'centre' of the cultural practice to the 'periphery'. The smaller the number of initiates the more socially prized and socially 'rewarding' the practice. In France the importance accorded a practice by a group was usually reinforced by the school, which at once disseminated the information that the activity was important and effectively restricted the number of persons with access to it, thus maintaining the idea of a common value attached to the practice, at least *in abstracto* ('classical music is 'better' than 'pop music' even though relatively few people listen to and enjoy the former), while also maintaining its social value for the initiates and making those who did not participate feel inferior or incapable as individuals. Crucially, cultural knowledge was an important part of school knowledge but was seldom imparted directly or most effectively by the school. In this way cultural preferences and activities constituted a justification for social, as well as cultural, privileges because, although open to all and 'valued' by all, they were practised by few. In their study of visitors to European, and particularly French, art galleries and museums in the mid-1960s Bourdieu and Darbel (1969) showed how the most prestigious and socially 'paying' practices had the most socially self-selected audiences. Even within the already limited museum-going public, differences by social group could be distinguished according to the 'difficulty' of the access of the items concerned. Hence the 'folk-lore' and object museums had the most heterogeneous publics, whereas the homogenous exhibitions of the Jeu de Paume and the Musée des Arts Décoratifs had the most 'aristocratic' visitors considered in terms of education and profession. The more cultural 'capital' could be translated into social 'capital' in that it became more socially visible, such as in special exhibitions (where the visitors could be 'seen' as well as the exhibits), the more limited the audience became (ibid.: 146 ff.).[7] Moreover, as cultural need 'redoubles as it is satisfied', absence of practice is accompanied by an unawareness of any lack.

Cultural differences were not simply a reflection of social differences, more precisely of social inequalities, but active ingredients in those differences as they accentuated, legitimated, and perpetuated inequalities; they accumulated with social and economic divisions and interacted with them. Family and school together provided the key for decoding cultural activities, but the most 'paying' ones (modern jazz, modern drama, modern painting) were essentially learned outside the school. Moreover, the process was dynamic. A cultural practice or item once generalized lost its value of distinction necessitating constant renewal. Photography soon came to be considered an *art moyen* by the cultivated, 'who spurned its "interference" with their appreciation of the object' (Bourdieu, *et al.*, 1965).[8]

'Physical culture'—sport

During the late 1950s and particularly the early 1960s, the French Government devoted considerable attention and monies to the development of sports facilities in France; even in the more remote rural *communes* there suddenly sprouted basket-ball courts and swimming pools, in urban areas sports stadia appeared and a Minister of Sport was

[7] Television could not act as a fully effective mechanism of cultural diffusion, for working-class families mostly lacked the linguistic code necessary to a proper understanding (Sainsaulieu, 1966).

[8] The phenomenon is early apparent in relation to consumer goods—once black and white television became available to all the 'cultivated' either abandoned it or turned to colour (INSEE, *Econ. et. Stat.*: 1974: 58 (46))

appointed. Sport in France was taken very seriously; clubs proliferated and children were encouraged, though mostly outside school hours, and therefore as fee-payers, thus doing little to diminish socially unequal access to physical activities, to practise sports. This practice, however, was less for pleasure or health than for competition purposes. The emphasis on excellence, and excellence only, was common both to scholastic and extra-scholastic activities, the ideology of the one spilling over by a process of contagion, undoubtedly linked to the self-esteem and status of the *professeurs* of both, into the other. Thus many junior-level swimming clubs in municipally provided pools would not teach children to swim, and rapidly eliminated from their ranks children not up to competition standard. Tennis teachers frequently would only take children who could already play, and music teachers take only children competent in their instrument, while the local *conservatoires* established programmes apparently designed to eliminate the vast majority of children without musical parents prepared to spend hours each week on their musical education.

Sporting events undoubtedly had a role to play in the encouragement of French national sentiment and chauvinism and discouraged attention on social divisions and problems. As a spokesman for the official *Haut Comité des Sports* himself expressed it in 1965,

Sport is often the cement of a group, of a particularly coherent structure, rejecting social barriers and differentiations . . . It satisfies the need for social participation and favours the appearance alongside the hierarchy of everyday life, suffered by the majority, of a parallel hierarchy, which ignores the first and guarantees to some the possibilities of achievement which modern society otherwise refuses them. (Quoted in Brohm, 1971: 75.)

By doing this, Brohm suggests, sport fulfilled a compensating and diverting function. Sport *mimed* equality to avoid tampering with the 'hierarchy of everyday life'. Sporting practice and training involve submission to a certain discipline and to exact timing,[9] and give a moral

---

[9] The importance of exact timing was also inculcated by the school system by its emphasis on the time for each task and the division of tasks into small units. It may be of interest to the reader to note here Michel Foucault's description of the development of the division of time into small units in the industrial sphere from that used by religious orders. In this we see the linkages between church, industry, army, and society. Foucault writes: 'the rigour of industrial time for long retained a religious aspect. In the seventeenth century the rules of the important *manufactures* made precise the exercises which should divide up the work to be done: "All persons arriving in the morning at their looms before beginning work will begin by washing their hands and by dedicating their work to

connotation to the notion of competition which was part of the ideology of the economic and other social spheres. Sport, whose ideology puts it above all divisions of 'class, creed, and nation', lent its language to other spheres of the society, leading to discussion of elections as 'matches' with 'scores', to description of firms as setting up 'records', and to negotiations as taking place in 'rounds', suggesting implicitly the same absence, or at least unimportance, of social divisions outside the sporting arena.

Cultural and consumption: needs and happiness

With the fast development of the French economy, particularly after 1960, 'cultural needs' came to some extent to be translated into 'consumption needs', particularly in relation to objects invested with the power of acting as signs.[10] As opposed to the appreciation of 'difficult'

God; they will then make the sign of the Cross and begin work." Still in the nineteenth century, when industry, wishing to use rural workers, had to accustom them to work in workshops, *congrégations* was called upon; workers were regimented in "factory convents". Major elements of military discipline in the Protestant armies . . . were developed through a time rhythm determined by the exercises of piety . . . for centuries the religious orders were the masters of discipline; they were the specialists of time, the great technicians of rhythm and regular activies . . . [their heirs] refined the procedures and began to count in quarters of an hour, then in minutes, then in seconds. First in the army . . . [then] in elementary schools the division of time became more rigid and activities more closely defined by orders to be executed at once. [J-B. de la Salle recommended] "on the last stroke of the hour a pupil will ring the bell, and on the first stroke of the bell all pupils will kneel, arms crossed and eyes lowered. Prayers over, the teacher will sound a signal for the pupils to rise, a second for them to salute Christ, a third for them to be seated." In the early nineteenth century a timetable such as the following was proposed: 8.45 a.m. entry of monitor, 8.52 a.m. roll-call by monitor, 8.56 a.m. entry of pupils and prayer, 9.00 a.m. pupils sit on benches, 9.04 a.m. first slate, 9.08 a.m. end of dictation, 9.12 a.m. second slate, etc." The progressive extension of wage labour involved a greater control of time: "if workers arrive more than a quarter of an hour after the striking of the bell", "if a workmate is called for during working hours and loses more than five minutes" etc. . . . [Employers] began to ensure the quality of the time worked . . . so as to institute a totally useful time: "it is expressly forbidden during working hours to amuse one's companions by gestures or otherwise, to play any game, to eat, to sleep, to tell stories and jokes" and even during meal breaks, "no stories of history, adventure, will be told or other conversations held which distract workers from their work" . . . The time measured and paid must be time without impurity or defect, time of good quality . . . exactitude and application are, with regularity, the fundamental virtues of disciplinary time' (1975: 151–3).

[10] It should also be emphasized here that the boom economy, and the concentration of industry and commerce, favoured the development of a new ideology, which rapidly became dominant. This ideology could be subsumed in the emphasis on 'efficiency' and 'expansion' as justification of first economic and

works of art, exhibited in museums or 'difficult' music, played in concerts and available only to a very limited audience, the ideology of consumption, in France as in other advanced industrial societies, was presented as essentially 'democratic' and open to all on the one criterion of ability to pay, to buy, an ability made increasingly widespread by the boom economy. 'Happiness', the dominant theme in the publicity of the society, was 'sold' as obtainable through goods which could be bought by 'anyone' (in the social sense) and whose appreciation did not require a long apprenticeship. Although not all members of the society could participate equally, even many of the less privileged could consume 'images', which bolstered their position in their own eyes, and were encouraged in the idea that those who could not consume today would be able to do so tomorrow, for the 'progress' of consumption was presented as constant.

This was the ideology. The practice, as Baudrillard pointed out, was different, for consumption objects and practices stemmed directly from social objectives and a social logic. Consumption differences,

far from breaking down the social hierarchy, result in radical discrimination, in a segregation of fact, which destine certain classes . . . to certain signs, to certain practices and contain them . . . inside this destiny, in a socially systematic way. The messages objects give us concern less the user and his technical practices then social claims and resignation, social mobility and inertia, social stratification and classification . . . if the objects seem to speak to all . . . it is only to put each person back into his place. (Baudrillard, quoted in Granou, 1971: 43–4.)

The social and class-based nature of this cultural logic was never manifest but always hidden. One way in which consumption presented itself as democratic, open to all, was through its claims to satisfy basic human needs and, at the same time, and for the same reasons, to mitigate, if not completely ultimately destroy, social inequalities.

the objects, goods, and services all claim to 'respond' to the universal motivation of the individual as social *anthropos*. On this basis . . . the leitmotiv of the ideologists of consumption [suggests] that the function [of consuming] is to correct the inequalities of a stratified society:

then social decisons, and for technocratic control, in 'scientific management', not only of the state administration (where it was exemplified by the actions and rapid rise to importance of ENA graduates), but also in the private business sector. In the latter the spread of the new ideology was encouraged by the creation from 1958 onwards of business schools, largely using American curricula and teaching methods, whose graduates went to fill the high levels of the most technologically advanced large-scale economically dominant industries and important sectors such as banking and finance.

opposed to the hierarchy of power and social origins there would be the democracy of leisure, of the motorway, and the refrigerator. (ibid.: 43–5)

The importance of universals in the ideological justification of a society is underlined by Baudrillard, who suggests that in modern bourgeois societies consumption takes the role of legitimator played in the past by the universals of religion or the humanist ideals of liberty and equality. 'The present day takes the absolute obviousness of the concrete seen in human needs and the material and cultural goods which satisfy them' (quoted Granou, 1971: 45).

The universal of consumption is particularly important because it contains a natural referent, needs, linked to a further one, happiness (*bonheur*), an essentially individual attribute and enterprise, even though ideally realized through the family. 'All discourse on needs is based on a naive anthropology; that of the natural propensity for happiness. Happiness, inscribed in letters of fire behind the slightest publicity for the Canary Islands or for bath salts, is the absolute reference of the consumer society; it is truly the equivalent of salvation' (Baudrillard, 1970: 59).

The notion of 'need' is 'equalizing' because seen as inherent in all men: implicit is the thesis that 'all men are equal in relation to the *use-value* of objects and goods (whereas they are unequal and divided in relation to their *exchange value*). Need being indexed on use-value, there obtains a relationship of *objective* utility or a natural goal (*finalité*) in relation to which there is no more social or historical inequality' (ibid.: 61).

Nature and society and nature and culture

A constant theme in most discussions of the role of different social institutions and ideologies in the attachment of French people to their society is the duality nature-society or nature-culture. This dual reference is especially evident in relation to those most pervasive value twins, consumption and happiness, but each institution or major sphere in the society seems to have related to the model 'what is natural is right' and therefore what was social had to be made to seem in some way natural, whether in education, in the values inculcated by the Catholic Church, in the family, or in cultural practices. The most important natural referents—'intelligence' (the 'gift') for education, 'taste' for culture, 'reproduction' for social roles in the family and the division of labour and others—were organized in varying combinations and given varying weights in different parts of the social structure.

The reference to 'nature' served a dual purpose. It denied a certain historicity and relativity to social organizations, for natural referents are essentially unchanging, or changing only by slow movements forward which could be qualified as 'progress' (as there are also slow improvements, evolution, in the natural world), and thereby tended to draw attention away from advocates of radical change, especially by political action. Equally important, the whole social organization could be given a basic natural referent and disguised as an 'organism', in which the different organs, if 'healthy', should function in harmony. In society, as in nature, big may eat small and have to be restrained, and as in nature there may be 'disease' which needs to be cured, but members of each social group could use this image and believe they recognized beneath an apparently hostile exterior a fundamental similarity of interest with their fellows in other groups. Most important of all, the prevalent acceptance of the natural referent went far to disguise the existence of social classes and to discourage active participation or adherence to class organizations. This is not to give a determinant role to ideology and ideological processes but it is important to stress the role played by representations of a society in reinforcing adherence to it by its less privileged members.

8. TOWARDS A NEW SOCIETY?

Economic growth, industrialization, and urbanization, carried out after 1945 first under bourgeois and then under monopoly capitalism manifestly failed to solve the basic problems of social inequality in French society. This failure is evident in relation to material and symbolic rewards as well as to the over-all position of individuals and groups within the opportunity structure. Bourgeois hegemony, bourgeois domination of the structure of the economy and the 'shape' of the society remained, and can be seen in control of the major institutions of production and distribution, of education, of information, of decision-making, at national, and frequently at local, level.

This hegemony suggests a reason for the persistence of inequalities. Economic growth does not have an inner momentum, an inherent logic which can mean, regardless of the political circumstances under which it occurs, that its results will be everywhere the same. The social groups who control the economic process are crucial to the direction taken by both economy and society, even if that control involves contradictions and works within important limitations. It is suggested, therefore, that bourgeois control of the major institutions of French society after 1945 in many ways made the persistence of inequality inevitable. Not only were the interests of controllers and workers frequently in conflict, but the whole ideology of the society rested on and encouraged inequalities. Inequalities, particularly in relation to income, and command of decisions were justified by dominant groups as essential to the 'progress' which would be made possible by economic growth and as an essential mechanism of that growth itself. This belief was expressed as the necessity for a steep hierarchy of incomes, high incomes being seen as reward for 'risk-taking' and 'responsibility', as recompense for 'rare skills' and as an encouragement to 'ambition', in both education and professional life. Continued bourgeois control and emphasis on such an ideology could mean little fundamental revision of the system at the same time as it could do little to reduce inequalities.

This is not to say that attempts were not made at change from below. Throughout the period considered in this book, protests about their situation were made, whether expressed in political movements or in strikes, by different sections of the population. Small shop-keepers, independents, artisans, and farmers expressed their discontent in political terms in the Poujadist movement of the mid-1950s; small, and young, farmers did so in a renovated syndicalism, in riots, and by less violent pressures in the late 1950s and throughout the 1960s. Regionalists took to bombs and sabotage in the late 1960s and early 1970s. These were people adversely affected by the logic of the capitalist development of the period and hit with particular force in France because of the speed of the process after 1945.

The slumps, for economic development was uneven and occurred in periods, particularly in the early 1950s, in 1958–9, and in the mid-1960s, culminating in 1968, were reflected in long and bitter strikes in shipyards, in mines, and in many industrial sectors where reconversion and a decrease in demand meant unemployment of workers. On the whole, however, successive Governments managed to fend off the threat from the Left, although the extreme Right was nearly more successful.

How this was managed raises complex questions, involving analysis on a number of levels. A complete explanation would demand more research than has yet been carried out, and far more space than is available here. A number of material and ideological factors were, however, clearly important. On the material level, it is evident that economic growth did improve over-all living standards. As a link between the material and ideological, the promise of consumption, magnified as in a mirror by the constant opening of new hypermarkets displaying a wide range of goods and offering easy credit—the typical conditions of a recent mass-consumption society—did much to foster public belief in rapid, or at least ultimate, betterment. If relative deprivation is an important component of attitudes, so too is relative improvement, both in relation to oneself and to others. Moreover, many sections of the more skilled and hence better paid, sections of the working class adhered to the bourgeois belief in the rightness of a hierarchy of reward related to skill and the rarity of a skill on the labour market.

In the social structure material and ideological factors were mixed. The increase in numbers in education and the continuous insistence in the mass media on the growth of tertiary sector, and therefore 'clean', jobs and of places for technicians and *cadres moyens*, suggested possibilities of social promotion for many, even though in reality these chances remained almost as limited as before and almost non-existent as far as 'long-distance' social mobility was concerned. Again, on the material level, the social reforms undertaken at the Liberation, such as the progressive extension of social security to virtually the whole population, insuring them, to some degree at least, against the most disastrous financial effects of sickness, old age, and unemployment, and the continuance of the Vichy-inspired 'family' policy, providing generous maternity and family allowances, undoubtedly had a 'stabilizing' social effect. Sheer ignorance on the part of the mass of people of some of the important inequalities which remained in spite of 'social protection' was also undoubtedly important. A study by the CERC in the early 1970s concluded that 'the French are ill-informed both on the evolution of income and the present level of income of their co-citizens'. The least well-off sections of the society—farmers, manual, and white-collar workers—grossly underestimated the high incomes earned particularly by people in non-salaried professions. The income of a PDG (Président Directeur Général) was under-estimated by half and the real range of incomes was twice as great as commonly supposed.[1]

On the political level, protest movements tended to be 'recuperated' by the Government in office, as was, for instance, the case with the young farmers' movement, the CNJA, after 1960. The relatively favourable economic situation much contributed to that recuperation, although other factors were also important, such as the low percentage of salaried workers in France and the continued political efficacy (for the Right) of tolling the 'red peril' bell. The latter was heard in 1968 when, after the most widespread and radical social movement since the nationwide strikes leading the Popular Front in 1936, the elections in June returned an enormously increased Gaullist majority, even in traditionally left-wing regions such as the Centre and the south-west.

Divisions within the working class

Returning now to more sociological factors, there exist two levels of analysis. On the one hand, there are the mechanisms, principally ideological, assisting the 'smooth' functioning of the system, even though the everyday experience of many members of the society might otherwise suggest the extent of their disadvantage in relation to other groups. On the other, there is the important role which seems to have been played in social conservation in France by real differences of situation, and hence of consciousness and ideology, between different sections of the working class. The 'images' or 'representations' each class fraction holds of itself and others have both been generated by differences of situation and contributed to those differences. The 'real'

[1] In 1973 *Le Nouvel Observateur* reported a strike by miners in the north of France because they had discovered that the *ingénieurs* got more free coal than than they did. Asked about the salaries of the those same *ingénieurs* and other *cadres*, the miners guessed far too low. The reader can only wonder what popular reaction with be if true incomes were widely known.

situation of different sections of the working class undoubtedly varied historically during the different periods of French industrialization, and there continued to be some variation, both in the situation and in interpretations of it, and support for different strategies and policies proposed for changing it throughout the period after 1945.

The principal differences, described notably by Mallet (1963) and Touraine (1966), were related to characteristics of the firm—technology used, size of enterprise (or establishment), and the type of its control—and to individual characteristics—the length of time a person had been in the manual working class, especially its industrial sections, his reasons for joining it (flight from the land, etc.), type of job held and the level of skill demanded, and his expectations of how long he would remain with it. The differences were, throughout the period, exemplified in trade union membership and in union policy. A three-fold division of the working class was suggested by Touraine; based historically on the phases of the industrialization process which created different types of job, and hence of worker, at different times, it also allows for the co-existence of the three types of worker at any one period. In the early stages worker response to industrialization was the creation of craft unions, *syndicats de métier*. These unions grouped together skilled workers who were essentially concerned with the erosion, caused by technological change, of their skills and the social position to which these gave a 'right'. Their principal aim was therefore ensuring job security. Mass industrialization and the growth of production-line techniques gave birth to the basically unskilled *ouvrier spécialisé* (OS), whose principal claims, expressed in union action, were economic—wage demands rather than demands concerning a modification of place in the production process or job security. The third stage, that of automated plants, saw the growth of a highly skilled but plant-specific labour force, highly unionized and militant, for these workers were conscious not only of their dependence on the firm but also of the hiatus between their position as full citizens outside working hours, confirmed by the consumption made possible by high earnings, and their subordinate position in the firm (Mallet, 1963). Touraine suggests that the first two types of unionism are incapable of generating suggestions for an alternative society, for they reject emerging forms of production and hence are reactionary; the third type, he says, belonging to the vanguard, the *nouvelle classe ouvrière*, is far more revolutionary and future-oriented.

All these types of worker and union existed in France from at least 1960 onwards, and the differences between them were reflected in union membership figures (low for craft and OS unions, high for the automated plants) and policies. Evidence from studies made after 1968, however, suggested the marginal importance only of the new demands made by the *nouvelle classe ouvrière* and its representatives (e.g. Dubois *et al.*, 1971), and suggests the continued importance of the three divisions within the working class.

Rising political awareness: Social contradictions and the effects of the slump

The socio-economic and associated political systems seem, however, to have bred an important number of internal contradictions and in the early 1970s to have aroused in an important part of the population the feeling that social inequalities were too flagrant and economic growth too blatantly favouring certain social groups. In spite of the economic boom in the last half of 1968 and afterwards, the major left-wing parties, socialist and communist, renewed contact in the late 1960s and early 1970s and came together in 1972 as the Union de la Gauche and as common signatories of the Programme Commun, a programme of common economic, social and political objectives. The political effectiveness of the Union of the Left was seen in the legislative elections of 1973 and in the presidential elections of the spring of 1974, caused by the death of Georges Pompidou, when the united Left candidate, François Mitterand, lost by less than 1 per cent of the votes to the 'majority' party (a mixture of the Gaullist UDR, Centrist and his own Républicains Indépendants parties), candidate Valéry Giscard d'Estaing. The French nation thus appeared for the first time in many years[2] to be divided into two almost equal camps—a political coalition of socialists and communists against a political coalition of the Right and Centre. The political style of the Right changed from one of hard-line anti-socialism to one of conciliation and, at least apparent, compromise in which the President appeared as more moderate and reformist than many of his Parliamentary supporters and the new ministers were presented as a cabinet of social reform.

This reformist movement coincided with the beginning of the worst social effects of the oil crisis and world recession in the autumn of 1973 and particularly with the beginning of widespread unemployment, low or negative economic growth, and a fall in the real living standards of many sections of the population, the latter caused not only by

[2] In late 1965 Charles de Gaulle, presidential candidate against Mitterand, was put in *ballotage* and only elected in the second round, and later resigned after the failure of the referendum on regions in 1969, but the victory of the Left was by no means a 'near thing'.

short-time work or loss of job but by continued inflation leading to steep price rises. At this point the failure of previous economic growth to solve many social inequalities was in the forefront of public attention and seemed allied to the incapacity of governments to control the economy in bad times in the same sense as they had under conditions of boom.

The long-term effects of the slump cannot be estimated here, although most sections of the French population, including representatives of (the most 'progressive') employers' associations, such as José Bidegain, seemed agreed that things 'will never the same again'. In 1975 production fell for the first time since 1945, and by the biggest amount since 1931–2 (Delors, 1976).[3] The President of the French *patronat* organization CNPF, in its general assembly in January 1976, declared that 1976 would be 'the year of truth'. Even if the low rate of economic growth apparent in late 1975 should continue, he said, unemployment would not disappear, for many firms had continued to employ as much labour as possible from 1973 to 1975, and even with a 5 per cent growth rate in 1976 only 150,880 new jobs would be created. Moreover, the crisis, and the measures taken to stem it, encouraged firms to invest in capital rather than in labour, thus accelerating a process already begun in the 1960s.

The effects of the crisis show, as might be expected, a continuation, and indeed an aggravation, of existing inequalities. Unemployment hit women (4·4 per cent unemployed as against 2·8 per cent men) and then workers (who in 1975 represented 51 per cent of the unemployed, but less than 40 per cent of total active population) the most, while it seems likely that its lessening will benefit *cadres* first (Seys, 1975; Lefournier, 1976). In spite of Government measures, only 105,000 persons, of over one million unemployed, received in the last quarter of 1975 the 90 per cent of their previous salary supposedly 'guaranteed' by the Government to all those laid off for 'economic reasons'; 400,000 others received only between 10 per cent and 35 per cent of their salaries, and 500,000 others at any one moment received nothing at all according to M. Bergeron, of *Force Ouvrière*, reported in *Le Monde* (8 January 1976, p. 24). The period of unemployment also lengthened considerably: the unemployed receiving some insurance payment, the

[3]   An immediately obvious effect of the crisis was unemployment, officially reaching 1,020,000 in the autumn of 1975, but estimated by INSEE as well as the CGT to be between 1,100,000 and 1,300,000 in 'reality'. At the same time, many small and medium-sized firms went bankrupt, causing innumerable social problems—the number of bankruptcies in Paris alone increased by 21 per cent in 1975 (*Le Monde*, 9 January 1976, p. 9), concerning over 1,000 firms in the capital.

only ones known with precision, had to wait on average seven months for a new job in 1975 instead of the four or five months previously necessary. At a maximum, unemployment benefit lasted twelve months—after that even *cadres* only received the 11 or 12 f. per day of public aid unless the ASSEDIC granted them exceptional benefit.

Reformist measures

After his election to the Presidency in 1974, Giscard d'Estaing constantly presented his Government as one of reform and social conscience. His highly successful election slogan had been the suggestion, and promise, that the Left did not have the monopoly of 'heart', and in the first eighteen months the President introduced a number of reforms. These reforms, however, could be characterized rather as 'useful' socially speaking, than as representing any fundamental changes in the structure of society or economy. The first was the liberalization of abortion, courageously carried through the National Assembly by Simone Weil, Minister of Health, in the autumn of 1974. The measure would not have been passed, however, except for the support of left-wing party deputies, for Giscard's own supporters (including members of the UDR) largely either opposed the measure or abstained from voting. Remembering the class background of the UDR and Républicains Indépendants, this lack of support even for a relatively minor social measure suggests the important limitations on any possibilities of action by the President. He would seem condemned to small measures, undoubtedly improving the everyday life of many, even millions of people, but doing little to alter their basic position in society.

Attempted reforms, which were apparently important, were in fact limited in scope. A telling example is that of education. The education system worked in France throughout our period as a basic mechanism of social selection and justification: it distributed the diplomas which were the 'tickets' to particular occupational levels[4] to children from backgrounds such that they would, in overwhelming majority, have reached those levels 'anyway' through the action of social institutions such as their family alone. Inequalities within education began early in the primary school. The Réforme Haby of 1975, named after the Minister of Education, merely consecrated *de facto* inequalities by making them an official part of the system, for he created two 'classes'

---

[4]   These levels are officially recognised; level V. is that of *ouvriers*, seen in the CAP 'professional' diplomas, III and IV are *technicien* (Brevet de Technicien or Brevet de Technicien Supérieur, D.U.T.), and I and II are *cadre supérieur* diplomas in higher education.

of children in primary schools; those who could 'naturally' go fast were henceforth to be able to 'miss out' some years, while the 'slow' will follow the two-year system in each class. In addition 'bright' children of five years of age will be admitted to primary schools instead of waiting to be six or nearly six. The 'fit' between social origins and intellectual 'ability' seemed likely to be even more clearly seen from the earliest days of education and even the *maternelles* officially changed their vocation. No attempt whatsoever was made to change the system in favour of working-class children nor to attack the bourgeois ideology underlying the whole educational process—seen in the emphasis on competition, isolated work by individual children, passive learning procedures, and the themes of the books used—and which, through the logic of the whole system, continued to reproduce, while diguising the true basis of that reproduction, the social relations of capitalist society. Any real reforms of the system would involve a 'cultural revolution' unlikely in a Giscardian régime.

Education, however, is perhaps one area where the contradictions inherent in the society and encouraged by the economic boom and the official ideology of opportunity through education were to become most apparent. The economy of France, even before the crisis, provided, as we saw, relatively few jobs which needed anything but elementary educational skills. Although technicians and *cadres* increased in number, their proportions in the total labour force remained tiny. At least 30—35 per cent of jobs remained totally unskilled, involving virtually no professional preparation. An increasing number of young people acquired educational diplomas, at many levels, but the 'ticket' by 1975 was no longer valid. Of course, as Grignon (1971) pointed out, for a long time this had been the case at the lower levels of the economic process; from 1968 onwards, but particularly after 1971—2, it became frequently the case at the level of the *licence.* The Government created a proliferation of 'new' diplomas,[5] both at the secondary and higher levels, in an attempt to maintain an equilibrium between diplomas and job offers, but that attempt manifestly failed, and the Government continued to rely on the high 'natural' drop-out rate (largely caused by the refusal of sufficient money to the universities, financed on a

[5] In January 1976 the reform of the second cycle (*licence* and *maitrise*) of university studies was published. Attempting to fit university diplomas more closely into the job market, it opened the way for business control of university diplomas and 'selection' by the quality of the university attended. Reaction by students, teachers, and even the presidents of universities was immediate and strong and expressed in a national university level strike lasting from February to May.

yearly basis, to make student conditions reasonable, and to students in the form of scholarships or loans) to maintain the problem within 'reasonable' bounds. Again, although 'education' was put forward in 1975–6 as a means of combating unemployment, and although state employment agencies from 1976 were to have the right to create their own Centres de Formation so that the unemployed could learn a trade, nothing guaranteed that the then shortages of certain forms of highly skilled labour would be more than temporary. On the contrary, the market for skilled labour seemed more likely to continue to function as Grignon (1971) described.

Perhaps because of these problems of education and unemployment, although presenting his campaign under the wider banner of 'the reduction of inequalities', Giscard d'Estaing announced towards the end of 1975 that he planned a series of measures designed to 'upgrade' the prestige and conditions of manual work. The first of these concerned the possibility for certain manual workers to retire at sixty years of age. However, this measure, announced as though it would affect vast sections of the manual working class, will in fact concern at most two million persons, and affect only 100,000 during the first two years; to qualify not only must a worker have undertaken 'hard' labour, but he must also have contributed for forty-three years to the social security system or, if a woman, have brought up three children as well as contributed for many years. The measure could thus, at its best, only concern persons who belonged to the long-established working class, being members of it at least since 1933 (although an amendment by the socialists forced the extension to certain agricultural workers). We have seen earlier how small that class was before 1939 and how many people were forced into it from farming, artisan, and independent sectors by the economic changes after 1945. Most of them could never benefit. Indeed, even for many members of the working class, it was not possible to contribute before 1939, and many would not have started a regular job with obligatory contributions by the maximum permissible age of seventeen years.

There were, then, severe limitations even to the overtly 'social' measures taken by the Government before the end of 1975. Much remained promised—the much heralded 'reform of the firm' had by then not even appeared in outline, for it inevitably received powerful opposition from employers.[6] Reform of the social security system,

[6] At their conference in late January 1976, the Petites et Moyennes Enterprises (PME) confirmed again their total opposition to any reform of the structure of enterprises.

whose total bankruptcy was predicted by *l'Humanité* for late January 1976, was strongly opposed by the *cadres*, who struck against it in December 1975, and by many 'liberal' doctors, represented in at least one of their *syndicats*, who refused to allow the creation of health centres which they feared would represent too strong a competition. Many doctors also opposed the extension of the system whereby a sick person paid directly only a small proportion of his medical bills, commonly the equivalent of £50 or £60, a measure which would directly benefit the low paid.

'Reform' of 'social' housing was also promised, and reports were commissioned. Towards the end of 1975 even the organizations responsible for HLM (Habitations à Loyer Modéré) building and management were emphasizing the limited possibilities of housing the poorer sections of the society. No progress was made in this during the boom period— HLM in 1973 housed the same proportion of low-income families as in 1963; in 1973, they represented only 11 per cent of 'principal dwellings', although 27 per cent of dwellings for rent (Durif and Marchand, 1975: 3—20). This proportion remained far below the needs of the population in spite of reforms allowing the attribution of HLM to the old and to young couples with no children. Most HLM had, for financial reasons, to be built in the outer suburbs of cities, thus increasing the social isolation of members of the working class and, while improving their housing conditions, making infinitely worse their working lives through an extension, frequently to two or more hours per day, of time spent travelling. This problem could not be touched by the Government without touching the interests of buildings and owners of land in urban areas. Although Giscard's Government did introduce in 1975 a measure to tax building values, it seemed likely to do little to solve social housing problems, and a public transport policy remained an urgent necessity.

Discussion earlier in this book pointed to the absence in France of capital gains tax. In January 1976 the President announced his intention of introducing such a tax. It seemed likely, however, that many would escape it, for inherited capital and items held 'for a long time' were to be exempt, as were profits on sales of principal dwellings. The precise provisions of the tax, and even more its effect, remained to be made clear, but at once the chorus of denunciation was strong, apparently uniting almost all sections of the population and political groupings. Further, there was no apparent inclination on the part of the Government to introduce any more specific wealth tax at all.

Much, it is evident, remained to be done in terms of the persistent and deep-set inequalities in France. Considerable doubt remains about the possibility of fundamental reforms under a Government, and a President, supported essentially by right-wing and centrist forces in French society. Where bourgeois control remains, the conditions of economic slump may prove as incapable as those of boom of instigating fundamental social and economic reforms.

Towards social change

In terms of the social forces acting for and against reform, the future balance was difficult to see. The working class remained in 1975 much divided in relation to ideology, to its perception of society, and to the means necessary to bring about social change. In 1971 Vidal diagnosed not three but six ideological representations expressed in union action and demands. Although, in Vidal's view, the ideological element had a certain autonomy, such that there existed a possible basis for unity over and beyond the particular situation of different sections of the working class, nevertheless the differences of situation remained important dividers:

Union action is the recapitulation, in the specific framework of worker militancy, of the social relations operating in the society. These social relations are of three orders: the relation which links the classes to each other; the relation which the working class constructs with the field in which it legitimates that action; the relation which the opposed class, symmetrically, develops with the field. (Vidal, 1971: 67)

In 1968 many observers were struck by the 'conservative' nature of the unions' demands, particularly those belonging to the CGT (and supported by the Communist Party which condemned 'adventurers'), and their 'braking' effect on union members, who were frequently overtaken by non-unionized colleagues in the decision to occupy factories and workshops. After 1968 unskilled workers became to some extent more radical, and immigrant workers, for instance, undertook a lengthy if unsuccessful strike at Renault in the spring of 1973. The crisis after 1973 and the success of the Lip watch firm strikers in 1974, led to a new wave of factory occupations, estimated at around 200 on any given day in 1975. These were frequently undertaken in desperation against proposed redundancies, and few were successful. It is possible that experience of redundancy and the temporary 'power' given by occupation of a place of work, may, if given coherent direction, lead to more radical demands, but it is not clear who would provide that direction.

On the whole it would seem that to the dominant class in France, even at the end of our period, there was opposed no unified working class. The middle class also remained divided, some sections of it being more attached to the dominant bourgeoisie than to the working class. Although there undoubtedly existed divisions between the different fractions of the bourgeoisie, they were not of the same importance; the dominant class had principally to ensure only the maintenance of the institutions of the society already in existence or, at most, to devise means of containing the most pressing demands from below for reform within 'acceptable' bounds. In the face of economic changes which did not always work to the immediate advantage of all sections of the industrial bourgeoisie, they had the possibility of operating 'reconversion' strategies.

The bourgeoisie did not have to make the two steps, first of increased consciousness and then of political action, which were necessary to the working class. They did not have to go beyond the dominant ideology of the society and legitimation of the existing social order so as to be able to construct an alternative. The first step is difficult, the second seems to happen only in particular circumstances which make the 'explosion of consciousness' possible (Lefèbvre, 1969). Even where consciousness is changed by a slow process of increasing awareness and developed by direct 'political' action, the question of the direction of that consciousness remains. The experience of 1968 showed perhaps the possibility of the creation of an alternative, but also the extent of the difficulty, even in a time of mass movement.

It is possible that the conditions of economic crisis of the middle 1970s, far more serious than those of 1968, allied to an already raised public consciousness of the need for major social reforms, may lend themselves to a real possibility for the construction of alternatives. By 1975, the conditions of crisis had, to some extent, encouraged the development of a polarization of attitudes. On the one hand, after the first wave of fear of unemployment, social protests in the form of strikes and factory occupations became again frequent. On the other hand, the Giscardian reforms, however moderate, were heartily disliked by important sections of the *patronat* who seemed to be partisans of the most conservative analysis of the situation of France expressed by the well-worn but still powerful suggestion that Western democracies have overprotected their members, undermining incentives to work and the spirit of enterprise. This book suggests, on the contrary, that much still remained to be done in social protection and in the reduction of social and economic inequalities. In spite of this, the stringent economic conditions of 1976 seemed more likely to lend more weight to the conservative approach than to the radical, and Government attempts at reform probably to content the middle ground. Public rhetoric largely preached moderation. An article in the business journal, *l'Expansion*, in January 1976 suggested that

rapid growth in gross terms, but growth which does not develop aggressive competition, growth which is more in the service of the disfavoured and the third world, resting less on inequality of reward as a factor of progress, would seem, in the present state of affairs, the most reasonable choice.

But this of course begs the question. By what means could this growth be achieved without important structural changes? Who would be prepared to undertake and who to accept such structural changes? How would they be carried out? These the classic questions of political action, remained very much open at the beginning of 1976 in France no less than in other industrialized countries of the Western world.

BIBLIOGRAPHY

ADAM, G. 1972. 'Introduction à un débat sur la nouvelle classe ouvrière , *Rev. française de science pol.*, 22 (3); 509–28.
— — BON, F., CAPDEVIELLE, J., and MOURIAUX, R. 1970. *L'Ouvrier français en 1970*. Paris: A. Colin.
ALTHUSSER, L. 1969. *For Marx*. Harmondsworth: Penguin.
— — 1970 'Idéologie et appareils idéologiques d'état', *La Pensée*, 157: 3–38. A similar article appears in translation in B. Cosin (ed.), 1972, *Education, Structure and Society* (Penguin, pp. 242–80), and this is the reference here.
Ambassade de France. 1971. *Education in France*, London.
— — 1973. *The Engineer's Training in France*, London.
ANDRIEUX, A., and LIGNON, J. 1960. *L'Ouvrier d'aujourd'hui*. Paris: Marcel Rivière. Republished 1966, Paris: Gonthier.
ARDAGH, J. 1968 and 1970. *The new French revolution*. London: Secker and Warburg. Published as *The New France*, 1970. Penguin.
ARON, R. 1960a. *France, Steadfast and Changing*. Cambridge Mass.: Harvard University Press.
— — 1960b. 'Classe sociale, classe politique, classe dirigeante', *Archs. europs. soc.*, 1 (2): 260–81.
— — 1962. 'Quelques problèmes des universités françaises', *Archs. europs. soc.*, 3: 102–22.
— — 1964. *La Lutte des classes: nouvelles leçons sur les sociétés industrielles*. Paris: Gillimard.
— — 1965. 'Catégories dirigeantes ou classe dirigeante?', *Rev. française de science pol.*, 15: 7–27.
Aspects de la Conjoncture. 1970. 'Les cadres dans la population active', Ministère de l'Éducation Nationale, Service Central des Statistiques, 13: 1–12.
AUGÉ-LARIBÉ, M. 1950. *La Politique agricole de la France de 1880– 1940*. Paris: P.U.F.
AVRIL, P. 1969. *Politics in France*. Harmondsworth: Penguin.
BACHY, J.-P. 1971. *Les Cadres en France*. Paris: A. Colin.
BAGÈS, R. 1974. 'L'exode rural et la mobilité sociale', *Population* 29: 121–31.
BALLÉ, C., and PEUCELLE, J.-L. 1972. *Le Pouvoir informatique dans l'entreprise*. Paris: Éditions d'Organisation.
BANDERIER, G. 1970. 'Répartition et évolution des revenus fiscaux des ménages 1956–65', *Écon. et stat.* 16: 29–41.
— — 1974. 'Les revenus fiscaux des ménages en 1970 et leur évolution depuis 1962', *Écon. et stat.* 52: 15–28.
BARBICHON, G. 1969. 'Mutations et migrations des agriculteurs', *Rev. écon. pol.* 79 (2): 341–74.
BARRIER, C. 1968. 'Techniciens et grèves à l'électricité de France', *Soc. du travail* 10 (1): 50–71.

—— 1975. *Le Combat ouvrier dans une entreprise de pointe.* Paris: Éditions Ouvrières.

BAUDELOT, C., and ESTABLET, R. 1971. *L'école capitaliste en France.* Paris: Maspéro.

—— ESTABLET, R., and MALEMORT, J. 1974. *La Petite Bourgeoisie en France.* Paris: Maspéro.

BAUDRILLARD, J. 1968. *Le Système des objects.* Paris: Gallimard.

—— 1970. *La Société de consommation.* Paris: Gallimard.

—— 1973. *Le Miroir de la production.* Paris: Casterman.

BEAUDEUX, P. 1975. 'Le prix des cadres, 1975', *Expansion* 86: 83–106.

BEAUJOUR, M., and EHRMANN, J. 1965. *La France contemporaine.* Paris: A. Colin.

BELDEN-FIELDS, A. 1970. *Student politics in France* (a study of l'UNEF). New York: Basic Books.

BELL, C. 1968. *Middle-class families.* London: Routledge and Kegan Paul.

BELLEVILLE, P. 1963. *Une nouvelle classe ouvrière.* Paris: Julliard.

BELLINI, J. 1970. *The new France: Heirs on trial.* Young Fabian pamphlet 21. London: Fabian Society.

BELORGEY, G. 1967. *Le Gouvernement et l'administration de la France.* Paris: A. Colin.

BEN-DAVID, J. 1963. 'The growth of the professions and the class system', *Current Soc.,* 12: 256–77. Reprinted 1967 in BENDIX, R., and LIPSET, S. M. (ed.), *Class, status and power.* London: Routledge and Kegan Paul.

BENGUIGUI, G. 1967. 'La professionalisation des cadres dans l'industrie', *Soc. du travail,* 9 (2); 134–43.

—— and MONJARDET, D. 1968. 'Profession ou corporation? Le cas d'une organisation d'ingénieurs., *Soc. du travail,* 10 (2): 275–90.

—— 1970. *Être un cadre en France . . .?* Paris: Dunod.

BERGER, I., and BENJAMIN, R. 1964. *L'univers des instituteurs.* Paris: Éditions de Minuit.

BERGER, S. 1972. *Peasants against Politics. Rural organisation in Brittany, 1911–1967.* Cambridge, Mass: Harvard University Press.

BERNARD, P. 1969. 'Revenus et salaires', *Rev. écon. pol.* 5: 1095–04

BERNOT, L., and BLANCARD, R. 1953. *Nouville, un village français.* Paris: Institut d'Ethnologie.

BERNOUX, P. 1974. *Les Nouveaux Patrons.* Paris: Éditions Ouvrières.

—— MOTTE, D., and SAGLIO, J. 1973. *Trois ateliers d'O.S.* Paris: Éditions Ouvrières.

BERSTEIN, S. 1969. *La Décolonisation et ses problèmes.* Paris: A. Colin.

BERTAUX, D. 1969. 'Sur l'analyse des tables de mobilité sociale', *Rev. française. soc.* 10: 448–90.

—— 1970. 'L'hérédité sociale en France', *Écon. et stat.,* 9: 37–47.

—— 1974. 'Mobilité sociale biographique: une critique de l'approche transversale', *Rev. française. soc.,* 15 (3): 329–62.

BETTELHEIM, C., and FRÈRE, S. 1950. *Auxerre: une ville moyenne française.* Paris: A. Colin.

BIAREZ, S., BOUCHET, C., DU BOIS BERRANGER, G., *et al.* 1973. *Institution communale et pouvoir politique. Les cas de Roanne.* Paris: Mouton.

BIGATA, G., and BOUVIER, B. 1974. *Les Conditions de vie des ménages en 1972,* Les collections de l'INSEE, Série M, 32.

BILLY, J. 1962. 'Les X dans les affaires', *Entreprise,* 24: 47–61.

— — 1963. *Les Techniciens et le pouvoir.* Paris: Presses Universitaires de France (P.U.F.).

BISSERET, N. 1968. 'La sélection à l'université et sa signification pour l'étude des rapports de dominance', *Rev. française. soc.,* 9 (4): 463–96.

— — 1972. 'Classes sociales, "capital culturel" et chances scolaires: forme nouvelle de l'idéologie dominante?', *Epistémologie Sociologique* 13: 71–86.

— — 1974. *Les Inégaux ou la sélection universitaire.* Paris: P.U.F. 208.

BLÉTON, P. 1966. *Le Capitalisme français.* Paris: Éditions Ouvrières.

BLONDEL, J. 1974. *Contemporary France: Politics, Society and Institutions.* London: Methuen.

BOLTANSKI, L. 1969. *Prime éducation et morale de classe.* Paris: Centre de Sociologie Européenne: Mouton.

— — 1972. '*L'espace positionnel: les professeurs des écoles du pouvoir et le pouvoir.* Centre de Sociologie Européenne. Paris. A shorter version of this paper was subsequently published in 1973 as 'L'espace positionnel. Multiplicité des positions institutionelles et habitus de classe', *Rev. française. soc.* 14 (1): 3–26.

BON, F., and BURNER, M.-A. 1966. *Les Nouveaux Intellectuels.* Paris: Cujas. Republished 1971, Paris: Le Seuil.

BOREL, N. 1974. 'Les bas salaires en juillet 1974', *Écon. et stat.,* 62: 3–12.

BORELLA, F. 1973. *Les Partis politiques dans la France d'aujourd'hui.* Paris: Le Seuil.

BOTTOMORE, T. 1952. 'La mobilité sociale dans la haute administration française', *Cahiers int. soc.,* 13: 167–178.

BOUDON, R. 1973. *L'Inégalité des chances.* Paris: A. Colin.

BOURDIEU, P. 1966a. 'L'école conservatrice: Les inégalités devant l'école et devant la culture'.*Rev. française. soc.,* 7: 325–47.

— — 1966b. 'Condition de classe et position de classe', *Archs. europs. soc.* 7: 201–29.

— — 1970. 'Les marché des biens symboliques'. Centre de Sociologie Européenne, unpublished.

— — 1971. 'Reproduction culturelle et reproduction sociale'. *Inf. sci. soc.,* 10 (2): 45–79.

— — 1972. *Esquisse d'une théorie de la pratique.* Geneva: Librairie Droz.

— — 1974a. 'Champ du pouvoir, champ intellectual et habitus de classe', *Scolies,* 1: 7–26.

— — 1974b. 'Avenir de classe et causalité du probable', *Rev. française soc.,* XV: 3–42.

— — BOLTANSKI, L., CASTEL, R., and CHAMBOREDON, J.-C. 1965. *Un Art moyen, essai sur les usages sociaux de la photographie.* Paris: Éditions de Minuit.

—— BOLTANSKI, L., and SAINT MARTIN, M. de. 1973. 'Les stratégies de reconversion; les classes sociales et la système d'enseignement', *Soc. sci. inf.*, 12 (5): 61–113.

—— and DARBEL, A. 1966. 'La fin d'un malthusianisme?', in Darras, 1966.

—— and DARBEL, A. 1969. *L'amour de l'art*. Paris: Minuit.

—— DELSAUT, Y., and SAINT MARTIN, M., de. 1970. 'Les fonctions du système d'enseignement; classes préparatoires et facultés.' Centre de Sociologie Européenne, unpublished paper.

—— and PASSERON, J.-C. 1964 a. *Les Héritiers. Les étudiants et la culture*. Paris: Minuit.

—— 1964b. *Les étudiants et leurs études*. Paris: Mouton.

—— 1967. 'Sociology and philosophy in France since 1945: Death and resurrection of a philosophy without a subject', *Social Research*, 34 (1): 162–212.

—— 1968. 'L'examen d'une illusion', *Rev. française. soc.* 9 (Special No.): 227–53.

—— 1970. *La Reproduction*. Paris: Minuit.

—— and SAINT MARTIN, M. de. 1965. *Rapport pédagogique et communication*. Cahiers du Centre de Sociologie Européenne, Paris: Mouton.

BOURRICAUD, F. 1961. 'Le "malaise patronal",' *Soc. du travail*, 3 (3): 221–35.

BOUVIER-AJAM, M., and MURY, G. 1963. *Les Classes sociales en France*, 2 vols. Paris: Éditions Sociales.

BRÉSARD, M. 1950. 'Mobilité sociale et dimension de la famille.' *Population*, 3: 533–66.

BRINDILLAC, C. 1953. 'Les hauts fonctionnaires', *Esprit*, 12: 862–77.

BROHM, J.-M. 1974. 'L'Innocence des stades', *Politique Aujourd'hui*, oct.–dec: 71–8.

BRUNET, R. 1965. *Les Campagnes toulousaines*. Faculté des lettres et sciences humaines de Toulouse.

BUTLER, M., GAUDEMAR, J.-P. de., PITOEFF, L., and TOURREAU, R. 1974. 'Formations et carrières professionnelles', *Soc. du travail*, 15 (1): 65–85.

CALOT, G., and DEVILLE, J.-C. 1971. 'Nuptualité et fécondité selon le milieu socio-culturel', *Écon. et. stat.*, 27: 3–42.

—— and HEMERY, S. 1969. 'La fécondité diminue depuis quatre ans', *Écon. et stat.*, 1: 33–44.

CAPDEVIELLE, J., and MOURIAUX, R. 1970. *Les Syndicats ouvriers en France*. Paris: A. Colin.

CAPECCHI, V. 1967. 'Problèmes méthodologiques dans la mesure de la mobilité sociale', *Archs. europs. soc.* 8 (2): 285–316.

CARRÉ, J.-J., DUBOIS, P., and MALINVAUD, E. 1972. *La Croissance française*. Paris: Le Seuil. (Also published in abridged form, 1973.)

CASANOVA, A., PREVOST, C., and METZGER, J. 1970. *Les Intellectuels et les luttes de classes*. Paris: Éditions sociales.

CASTLES, S., and KOSACK, G. 1973. *Immigrant Workers and Class Structure in Western Europe*. Oxford: Oxford University Press.

CAUTE, D. 1964. *Communism and the French intellectuals 1914–1960*. London: Deutsch.

CAYROL, R., PARODI, J.-C., and YSMAL, C. 1973. *Les Députés français*. Paris: A. Colin and Fond. Nat. des Sci. Pol.

Centre d'études des Revenus et des Coûts. 1974. 'Ce que les français savent de leur revenu', *Écon. et stat.*, 54., 35–40.

CÉZARD, M. 1972. 'O.S. et manœuvres forment un tiers des salariés de l'industrie', *Écon. et stat.*, 38' 49–51.

—— 1973. 'Les cadres et leurs diplômes', *Écon. et stat.* 42: 25–41.

CHAMBOREDON, J.-C. 1971. 'La délinquance juvénile, essai de construction d'objet., *Rev. française. soc.*, 12 (3): 335–77.

CHAMPAGNE, P., and GRIGNON, C. 1969. 'Rapport d'enquête sur le public du Conservatoire National des Arts et Métiers' Unpublished.

CHAPOULIE, J.-M. 1973. 'Sur l'analyse sociologique des groupes professionnels', *Rev. française. soc.*, 14 (1): 86–114.

—— 1974. 'Le corps professoral dans la structure de classe', *Rev. française. soc.*, 15 (2): 155–200.

CHARLOT, J. 1973. 'Les élites politiques en France de la IIIe à la Ve république', *Archs. europos. soc.* 14 (1): 78–92.

CHARRAUD, A. 1975. 'Les revenus fiscaux de 5,000 foyers suivis pendant trois ans', *Écon. et stat.*, 66: 53–9.

—— and SAADA, K. 1974. 'Les écarts de salaires entre les hommes et les femmes', *Écon. et stat*, 59: 3–17.

CHATELAIN, P. 1967. 'Scolarisation et activité professionnelle des adolescents en France', *Annales de géographie*, 76 (416): 385–410.

CHAZELLE, J. 1968 (2nd edn.). *La Diplomatie*. Paris: P.U.F.

CHEVALIER, M. 1956. *La Vie humaine dans le Pyrénées Ariégeoises*. Paris: Génin (Médicis).

CHOMBART de LAUWE, P.-H. 1956, *La Vie quotidienne des familles ouvrières*. Paris: Centre National de la Recherche Scientifique.

—— 1960. 'Y-a-t-il encore une classe ouvrière?' *Rev. de l'action pop.*, 135: 195–203.

CLAUDE, H. 1965. *La Concentration capitaliste. Pouvoir économique et pouvoir gaulliste*. Paris: Éditions Sociales.

—— 1966. 'Les groupes financiers', *Écon. et pol.*, 139: 112–20.

—— 1972. *Le Pouvoir et l'argent*. Paris: Éditions Sociales.

CLÉMENT, P., and XYDIAS, N. 1955. *Vienne-sur-le-Rhône*. Paris: A. Colin.

CLERC, P. 1964a. 'La famille et l'orientation scolaire au niveau de la 6e; enquête de juin 1963 dans l'agglomération parisienne', *Population*, 4: 627–72.

—— 1964b. 'Changements dans la structure socio-professionnelle de la France entre 1954 et 1962', *Population*, 4: 683–705.

COLLINET, N. 1969. 'Le mouvement ouvrier, le législation sociale et les événements de mai', *Rev. écon. pol.* 5: 1154–79.

Communauté Économique Européenne. 1964. *La Politique régionale dans la C.E.E.* Bruxelles.

Confédération Générale du Travail. 1973. *Les femmes salariées*. Paris: Éditions Sociales.

Le Conseiller Scientifique. 1973. *The engineers' training in France*. London. Ambassade de France.

CORNU, R., and LAGNEAU, J. 1969 *Hiérarchies et classes sociales*. Paris: A. Colin.

COSSON, J. 1971. *Les Industriels de la fraude fiscale*. Paris: Le Seuil.

COSTON, H. 1955. *Les Financiers qui mènent le monde*. Paris: La Librairie Française.

COUTROT, A., and DREYFUS, F. 1965. *Les Forces religieuses dans la société française*. Paris: A. Colin.

COX, H., and MORGAN, D. 1973 and 1974. *City Politics and the Press*. Cambridge: University Press.

CROZIER, M. 1955. *Petits Fonctionnaires au travail*. Paris: Centre National de la Recherche Scientifique.

—— 1960. 'Classes sans conscience ou préfiguration de la société sans classes', *Archs. europos. soc.* 1 (2):

—— 1963. *Le Phénomène bureaucratique*. Paris: Le Seuil.

—— 1965. *Le Monde des employés de bureau*. Paris: Le Seuil.

—— 1970. *La Société bloquée*. Paris: Le Seuil.

—— 1973. *L'ère des technocrates*. Paris: Éditions d'Organisation.

—— *et al.* 1975. *Où va l'administration française*? Paris: Éditions d'Organisation.

DARBEL, A. 1967. 'Inégalités régionales ou inégalites sociales?' *Rev. française. soc.*, 8 (Special No.): 140–66.

—— 1975. 'L'évolution récente de la mobilité sociale', *Écon. et. stat.* 71: 3–22.

—— and SCHNAPPER, D. 1969. 'La probabilité d'entrer dans la fonction publique', *Écon. et stat.*, 4: 43–50.

—— 1969 and 1972. *Les Agents du système administratif. Morphologie de la Haute Administration Française*. Vol. 1: Paris: Mouton, 1969. Vol. 2: Paris: Mouton, 1972.

DARRAS. 1966 (collective pseudonym). *Le Partage des bénéfices*. Paris: Éditions de Minuit.

DAUMARD, A. 1958. 'Les élèves de l'Ecole Polytech. de 1815 à 1848', *Rev. d.histoire moderne et contemp.*, 5: 226–34.

—— 1963. *La Bourgeoisie parisienne de 1815 à 1948*. Paris: SEVPEN

DAUZAT, A. 1961. *La Vie rurale en France*. Paris: P.U.F.

DEBATISSE, M. 1963. *La Révolution silencieuse*. Paris: Calmann-Lévy.

DELEFORTRIE-SOUBEYROUX, N. 1961. *Les dirigeants de l'industrie française*. Paris. A. Colin.

DELORS, J. 1976. 'L'État, c'est l'autre', *Expansion*, jan.: 33.

DELPHY C. 1969. 'Le patrimoine et la double circulation des biens dans l'espace économique et le temps familial', *Rev. française. soc.*, 10 (Special No.): 664–86.

DERRUAN-BONIOL, S. 1967. 'Le département de la Creuse; structure sociale et évolution politique', *Rev. française. science pol.* 7 (1): 38–66.

DESPLANQUES, G. 1973. 'À 35 ans, les instituteurs ont encore 41 ans à vivre, les manœuvres 34 ans seulement', *Écon. et stat.* 49: 3–19.

DESTRAY, J. 1971. *La vie d'une famille ouvrière*. Paris: Le Seuil.

DETRAZ, A. *et al.* 1959. 'Qu'est-ce que la classe ouvrière française?' *Arguments*, 12–13. Entire number.

DIDIER, M., and MALINVAUD, E. 1969. 'La concentration de l'industie s'est-elle accentuée depuis le début du siècle?', *Écon. et stat.*, 2: 3–10.

DIMAN, D. 1972. 'Évolution des structures de bilan des entreprises industrielles entre 1961 et 1969', *Écon. et stat.*, 36: 21–38.

DION, M., and M. 1972. *La Crise d'une société villageoise*. Paris: Éditions Anthropos.

DOGAN, M. 1961. 'Political ascent in a class society: French deputies 1870–1958', in D. Marvick (ed.), *Political Decision Makers*. Chicago: Chicago Free Press.

–– 1965 *L'Origine sociale de personnel parlementaire français*. Paris: A. Colin.

–– 1967. 'Les filières de la carrière politique en France', *Rev. française. soc.*, 8: 468–92.

–– and ROSE, R. 1971. *European politics–a reader*. London: Macmillan.

DRANCOURT, M. 1973. 'Les trois profils du manager', *Entreprise*, 912; 72–3.

DUBOIS, N. 1937. *Que deviennent les étudiants?* Paris: Sirey.

DUBOIS, P. *et al.* 1971. *Grèves revendicatives ou grèves politiques?* Paris: Anthropos.

DUHAMEL, A. 1971. 'Qui gouverne en France?' *Les Informations*, 138: 48–54.

DULONG, R. 1974. 'L'église de l'ouest et luttes de classe dans la paysannerie', *La Pensée*, 175: 82–103.

–– 1975. *La Question bretonne*. Paris: A. Colin.

DUPARC, C. 1971. 'Le jeudi de la vie', *Le Nouvel Observateur*, 366: 55–68.

DUPEUX, G. 1964. *La Société française–1789–1960*. Paris: A. Colin.

–– 1969. *La France de 1945–1965*. Paris: A. Colin.

–– 1974. 'La croissance urbaine en France au XIXe siècle', *Rev. d'histoire et d'écon. soc.*, 52 (2): 173–89.

DURAND, C., and M. 1971. *De l'O.S. à l'ingénieur–carrière ou classe sociale?* Paris: Éditions ouvrières.

–– and DUBOIS, P. 1975. *La grève*. (Fondation Nationale des Sciences Politiques.) Paris: A. Colin.

DURIEUX, B. 1973a. 'La décentralisation des emplois ne touche que l'industrie', *Écon. et stat.*, 46: 57–61.

–– 1973 b. 'La situation de l'emploi en 1972', *Écon. et stat.*, 48: 27–43.

–– and SEIBEL, C. 1973. 'Ages et revenus de retraite', *Écon. et stat.*, 46: 3–25.

DURIF, P. 1974. 'Ménages et familles dans les recensements', *Écon. et stat.*, 60: 62–70.

–– and MARCHAND, O. 1975. 'Les locataires des HLM en 1973', *Écon. et stat.*, 73: 3–20.

DURRIEU, Y. 1973. *L'impossible régionalisation capitaliste*. Paris: Anthropos.

DUTAILLY, J.-C., 1973. 'Deux logements sur trois ont été achevés avant 1948' *Écon. et. stat.,* 49: 59–63.

DUVERGER, M. 1964. *Les Partis politiques,* Paris: A. Colin.

EGGENS, J. 1970. 'Le prix des cadres, 1970', *Expansion,* 31: 125–37.

EHRMANN, H. 1957. *Organized Business in France.* Princeton, N.J.: Princeton University Press.

–– 1961. 'French bureaucracy and organized interests', *Administrative Science Quarterly,* March: 534–55.

–– 1971. *Politics in France.* London: Little, Brown & Co.

ELOY, J.-Y., and VANDERPOTTE, G. 1972. 'Une nouvelle représentation du chômage', *Rev. française des affaires soc.*: 15–33.

Entreprises. 1966. 'Où sont les polytechniciens?' 562: 85–91.

EUVRARD, F. 1973. 'Les plans français: Quelques aspects de la redistribution', *Analyse et Prévision,* 15 (6): 683–717.

EYMARD-DUVERNAY, F. 1974. 'Le chômage a augmenté de 12% entre mars 1973 et mars 1974', *Écon. et stat.,* 62: 39–43.

FARCY, H. de. 1971. 'La reconversion des agriculteurs', *Études,* fév.: 225–235.

FAURE, M. 1966. *Les paysans dans la société française.* Paris: A. Colin.

FAUVET, J., and MENDRAS, H. 1958. *Les Paysans et la politique.* Paris: A. Colin.

FLOWER, J. E. 1971. *France to-day–introductory studies,* 2nd ed. London: Methuen.

FOHLEN, C. 1966. *La France de l'entre-deux-guerres–1917–1939.* Paris: Castermann.

Fondation Nationale des Sciences Politiques (Many authors). *L'univers politique des paysans dans la France contempraine.* Paris: A. Colin.

FOUCAULT, M. 1975. *Surveiller et punir–naissance de la prison.* Paris: Gallimard. (Most of Foucault's other work has been translated into English. The other works are fascinating but less directly relevant to the present theme and therefore do not appear here.)

FOURASTIÉ, J. 1972. 'Enquête sur la scolarité d'enfants appartenant à des milieux favorisés', *Analyse et Prévision,* 14 (1–2): 803–31.

FOX, T., and MILLER, S. 1967. 'Intra-country viarations: occupational stratification and mobility', in BENDIX, R., and LIPSET, S. *Class, Status and Power.* London: Routledge and Kegan Paul (2nd ed.): 574–81.

FRASER, W. R. 1963. *Education and Society in Modern France.* London: Routledge and Kegan Paul.

FRÉMONTIER, J. 1971. *La Forteresse ouvrière.* Paris: Fayard.

FRIEDMANN, G. *Villes et campagnes.* Paris: A. Colin.

–– and NAVILLE, P. (eds.) 1961. *Traité de sociologie du travail.* Paris: A. Colin.

FRISCH, J. 1966. 'Les comportements ouvriers de mobilité', *Année sociologique,* 17: 499–53.

–– 1971. 'L'importance des diplômes pur la promotion', *Écon. et stat.,* 21: 33–44.

FRITSCH, P. 1971. *L'Éducation des adultes.* Paris: Mouton.

–– and DE MONTLIBERT, C. 1972. 'Le cumul des désavantages: les élèves des centres ménagers', *Rev. française soc.* 13 (1): 80–93.

GARNIER, M., and HAZELRIGG, L. 1974. 'La mobilité professionnelle en France comparée à celle d'autres pays', *Rev. française. soc.* 15 (3): 363–378.

GAVI, P. 1970. *Les Ouvriers.* Paris: Mercure de France.

GAXIE, D. 1973. *Les Professionnels de la politique.* Paris: P.U.F.

GÉLINIER, O. 1972. *L'entreprise créatrice.* Paris: Hommes et Techniques.

GENG, J.-M. 1973. *Information. Mystification.* Paris: Epi.

GEORGE, P. 1964. 'Anciennes et nouvelles classes dans les campagnes françaises', *Cahiers int. soc.,* 37 (2): 3–22.

GÉRARD, M.-C., and HÉMERY, S. 1973. 'La mortalité infantile en France suivant le milieu social', *Écon. et stat.,* 48: 33–41.

GERVAIS, M., SERVOLIN, C., and WEIL, J. 1965. *Une France sans paysans.* Paris: Le Seuil.

GIRARD, A. 1951. 'Mobilité sociale et dimension de la famille: enquête dans les lycées et les facultés', *Population,* 6: 103–124.

—— 1961. *Le réussite sociale en France.* Cahiers de l'INED No. 38, Paris: P.U.F.

—— 1964. *Le Choix du conoint.* Paris: P.U.F. (2nd edn. 1974.)

—— 1974. *"Population" et l'enseignement.* Cahiers de l'INED, Paris: P.U.F.

—— and BASTIDE, J. 1963. 'La stratification sociale et la démocratisation de l'enseignement', *Population,* 18: 435–72.

—— 1973. 'De la fin des études élémentaries à l'entrée dans la vie professionnelle ou à l'université. La marche d'une promotion de 1962 à 1972', *Population,* 28 (3): 571–93.

—— and CLERC, R. 1964. 'Nouvelles données sur l'orientation scolaire au moment de l'entrée en 6e', Part 1: Åge, orientation scolaire et sélection', *Population,* 5: 829–64.

—— BASTIDE, J., and POURCHER, G. 1963. 'Enquête nationale sur l'entrée en sixième et la démocratisation de l'enseignment', *Population,* 18: 9–48.

GIROD, R. 1971. *Mobilité sociale. Faits établis et problèmes ouverts.* Geneva: Droz.

GODARD, F. 1972. 'De la notion de besoin au concept de pratique de classe. Notes pour une discussion', *La Pensée,* déc.: 82–108.

GODSON, R. 1973/4. 'Non-governmental organizations in world politics; the American Federation of Labor in France, 1945–52', *World Affairs,* winter: 208–27.

GOGUEL, F., and GROSSER, A. 1964. *La Politique en France.* Paris: A. Colin.

GOLDTHORPE, J. 1964. 'Social stratification in industrial society', in HALMOS, P. (ed.). *The Sociological Reveiw,* Monog. 8: 97–122. Reprinted in 1967, BENDIX, R., and LIPSET, S. (eds.), *Class, Status and Power.* London: Routledge and Kegan Paul.

—— and HOPE K. 1974. *The Social Grading of Occupations.* Oxford University Press.

GOMBERT, M. 1974. 'Combien y-a-t-il d'agriculteurs en France?' *Écon. et stat.,* 61: 62–76.

GONTIER, G., BIDOU, D. and VRAIN, P. 1970. 'Carrière universitaire et perspectives professionnelles', *Population*, 25 (Special No.): 37 37–78.

GORCE, P.-M. de la. 1965. *La France pauvre*. Paris: Grasset.

GORGÉ, J-P. 1975. '1974: nouvelle vague de restructuration dans les groupes industriels et financiers', *Écon. et stat.*, 67: 65–8.

— and TANDÉ, A. 1974. 'L'équipement des ménages au début de 1974', *Écon. et stat.*, 58: 45–60.

GORZ, A. 1964. *Stratégie ouvrière et néocapitalisme*. Paris: Le Seuil.

— 1973. *Critique de la division du travail*. Paris: Le Seuil.

GOURNAY, B. 1964. 'Un groupe dirigeant de la société française: les grands fonctionnaires', *Rev. française. science pol.*, 14: 214–42.

GOUX, C. 1969. 'Productivité, production et revenu brut', *Rev. d'écon. pol.* 5: 946–52.

GRIAS, B. 1969. 'Sur 100 personnes actives, 15 paysans, 38 ouvriers', *Écon. et stat.*, 2: 41–9.

GRANICK, D. 1962. *The European Executive*. London: Weidenfield and Nicolson.

GRANOTIER, B. 1973. *Les Travailleurs immigrés en France*. Paris: Maspéro.

GRANOU, A. 1971. 'Le règne de la marchandise', *Politique Aujourd'hui*, October: 37–50.

GRATTON, P. 1971. *Les Luttes de classes dans les campagnes (période 1870–1921)*. Paris: Anthropos.

GRAUBARD, S. 1963. *A New Europe?* London: Oldbourne Press.

GRENADOU, E., and PRÉVOST, A. 1966. *Grenadou, paysan français*. Paris: Le Seuil.

GRIGNON, C. 1968. 'L'orientation scolaire des élèves d'une école rurale', *Rev. française. soc.*, 9 (Special No.): 218–26.

GRIGNON, C. 1971. *L'Ordre des choses*. Paris: Éditions de Minuit.

— and PASSERON, J-C. 1970. *Innovation in higher education: French experience before 1968*. Paris: O.E.C.D.

GRIMAL, H. 1965. *La Décolonisation 1919–1963*. Paris: A. Colin.

GROS, J.-P., CHAROY, X. 1972. 'D'après le recensement de l'agriculture la concentration des exploitations agricoles s'accentue', *Écon. et stat.*, 32: 44–8.

Groupe de Recherches Sociologiques. 1974. *Société paysanne ou lutte de classes au village*. Paris: A. Colin.

GUIGNON, N., and LÉRY. A. 1973. 'Les comportements de loisirs des français', *Écon. et stat.*, 51: 41–9.

GUILBERT, M. 1966. *Les Fontions des femmes dans l'industrie*. Paris: Mouton.

GUILLEMARD, A.-M. 1972. *La Retraite, une mort sociale. Sociologie des conduites en situation de retraite*. Paris: Mouton.

GUIRAL, P. 1969. *La société française 1815–1914 vue par les romanciers*. Paris: A. Colin.

GURVITCH, G. 1966. *Études sur les classes sociales*. Paris: Gonthier.

GUYARD, J. 1965. *Le Miracle français*. Paris: Le Seuil.

HACKETT, J., and A.-M., 1963. *Economic planning in France*. London. Allen and Unwin.

HALL, D., and BETTIGNIES, H.-C. de 1968. 'The French business élite', *European Business* 19: 1–10.

—— and AMADO-FISCHGRUND, G. 1969. 'The European business élite', *European Business* 23: 45–55.

HALLS, W. D. 1965. *Society, Schools and Progress in France*. London: Pergamon.

HAMILTON, R. 1967. *Affluence and the French worker in the Fourth Republic*. Princeton, N.J.: Princeton University Press.

HAMON, L. (ed.) 1962. *Les nouveaux comportements politiques de la classe ouvrière*. Paris: P.U.F.

L'HARDY, P. 1973. 'Les disparités du patrimoine', *Écon. et stat.*, 42: 3–23.

HARVET, J.-C. 1972. 'Où va l'argent de la France?' *Le Nouvel Observateur*. 416: 31–3.

HÉMERY, S. 1969. 'L'évolution démographique', *Rev. écon. pol.*, 5: 861–872.

— 1974. 'La baisse de la fécondité est observée dans tous les pays développés', *Écon. et stat.*, 56: 41–44.

HERVO, M., and CHARRAS, M.-A. 1971. *Bidonvilles*. Paris: Maspéro.

HOFFMAN, S. 1956. *Le Mouvement Poujade*. Paris: A. Colin.

—— et. al., 1963. *France: Change and Tradition*. London: Gollancz.

HOUSSIAUX, J. 1958. *Le Pouvoir des monopoles*. Paris: Sirey.

d'HUGUES, P., and PESLIER, M. 1969. *Les Professions en France*. Cahiers de l'INED, No. 56, Paris: P.U.F.

HUMBLET, J. 1966. *Les Cadres d'entreprise*, Paris: Éditions Universitaires.

IDIART, P. 1962. 'Phénomène ouvrier et phénomène de classe', *Cahiers int. soc.*, 30 (7): 105–124.

—— and GOLDSTEIN, R. 1965. *L'Avenir professionnel des jeunes du milieu populaire*. Paris: Éditions Ouvrières.

Informations Sociales. 1973. 'Où va la famille française?', 4 (entire number).

INSEE. 1970. 'Données essentielles sur l'industrie française', *Écon. et stat.*, 14: 33–50.

INSEE. 1971. 'En 1968 29% des jeunes travailleurs déclarent n'avoir aucun diplôme', *Écon. et stat.*, 20: 47–8.

INSEE. 1972a. 'Les revenus des personnes âgés'. *Écon. et stat.*, 39: 53–7.

INSEE. 1972b. 'Un million de cadres supérieurs dénombrés au recensement de 1968', *Écon. et stat.*, 40: 50–4.

INSEE. 1973a. 'La main d'œuvre étrangère en 1971 dans les établissements industriels et commerciaux', *Écon. et stat.*, 47: 57–64.

INSEE. 1973b. 'Les comportements de loisirs des français', *Écon. et stat.*, 51: 39–43.

INSEE. 1974 L'équipement des ménages au début de 1974, *Écon. et stat.*, 58: 45–8.

Institut d'Études Politiques. 1970. *Aménagement du territorie et développement régional*, vol. 3., Grenoble: I.E.P.

ISAMBERT-JAMATI, V. 1968. 'Les objectifs de l'enseignement second-

aire français, esquisse d'une étude diachronique', in BALANDIER, G. *et al. Perspectives de la Sociologie Contemporaine.* Paris: P.U.F.
—— 1970a. 'Educational development and economic development; comparisons between two regions of France', British Sociological Association, Annual Conference, *The Sociology of Education.*
—— 1970b. *Crises de la société, crises de l'enseignement.* Paris: P.U.F.
JACQUIN, F. 1955. *Les Cadres de l'industrie et du commerce.* Paris: A. Colin.
JANCO, M., and FURJOT, D. 1972. *Informatique et capitalisme.* Paris: Maspéro.
JEGOUZO, G. 1974. 'De nouvelles conditions de renouvellement de la population paysanne', *Écon. et stat.,* 61: 21—8.
—— 1975. 'Paupérisation en agriclture', *Écon. et stat.,* 65: 45—8.
—— and BRANGEON, J.-L. 1974. 'Célibat paysan et pauvreté', *Écon. et stat.,* 58: 3—13.
—— 1975. 'Les chances scolaires des enfants de paysans', *Écon. et stat.,* 67: 3—21.
JENNY, F., and WEBER, A.-P. 1974. 'L'évolution de la concentration industrielle en France de 1961 à 1969', *Écon. et stat.,* 60: 45—8.
KAES, R. 1963. 'Les ouvriers et la culture ouvrière', *Soc. du travail* 5 (3): 247—61.
—— 1964. *Quelques attitudes ouvrières à l'égard de l'école et de l'enseignement.* Institut de Travail, Strasbourg: Université de Strasbourg.
KAHN, J. 1967. 'Les salaires et les salariés', *Écon. et pol.,* 153/4/5: 169—81.
KARPIK, L. 1965. 'Trois concepts sociologiques: le projet de référence, le statut social, et le bilan individuel', *Archs. europs. soc.,* 6 (2): 191—222.
KOSCIUSKO-MORIZET, J. 1973. *La Mafia polytechnicienne.* Paris: Le Seuil.
KRYN, J. 1971. *Lettres d'un maitre de village.* Paris: Le Seuil.
LABBENS. J. 1969. *Le Quart monde—la condition sous-prolétarienne.* Paris: Éditions Science et Service.
LACOMBE, E-H. 1971. *Les Changements de la société française.* Paris: Éditions Ouvrières.
LAFOREST, P. 1974. 'Le pouvoir d'achat des actions, des obligations et de l'or en 1973', *Écon. et stat.* 59: 51—5.
LALUMIÈRE, P. 1959. *L'Inspection des finances.* Paris: P.U.F.
LAMBERT, B. 1970. *Les Paysans dans la lutte des classes.* Paris: Le Seuil.
LAMBERT-DANSETTE, J. 1954. *Quelques Familles du patronat textile de Lille-Armentières, 1789—1914.* Lille: E. Raoust.
LANCOURT, B. 1967. 'Le chômage en 1967', *Écon. et pol.,* 157/8: 61—74.
LANGLOIS, D. 1971. *Les Dossiers noirs de la police française.* Paris: Le Seuil.
LANGLOIS, F. 1962. *Les Salariés agricoles en Frances.* Paris: A. Colin.
LAUNAY, J.-P. 1970. *La France sous -développée.* Paris: Dunod.

LAURENT, S. 1968. 'Les classes sociales dans la France d'aujourd'hui', *Nouvelle Critique*, 2: 3—12.

LAUTMAN. J., DION, M., and DELPHY, C. 1974. *La Transmission du patrimoine. Enquête sur les indépendants.* Centre d'Ethnologie Française, roneogr.

LECAILLON, J. 1970. *L'Inégalité des revenus.* Paris: Cujas.

LEDRUT, R. 1966. 'Les risques de chômage dans une société de capitalisme avancé', *Cahiers Int. Soc.* 40: 43—56.

LEENHARDT, J. 1968. 'La nouvelle classe ouvrière en grève, *Soc. de travail* 10(4): 441—9

LEFEBVRE, H. 1961. 'Changements dans les attitudes morales de la bourgeoisie; contribution à une sociologie de la classe bourgeoise', *Cahiers int. soc.* 8 (31): 15—40.

—— 1969. *The explosion—marxism and the French upheaval.* London Modern Reader. First published, Anthropos. 1968.

LEFOURNIER, P. 1976. 'Reprise sans emballement', *L'Expansion*, 93: 11—13.

LEGOUX, Y. 1959. 'Les techniciens et la culture', FLOUD, J., *et al.* (eds.), *École et Société.* Paris: Marcel Rivière, 1959.

LEMEL, Y., and PARADEISE, C. 1974. 'Appartenance et participation à des associations', *Écon. et stat.*, 55: 41—6.

LE RECLUS, F. 1969. 'Le Sénat républican., *Politique*, 12 (45—8): 45—56.

LE ROUX, P. 1970. 'Le développement des vacances est inférieur aux prévisions', *Écon. et stat.*, 14: 11—17.

LEROY, J. 1970. 'Le portrait robot du P.D.G. français', *Entreprise* 791: 159—67.

LÉRY, A. 1972. 'L'évolution de la fécondité avant et après la dernière guerre', *Écon. et stat.*, 37: 21—33.

LÉVY-LEBOYER, C. 1971. *L'ambition professionnelle et la mobilité sociale.* Paris: P.U.F.

LEWANDOWSKI, O. 1974. 'Différenciation et mécanismes d'intégration de la classe dirigeante. L'image sociale de l'élite d'après le *Who's who in France*', *Rev. française. soc.*, 15 (1): 43—73.

LEWIS, E. 1970. 'Social backgrounds of French ministers, 1944—67', *Western Political Quarterly*, 23(3): 564—78.

L'HARDY, P. 1976. 'Patrimoine des ménages: permanences et transformations', *Écon. et stat.*, 76: 3—25.

L'HOMME, J. 1960. *La grande bourgeoisie au pouvoir (1830—1880).* Paris. P.U.F.

LIPSET, S., and ROGOFF. N. 1954. 'Class and opportunity in Europe and the U.S.A', *Commentary* 18: 563—8.

LOCKWOOD, D. 1958. *The black-coated worker.* London: Allen and Unwin.

LONGEPIERRE, M. 1970. 'Permanence des conseillers généraux et renouveau des traditions administratives départementales' in *Aménagement du territoire et développement régional*, vol. 3: Grenoble: Institut d'Études Politiques: 3—32.

MAGAUD, J. 1974. 'Vrais et faux salariés', *Soc. du travail* 1: 1—17.

MAILLET, P. 1967. *La Structure économique de la France.* Paris: P.U.F.

MALLET, S. 1962. *Les Paysans contre le passé.* Paris: Le Seuil.

—— 1963. *La Nouvelle Classe ouvrière.* Paris: Le Seuil (4th ed., 1969).

MANN, M. 1973. *Consciousness and action among the western working class.* London: Macmillan.

MARCEAU, J. 1974. 'Education and social mobility in France', in PARKIN, F. (ed.) *The social analysis of class structure.* London: Tavistock.

—— 1975. *The Social Origins, Educational Experience and Career Paths of a Young Business Élite,* Final Report for the Social Science Research Council, June. INSEAD Monograph 1/76.

—— 1976. 'Role division and social cohesion; the case of some young French upper-class families., in ALLEN, S., and BARKER, D. (eds.) *Dependence and exploitation in work and marriage.* Harlow: Longmans.

MATHIEU, G. 1962. 'Les réponse des chiffres', *Les Temps Modernes,* 196/7: 401—58.

MAUPÉOU, N. de. 1968. *Les Blousons bleus. Étude sociologique des jeunes ouvriers de la région parisienne.* Paris: A. Colin.

MAURICE, M. *et al.* 1967. *Les cadres et l'entreprise.* Université de Paris—Institut des Sciences Sociales du Travail.

MENDÈS-FRANCE, P. 1963. *A Modern French republic.* London: Weidenfeld and Nicolson.

MENDRAS, H. 1953. *Études de sociologie rurale.* Paris: A. Colin.

MEYNAUD, J. 1962. *Nouvelles études sur les groupes de pression en France.* Cahiers de la Fond. Nat. des Sciences Pols. 118. Paris: A. Colin.

MEYRIAT, J. 1969. *Guide sommaire des ouvrages de référence en sciences sociales.* Paris: A. Colin.

MICHAL, M.-G. 1973. 'Les femmes jeunes travaillent de plus en plus fréquemment', *Écon. et stat.* 51: 33—8.

MICHEL, A. *Famille, industrialisation, logement. Thèse principale.* No date, no publisher, no place of publication given.

—— and TEXIER, G. 1964. *La condition de la Française d'aujourd'hui.* Geneva: Gonthier.

MICHELAT, G., and SIMON, M. 1968. 'Catholiques déclarés et irréligieux communistes: vision du monde et perception du champ politique', *Archs. des sciences soc. des religions.* 85: 57—111.

MINCES, J. 1967. *Le Nord.* Paris: Maspero.

—— 1969. *Un Ouvrier parle. Enquête.* Paris: Le Seuil.

—— 1973. *Les Travailleurs étrangers en France.* Paris: Le Seuil.

Ministère de L'Éducation Nationale. 1969. 'Les étudiants en France . . .', *Notes et Études Documentaires,* 3577.

Le Monde. 1973. *Les forces politiques et les élections de mars 1973.* (Dossier du Monde.)

Le Monde de L'Education. 1975. 'La réforme Haby'.

MONJARDET, D. 1972. 'Carrière des dirigeants et contrôle de l'entreprise', *Soc. du travail,* 13 (2): 131—44.

MORAZÉ, C. 1957. *Les Bourgeois conquérants.* Paris: A. Colin.
  Translated in 1966 as *The Triumph of the Middle Classes.* London:
  Weidenfeld and Nicolson.
MORIN, E. 1967. *Commune en France—la métamorphose de Plodémet.*
  Paris: Fayard.
—— 1969. *La Rumeur d'Orléans.* Paris: Le Seuil.
MORIN, F. 1974. *La Structure financière du capitalisme française.*
  Paris: Calmann-Lévy.
—— 1973. *Le Métier de militant.* Paris: Le Seuil.
—— 1972. *Les O.S.–objectifs.* Paris: Le Cerf.
MOTHÉ, D. 1973. *Le Métier de militant.* Paris: Le Seuil.
NATANSON, J., and PROST, A. 1963. *La Révolution scolaire.* Paris:
  Éditions Ouvrières.
NEGRONI, F. de. 1974. *La France noble.* Paris: Le Seuil.
NÉRÉ, J. 1967. *La Trosième République 1914–1940.* Paris: A. Colin.
NIAUDET, J. 1969. 'La consommation des ménages de 1962–1968',
  Rev. écon. pol. 5: 1105–53.
NOLLEAU, H. 1970. 'Données sur l'évolution du pouvoir d'achat des
  ouvriers depuis 1968', *Écon. et pol.,* 196/7: 141–66.
Le Nouvel observateur. 1973. 'Le prix d'un Français' par Josette Alia,
  Claudine Serem, *et al.,* 463/4/5.
—— 1974. 'Le prix d'un Français' par François Henri de Virieu,
  514/5/6/7.
PADIEU, R. 1972. 'Les bas salaires', *Écon. et stat.* 39: 17–29.
PAGÉ, J.-P. 1966. 'L'utisation des produits de la croissance., in
  DARRAS, *Le Partage des Bénéfices.* Paris: Minuit.
PAILLAT, P. *Old people.* International Trade Union Seminar on Low
  Income Groups. Paris: O.E.C.D.
PARKIN, F. 1971. *Class Inequality and Political Order.* London:
  MacGibbon and Kee.
PARODI, M. 1964. 'Agriculteurs menacés et agriculteurs menaçants',
  Études Rurales 12: 5–55.
—— 1966. *Low incomes groups and methods of dealing with their
  problems.* O.E.C.D. report (Trade Union Conference).
—— 1971. *L'Économie et la société française de 1945–1970.* Paris:
  A. Colin.
PAUTARD, J. 1965. *Les Disparités régionales dans le croissance de
  l'agriculture française.* Paris: Gauthier-Villars.
PERROT, M. 1961. *Le Mode de vie des familles bourgeoises, 1873–
  1953.* Paris: A. Colin.
—— 1967. 'Salaires, prestations sociales et pouvoir d'achat de 1964 à
  1966', *Études et Conjoncture,* 1: 97–129.
—— 1971. 'Les salaires publics et privés depuis 1968', *Écon. et stat.,* 20:
  15–22.
—— 1975. 'L'évolution récente des salaires, jusqu'en 1974', *Écon. et
  stat.,* 63: 37–45.
PÉTONNET, C. 1968. *Ces gens-là.* Paris: Maspéro.
PEYRE, C. 1959. 'L'origine sociale des élèves de l'enseignement
  secondaire en France', in FLOUD, J., *et al., École et Société.* Paris:
  M. Rivière.

PIEMME, J.-M. 1974. 'Le tissu idéologique dans le feuilleton télévisé', *Politique Aujourd'hui*, oct.–déc.: 18–44.

PINNEAU, M.-R. 1973. *Les O.S.* Paris: Éditions Sociales.

PITROU, A. 1972. *La Famille dans la vie de tous les jours*. Paris: Privat.

PLANCHAIS, J. 1970. *Les Provinciaux ou la France sans Paris*. Paris: Le Seuil.

PLEVEN, R. 1961. *Avenir de la Bretagne*. Paris: Calmann-Lévy.

POHL, R., LAULHÉ, P., and EYMARD-DUVERNAY, F. 1973. 'La population active en 1972', *Écon. et stat.* 44: 35–51.

–– and LIONNET, R. 1972. 'La population active en mars 1971., *Écon. et stat.* 34: 3–11.

POLACK, J.-C. 1972. *La Médecine du capital*. Paris: Maspéro.

POSNER, C. (ed.) 1970. *Reflections on the Revolution in France 1968*. London: Penguin.

POULANTZAS, N. 1973. 'On social classes', C.F.D.T. brochure reproduced in translation in *New Left Review*, 78: 27–54.

–– 1974. *Les Classes sociales dans le capitalisme aujourd'hui*. Paris: Le Seuil.

–– 1968. (vol. 1) and 1971 (vol. 2) *Pouvoir politique et classes sociales I*. Paris: Maspéro.

PRADERIE, M. 1968. *Ni ouvriers, ni paysans; les tertiaires*. Paris: Le Seuil.

–– and PASSAGEZ, M. 1966. 'La mobilité professionnelle en France entre 1959 et 1964', *Études et Conjoncture*, 21 (10): 1–166.

–– SALAIS, R., and PASSAGEZ, M. 1967. 'Une enquête sur la formation et la qualification des Français (1964)', *Études et Conjoncture*, 22 (1): 3–109.

PRIOURET, R. 1963. *Origines du patronat français*. Paris: Bernard Grasset.

PROST, A. 1968. *L'enseignement en France 1800–1967*. Paris: A. Colin.

QUOIST, M. 1952. *La ville et l'homme–Rouen*. Paris: Éditions Ouvrières.

RAMBAUD, P. 1962. *Economie et sociologie de la montagne*. Paris: A. Colin.

–– 1969. *Société rurale et urbanisation*. Paris: Le Seuil.

RÉMOND, R. 1966. *Atlas historique de la France contemporaine*. Paris: A. Colin.

REVOIL, J.-P. 1975. 'L'évolution de l'emploi en 1974 et au début de 1975', *Écon. et stat.* 69: 59–64.

REYNAUD, J.-D. 1963 and 1974. *Les Syndicats en France*. Paris: A. Colin. Revised in 1974. Paris: Le Seuil.

–– and TOURAINE, A. 1956. 'Deux notes à propos d'une enquête sur les étudiants en médecine', *Cahiers int. soc.*, 16: 124–48.

REZO, A. 1972. 'Le chômage–structure et évolution rêcentes', *Écon. et pol.*, 210: 93–110.

RIDLEY, F., and BLONDEL, J. 1964. *Public administration in France*. London: Routledge and Kegan Paul.

RIVIER, J. 1969. 'La place des entreprises publiques dans l'économie française', *Écon. et stat.* 6: 33–44.

RIVIÈRE, C. 1970. 'Ces maréchaux d'industrie qui arrivent par les salons . . .', *Entreprise* 785: 81–5.

ROZE, H. 1971. 'Prestations sociales, impôt direct et échelle des revenus', *Écon. et stat.* 20: 3–14.

—— 1972. 'La composition du revenu des diverses catégories socio-professionnelles', *Écon. et stat.* 31: 39–42.

—— 1974. 'Impôts directs et transferts sociaux: effets sur l'échelle des revenus de 1962–1970', *Écon. et stat.* 59: 19–31.

SAADA, K. 1972. 'Premiers regards sur la mensualisation', *Écon. et stat.* 30: 29–38.

SAINSAULIEU, R. 1966. 'Les classes sociales défavorisées en face de la télévision; quelques hypothèses', *Rev. française. soc.* 7: 201–14.

SAINT-MARTIN, M. de. 1968. 'Les facteurs de l'élimination et de la sélection différentielles dans les études de sciences', *Rev. française. soc.* (Special No.): 167–184.

—— 1971. *Les fonctions sociales de l'enseignement scientifique.* Paris: Mouton.

SALAIS, R. 1969. 'La population active., *Rev. d'écon. pol.* 5: 872–93.

—— 1970. 'Les niveaux de diplômes dans chaque catégorie socio-professionnelle', *Écon. et stat.* 9: 49–57.

—— 1972. 'La sensibilité de l'activité de la population aux variations du chômage', *Écon. et stat.* 38: 45–8.

—— and MICHAL, M.-G. 1971. 'L'activé des femmes mariées', *Écon. et stat.* 26: 27–36.

SAUVY, A., and GIRARD, A. 1965. 'Les diverses classes sociales devant l'enseignement; mise au point générale des résultats', *Population,* 20 (2): 205–32.

SCARDIGLI, V. 1970. *Social Policies and the working poor in France.* Paris: CREDOC.

—— 1975. 'Lifestyles, inequalities and the process of social change in France', *Futures:* 197–208.

SCHIÉLÉ, R., and MONJARDET, A. 1964. *Les Apprentis scolarisés.* Paris: Éditions Ouvrière.

SCOTFORD-ARCHER, M., and GINER, S. 1971. *Contemporary Europe, class and status and power.* London: Weidenfeld and Nicholson.

SÉGRE-BRUN, M., and TANGUY, L. 1967. 'Quelle unité d'analyse retenir pour étudier les variations géographiques de la scolarisation?' *Rev. française. soc.* 8 (Special No.): 117–39.

SERVAN-SCHREIBER, J.-J. 1967. *Le Défi américain.* Paris: Denoël. Translated in 1969 as *The American Challenge.* London: Penguin.

SEYS, B. 1975. 'Le chômage d'après l'enquête emploi d'avril 1975', *Écon. et stat.* 73: 43–52.

SIEGFRIED, S. 1957. 'Les écoles qui mènent la France', *Réalités,* avril: 82–5.

SIMON, M. 1963. 'Attitudes politiques ouvrières dans le département du Nord', *Cahiers int. soc.* 36, jan.–juin: 57–74.

Société Française de Sociologie. 1966. *Tendances et volontés de la société française.* Paris:

SPECKLIN, A. 1954. *Altkirch, type de petite ville*. Paris: Centre de Documentation Universitaire.

STANWORTH, P., and GIDDENS, A. 1974. *Élites and power in British society*. Cambridge: Cambridge University Press.

SULEIMAN, E. 1972. 'Sur les limites de la mentalité bureaucratique: conflits des rôles entre cabinets ministériels et directeurs', *Soc. du travail*, 14 (4): 388–409.

— — 1973. 'L'administrateur et le deputé en France', *Rev. française. science pol.*, 23 (4): 729–57.

— — 1974. *Politics, power and bureaucracy in France*. Princeton, N.J.: Princeton University Press.

SULLEROT, E. 1973. *Les Françaises au travail*. Paris: Hachette.

TAVERNIER, J. 1966. 'Le syndicalisme paysan et la Cinquième République 1962–1965', *Rev. française. science pol.*, 16 (5): 869–912.

TEMPLÉ, P. 1974. 'Répartition des gains de productivité et hausses des prix de 1959–1973', *Écon. et stat.* 59: 38–42.

THÉLOT, C. 1973a. 'Les tableaux de l'enquête "Formation et qualification professionnelles" sont disponibles', *Écon. et stat.* 41: 59–64

— — 1973b. 'Mobilité professionnelle plus forte entre 1965 et 1970', *Écon. et stat.* 51: 3–32.

THOENIG, J.-C. 1973. L'ére des technocrates; le cas des Ponts-et-Chaussées. Paris: Éditions d'Organisation.

TOPALOV, C. 1973. *La Promotion immobilière. Contribution à l'analyse de la production capitaliste du logement en France*. Paris: Mouton.

TORÉ, A. 1973. 'Forte hausse des prix des terres agricoles en 1972., *Écon. et stat.* 49: 43–5.

TOURAINE, A. 1965. *Sociologie de l'action*. Paris: Le Seuil.

— — 1966. *La Conscience ouvrière*. Paris: Le Seuil.

— — 1968. 'Anciennes et nouvelles classes sociales', in BALANDIER, G. et al. *Perspectives de la sociologie contemporaine*. Paris: P.U.F.

— — 1969. *La Société post-industrielle*. Paris: Denoël-Médiations.

— — 1973. *Production de la société*. Paris: Le Seuil.

— — and RAGAZZI, O. 1961. *Ouvriers d'origine argricole*. Paris: Le Seuil.

TOUZARD, H. 1967. *Enquête psychosociologique sur les rôles conjugaux et la structure familiale*. Paris: Centre National de la Recherche Scientifique.

TRIBALLAT-SELIGMAN, N. 1969. 'Le patrimoine immobilier et les ménages', *Rev. d'écon. pol.* 5: 894–906.

TROGAN, P. 1973. 'Les accidents du travail sont plus fréquents chez les immigrés', *Écon. et stat.* 48: 53–9.

TURC, A. 1973. 'La clientèle de l'assurance-vie en 1970', *Écon. et stat.*, 49: 46–51.

TURNER, R. 1960. 'Modes of social ascent through education', *American Soc. Rev.* 25: 121–39. Reprinted in BENDIX, R., and LIPSET, S. (eds.), 1967. *Class, Status and Power*. London: Routledge and Kegan Paul.

UNEDIC. June 1970. *Bulletin de liaison*.

UNEDIC. September 1973. *Bulletin de liaison.*
—— November 1973. *Bulletin de liaison.*
Union des Industries Métallurgiques et Minières. 1970. *Ingénieurs et cadres.* Paris.
URRY, J., and WAKEFORD, J. 1973. *Power in Britain.* London: Heinemann.
VANGREVELINGHE, G. 1969. 'Les Niveaux de vie en France 1956 et 1965', *Écon. et stat.* 1: 7–21.
VARENNES, H. 1971. 'Quelle classe ouvrière?', *Politique aujourd'hui,* 5: 3–11.
VIDAL, D. 1971. *Essai sur l'idéologie.* Paris: Anthropos.
VINCENT, G. 1967. *Les Professeurs du second degré.* Paris: A. Colin.
VINCIENNE, M., and RAMBAUD, P. 1964. *Les Transformations d'une société rurale: la Maurienne 1561–1962.* Paris: A. Colin.
VOLKOFF, S. 1970. 'Les salaires en 1968, année de Grenelle', *Écon. et stat.,* 14: 3–9.
—— 1974 a. 'Les salaires en 1971', *Écon. et stat.,* 54: 52–5.
—— 1974b 'Les salaires dans les grandes agglomérations', *Écon. et stat.,* 54: 48–51.
—— 1974c. 'Les hauts salaires en 1971', *Écon. et stat.,* 56: 56.
VOYENNE, B. 1962. *La Presse dans la société contemporaine.* Paris: A. Colin.
WARCK, R., and WAGNER, K. 1973. *Les Déshérités de l'école.* Paris: Maspéro.
WERTH, A. 1956. *France–1940–1955.* London: Robert Hale.
—— 1965. *Political leaders of the twentieth century–De Gaulle.* London: Penguin.
WILLARD, C. 1967. *Socialisme et communisme français.* Paris: A. Colin.
WILLIAMS, P. 1964. *Crisis and compromise: politics in the Fourth Republic.* London: Longmans.
—— GODLEY, D., and HARRISON, M. 1970. *French politicians and elections 1957–1969.* Cambridge: Cambridge University Press.
WRIGHT, G. 1964. *Rural revolution in France. The peasantry in the twentieth century.* Oxford: Oxford University Press.
WYLIE, L. 1957. *Village in the Vaucluse.* Cambridge, Mass: Harvard University Press.
—— 1966. *Chanzeaux: a village in Anjou.* Cambridge, Mass.: Harvard University Press.
ZELDIN, T. 1970. *Conflicts in French society.* London: Allen and Unwin.
—— 1973. *France 1848–1945.* Oxford: Clarendon Press.

INDEX